Re-imagining Educational Leadership

Re-imagining Educational Leadership

BRIAN J. CALDWELL

SAGE Publications

London • Thousand Oaks • New Delhi

First published ACER Press, Australia 2006
and by Sage Publications, London 2006

SAGE Publications Ltd
1 Oliver's Yard
55 City Road
London EC1Y 1SP

SAGE Publications Inc.
2455 Teller Road
Thousand Oaks, California 91320

SAGE Publications India Pvt Ltd
B-42, Panchsheel Enclave
Post Box 4109
New Delhi 110 017

British Library Cataloguing in Publication data

A catalogue record for this book is available from the British Library

ISBN-10 1-4129-3469-9 ISBN-13 978-1-4129-3469-5
ISBN-10 1-4129-3470-2 ISBN-13 978-1-4129-3470-1 (pbk)

Library of Congress Control Number: 2006928135

Typeset by J&M Typesetting
Printed in Great Britain by Athenaeum Press Ltd, Gateshead,
Tyne & Wear
Printed on paper from sustainable resources

Foreword

In 1988 when *The Self-managing School* by Brian Caldwell and his colleague Jim Spinks was published, it was a revelation to me. At the time I was on the staff of a teacher union in England and caught up in the conflicts over the Education Reform Act 1988 (UK) that followed several years of bitter industrial strife. Yet here in *The Self-managing School*, I glimpsed an insight into the future; a way in which the teaching profession could regain its self-respect by leading where it really matters to children and their parents—in the school. The Education Reform Act, building on some English experiments, proposed to devolve budgets to every school. At the time it was highly controversial and no-one was quite sure how it could be made to work. In relation to this major innovation, Caldwell and Spinks provided both the rationale and the practical guidance we all craved. Not least because of them, local management became one of the most successful and least contested of the reforms of the next decade.

Caldwell and Spinks hadn't finished contributing to education reform. *The Self-managing School* developed into a series in which the authors remained true to the original vision but refined the practice in the light of the emerging international evidence.

Brian Caldwell became a celebrity among educators in England partly because of his enduring knowledge, wisdom and good nature, and partly (I think he would agree) because it was in England that his vision had most impact. Government and headteachers working together implemented a radical interpretation of what the self-managing school might mean in practice. When Labour was elected in 1997 it drove devolution to an even more radical position. From 2006 this will mean each school receiving a delegated three-year budget.

Meanwhile, some headteachers working in loose collaboration, often associated with the Specialist Schools and Academies Trust, took advantage of the freedom and funding they were given to—quite literally—reinvent secondary education. Heads such as Tom Clark, Dexter Hutt, Pat Collarbone, Kevin Satchwell and David Triggs set ambitious goals, achieved standards that had seemed unobtainable a few years before, reorganised their timetables and their staffing models, and deployed technology as an agent of transformation. It was striking to me, whenever I discussed education with heads such as these, how often the name Brian Caldwell came up in the conversation. For Brian, himself a school leader by background, was never a pure academic. He was always connected to schools, always seeking out the leading edge, always learning from practitioners and always providing them with insights, ideas and a rationale.

In 1998, Brian wrote a seminal article in the *Times Educational Supplement*. Addressed to the Prime Minister, it was headlined 'The world is watching, Tony'. Ever since, Brian and many other education reformers have indeed been watching what we're doing in England. We often forget, caught up as we inevitably are in the day-to-day, just how radical and expansive our program of reform continues to be. The 2006 legislation will take this revolution a further step forward. We've had our ups and downs for sure but the evidence suggests many more ups. Above all, more students are achieving better results than ever before, though of course every educator in England knows we can do better still.

In my view the key to continued success is strong collaboration between government and headteachers at the leading edge of change. Brian Caldwell will no doubt continue to foster and inspire such collaboration. His work will always provide challenges and insights for all of us. Long may the conversation between Brian Caldwell and the English education system continue. The fact that we know you are watching, Brian, helps all of us both to perform well in the present and to invent a future in which we perform better still.

For these reasons, I commend Brian's writings to anyone committed to world-class public education.

Professor Sir Michael Barber
Expert Partner, Global Public Sector Practice, McKinsey and Company
Former Head of Prime Minister's Delivery Unit at 10 Downing Street, London, UK

November 2006

Contents

To Marie

Preface

This book spans 50 years in its coverage of leadership in education—25 years in the past and 25 years in the future. It is anchored in the present, at a point when certainty, coherence and continuity are under challenge, and there is need for a new perspective on purpose, policy and practice in the profession. Expressed simply, it is time to re-imagine educational leadership.

Henry Mintzberg is pre-eminent in his writing on strategy. He is an advocate of strategic thinking, which he describes as 'seeing': seeing ahead, seeing behind, seeing above, seeing below, seeing beside, seeing beyond, and above all, seeing it through. That is what this book endeavours to do for educational leadership. In imagining what leadership will be like in the future ('seeing ahead'), we need to see where it has come from ('seeing behind'). We need to understand strategy at the most senior levels ('seeing above') but also empathise with those who work at the front-line in achieving the outcomes ('seeing below'). We can learn much by observing what others are doing in our own countries ('seeing beside') but also from the study of how things are done elsewhere ('seeing beyond'). We must ensure that those who have the privilege to serve as leaders in education can sustain the effort ('seeing it through').

My journey began in 1981 when I returned to Australia after completing doctoral work in Canada on the decentralisation of decision-making in education. My immediate engagement in a project of national significance revealed how schools in what had traditionally been highly-centralised systems of public education could be self-managing. This led to my professional partnership with Jim Spinks, now extending over two decades, as we shared what we learnt around Australia and other nations where momentum was building for the adoption of such an approach. Sir Michael Barber has written of our work in England in the foreword that he kindly agreed to write for this book. There were powerful implications for leaders at all levels. The outcome is that self-management is now part of the culture, and the tipping point was passed at the turn of the twenty-first century. In the strategic frame under consideration, we were able to discern in limited practice a quarter of a century ago what has become part of the scene in the first decade of the 2000s.

I believe that the main features of what education will be like in the next quarter-century are now starting to emerge in the best of current practice. It is one purpose of this book to describe what is unfolding. The Specialist Schools and Academies Trust in England provided the launching pad for the project by engaging me to write three pamphlets which drew from experience in several countries, and these were the starting points for a series of workshops, each of which informed the next publication. These pamphlets constitute the heart of this book which becomes, in turn, the starting point for 18 workshops in every state and territory of Australia, organised by the Australian College of Educators. More will be learnt from these experiences.

We do not know the precise form that education will take in different settings in 25 years' time. No-one does. No-one should claim to have this foresight. Leadership is required, however, regardless of the form that education takes. This book describes leadership that is changing the world of education with moral purpose on a scale that can best be described as transformation. Such leadership differs in important ways from what has been expected in the past. It requires a change in role at all levels. It shifts the balance from what is often a dispiriting and discouraging experience to one that is exhilarating. It energises those who work at the system level in the support of schools.

I express my thanks to the Specialist Schools and Academies Trust for providing the framework within which this book could emerge, and for allowing the contents of pamphlets I wrote for its project on International Networking for Educational Transformation to be incorporated in this book. I am grateful for the scores of school leaders on three continents who shared their successes in formal presentations in 14 workshops in 2005, and the hundreds of others who participated and offered their insights. I acknowledge the interest and support of the Australian Council for Educational Research through ACER Press for its decision to publish the book, and the Australian College of Educators for organising a national program to work with educational leaders in re-imagining their roles. I have no doubt that more will follow on an even larger stage.

The eminent playwright and philosopher Václav Havel, who served as President of the Czech Republic following the Velvet Revolution, distinguished between 'hope' and 'optimism'. This book is written in the spirit of optimism, and is dedicated to my Czech partner and soul mate Marie, who has given me unstinting support along the way and helped keep my feet on the ground.

Brian J. Caldwell
Melbourne
November 2006

Introduction

CHAPTER 1

Imagination and re-imagination

Imagination lies at the heart of all that is best in education. It has always been so in the way we nurture the creative arts. Advances in medicine and science are often stimulated by the imagination. The great social movements that have freed the human spirit and lifted people out of material deprivation have required heroic effort by those who have imagined a better world, and done something about it. Imagination is central to the spiritual life. There are few societies around the world that are not committed to building a capacity for creativity at all levels of education, and stimulating the imagination is central to the endeavour.

Re-imagination in education

Imagination is positive and uplifting. It is also never ending, and that is why the idea of re-imagination is important, especially when emotions have been dulled, scientific effort has stalled, deprivation is evident, and learning is impaired.

The need for re-imagination in education was presented by Tom Peters in *Re-imagine!* (Peters 2003). Peters gained fame in the early 1980s with his co-authored and influential *In Search of Excellence* (Peters and Waterman 1982). He takes aim at virtually every institution in the public and private sectors, and singles out education as a prime target for re-imagination. Writing of the United States, he declares that 'I despair of the education system more than any other part of our society' (p. 290). His re-imagination of schools involves a change in image from the school as a factory, with a focus on units of mass production, to the school as a studio, with a focus on uniqueness and the needs and accomplishments of individuals. As far as pedagogy is concerned, he contends that 'teachers need enough time and flexibility to get to know kids as individuals. Teaching is about one and only one thing: Getting to know the child. Getting inside his or her psyche. Getting close enough to learn something about his or her learning trajectory' (p. 284). As far as curriculum is concerned, he believes that there should be 'a school curriculum that values questions above answers...creativity above fact regurgitation...individuality above uniformity...and excellence above standardised performance' (p. 277). Peters's line of argument is consistent with the call to personalise learning in plans for the transformation of schools in several nations.

Peters's view of the education system in the United States is a depressing one. However, even if one does not subscribe to the view that schools are in dire straits, it is still worthwhile to imagine or re-imagine a future that is different and even better than the present. This has been proposed for Australia. The theme of *Imagining Australia* (Duncan, Leigh, Madden and Tynan 2004) is that, while Australia is doing remarkably well in many fields, including education, the project of building the nation is unfinished. The authors contend that 'beneath the facade of confidence and optimism, there is a certain insecurity about the nation's purpose and an uncertainty about the nation's future' (p. 1). The 'central conviction' of the book is that 'the path towards the future is not through the past' (p. 6). The authors include schools in their invitation to imagine or re-imagine if Australians are to seize the opportunity to 'forge a great nation' (p. 3).

The challenge to re-imagine has been taken up in different ways in Singapore (re-imagining the nation), England (re-imagining a system of secondary education) and Australia (re-imagining a school).

Singapore celebrated its 40th anniversary in 2005. Addressing the National Day Rally on 21 August, shortly after becoming Prime Minister, Lee Hsien Loong (son of founding prime minister Lee Kuan Yew), issued a challenge 'What will Singapore be like 40 years from now? I can't tell you. Nobody can. But I can tell you it must be a totally different Singapore because if it is the same Singapore as it is today, we're dead. We will be irrelevant, marginalised, the world will be different. You may want to be the same, but you can't be the same. Therefore, we have to remake Singapore—our economy, our education system, our mindsets, our city' (Lee, LH 2005).

In 2005 the Ministry of Education in Singapore released *Nurturing Every Child: Flexibility & Diversity in Singapore Schools*, a policy that called for a more varied curriculum, a focus on learning rather than teaching, the creation of specialist schools, and more autonomy for schools and teachers (Ministry of Education, Singapore 2005). Many would ask why Singapore should embark on such a change. After all, Singapore ranked first among 49 nations in each of Grade 4 and Grade 8 for both mathematics and science in the 2003 program of the Trends in Mathematics and Science Study (TIMSS).

Singapore is a nation whose chief if not sole resource is its human resource. It realises there is a need to 're-make the nation' and accepts that it must also 're-make the school' if it is to achieve that end. Prime Minister Lee expressed it this way in his contribution to a special edition of *Newsweek* on the theme 'The Knowledge Revolution: Why Victory will go to the Smartest Nations & Companies': 'We are remaking ourselves into a key node in the global knowledge network, securing our place under the sun' (Lee LH 2006).

These intentions are remarkable given that Singapore was established as a nation in its own right in 1965. It has been transformed from a struggling colony to one of the world's most successful multi-cultural nations, with a thriving economy, as described in *From Third World to First* by founding Prime Minister Lee Kuan Yew (Lee KY 2000). Singapore's vision of 'Thinking Schools, Learning Nation' captured the imagination of educators around the world when it was announced by former Prime Minister Goh Chok Tong at the 7th International Conference on Thinking in June 1997 (Goh 1997).

One of the most successful efforts to re-imagine a school system has occurred in England. The secondary level been transformed in barely a decade from about 3100 standard comprehensive schools to 2502 specialist schools (as at January 2006) with the others to follow very soon. Each offers at least one of eleven specialisms while still addressing the broad national curriculum. As indicated by the proportion of students gaining five good passes in examinations for the General Certificate of Secondary Education (GCSE), achievement in specialist schools is 11 percentage points higher than in non-specialist schools, with these gains being highest in disadvantaged settings. Accompanying this change has been unprecedented partnership between schools and business and industry in areas of specialism, for example, partnership between organisations in the arts or sport and schools that specialise in these areas. The government is committed to a target of all secondary schools becoming specialist schools. It is arguably the most far-reaching change in secondary education in any nation. Examples from specialist schools in England are contained in a number of chapters.

There are many examples of re-imagination at the school level, especially where student achievement was once low and is now high. The case of Bellfield Primary School in the Melbourne suburb of West Heidelberg is a case in point. In the late 1990s, barely 30 per cent of students in the early years could read at a satisfactory level. Like many counterparts in school systems around the world, it was expected to lift its game, but the context seemed to thwart the effort. There were many single parent families, much poverty and high levels of crime in the community. An imaginative effort by former principal John Fleming and his colleagues has turned things around so that by the mid 2000s, nearly 100 per cent of students are achieving success. Assumptions changed and new professional capacities acquired. Chapter 13 contains a report of a master class by John Fleming, along with others by leaders who demonstrate a capacity for imagination and re-imagination.

This book celebrates success in the exercise of imaginative leadership, builds a case for much more, and proposes a range of strategies to accomplish it. It is not written because it is simply a nice-sounding concept. It is written because there is dire need in many settings.

To describe that need in the bluntest of terms: leadership has quite literally 'hit the wall', especially at the system level where governments and the community at large are losing patience with the perceived failure of some schools to meet expectations, and seemingly endless re-structuring has failed to achieve those expectations. There is also a crisis at the school level, as indicated in places where there are few applicants for the principalship and many leave because the work is unsatisfying and stressful. It ought not to be this way in a profession that is developing the most valuable resource in the nation.

Affirming good theory

There is nothing wrong with theory in leadership. Long-standing concepts and distinctions between leadership and management hold up well. The framework of John Kotter (1990) is helpful and affirmed. Leadership is a process for establishing direction, aligning people, motivating and inspiring, and achieving change. Management is a process that calls for planning and budgeting, organising and staffing, controlling and problem solving, and producing a degree of predictability. Elements of leadership line up with elements of management, so that the counterpart of establishing direction (leadership) is planning and budgeting (management). Aligning people (leadership) matches up with organising and staffing (management), motivating and inspiring (leadership) with controlling and problem solving (management), and achieving change (leadership) with producing a degree of predictability (management).

Research on leadership in education is sound and getting better, as is highlighted in several chapters. This research is most impressive in establishing the links between leadership and learning. The effort is aided by a data-rich environment.

What this book does is describe and learn from the experience of leaders who have succeeded in or are on the path to success in the transformation of schools. Transformation is considered here and throughout the book as significant, systematic and sustained change that results in high levels of achievement by all students in all settings, thus contributing to the wellbeing of the individual and of society. What this achievement is about and how it is measured varies from setting to setting, and is invariably contentious. Transformation is an appropriate word because such an outcome ('all students in all settings') has never been accomplished in any society in the history of education. It has, however, been accomplished in some settings, and this book draws on such success. It also listens to the voices of leaders who have transcended those aspects of the work that are boring, depressing, discouraging and dispiriting to experience a sense of exhilaration in their work.

The book is intended to challenge the context in which leadership at the system and school levels is exercised. It challenges the view that systems of education should be highly centralised. Indeed, it provides a wealth of evidence to support the concept of the self-managing school, moving toward autonomy. It challenges the notion that the key unit of organisation is the school or the classroom. Henceforth the key unit of organisation is the student. It challenges the long-standing assumption that schools can achieve transformation by acting alone. The reality is that transformation can only be accomplished through the networking of a complex array of services. It challenges the view that initial preparation and occasional professional development are sufficient to ensure that the professional is at the forefront of knowledge. Transformation calls for schools to be powerful learning organisations.

The proposed changes are so dramatic that some would argue that a new conception of education is required. David Hargreaves calls for a new 'education imaginary' that is a counterpart or consequence of the new 'social imaginary' that has taken shape over a hundred years or more (Hargreaves, D 2004). Hedley Beare, author of *Creating the Future School* (Beare 2001), has described what the new 'education imaginary' will be like in practice (Beare 2006). What is proposed in the pages that follow is consistent with the view that change on this scale is underway and, while current realities are challenged, it shows how imagination and re-imagination can do wonders in current contexts.

Points of departure

There is harmony with recent literature that takes up the theme of sustainability in leadership and change, but there are also points of departure. Andy Hargreaves and Dean Fink drew extensively on a study of change over three decades in eight high schools in New York State and Ontario, Canada. It therefore has more than a ring of authenticity, at least in these kinds of schools. They acknowledge at the outset that 'change in education is easy to propose, hard to implement, and even harder to sustain' (Hargreaves and Fink 2006, p. 1). They base their work on seven principles of sustainable leadership:

1. depth— sustainable leadership matters;
2. length—sustainable leadership lasts;
3. breadth—sustainable leadership spreads;
4. justice—sustainable leadership does no harm to and actively improves the surrounding environment;
5. diversity—sustainable leadership promotes cohesive diversity;
6. resourcefulness—sustainable leadership develops and does not deplete material and human resources;
7. conservation—sustainable leadership honours and learns from the past to create an even better future (Hargreaves and Fink 2006, pp. 18–20).

Hargreaves and Fink provide a compelling argument that much that is unsustainable derives from excesses in recent attempts at change. 'The past decade and more has seen the educational reform and standards movement plummet to the depths of unsustainability, taking educational leadership down with it'. They note that 'although it may not look or feel like it, the educational standards bubble [like the stock market, IT and property bubbles] is about to burst. In fact, in a number of places—the United Kingdom, Australia, and many parts of Canada—it already has' (Hargreaves and Fink 2006, pp. 9–10). The point of departure is this author's view that it is a bigger bubble that is about to burst in these and other settings, namely, the era of large centralised school systems that instigated what Hargreaves and Fink describe as 'the rapid, relentless, and pervasive spread of standardisation in educational reform' (p. 10). When things settle, standards will find their place, but principle 5 above will prevail, that is, there will be 'cohesive diversity'.

Michael Fullan has also written with great insight on sustainability, defined as 'the capacity of a system to engage in the complexities of continuous improvement consistent with deep values of human purposes' (Fullan 2005, p. ix). His involvement in several stages of large-scale educational reform ensures the authenticity of his work. This ranges from policy advice to evaluating the impact of reform. He identifies eight elements of sustainability:

1. public service with a moral purpose;
2. commitment to changing context at all levels;
3. lateral capacity building through networks;
4. intelligent accountability and vertical relationships;
5. deep learning;
6. dual commitment to short-term and long-term results;
7. cyclical energising;
8. the long lever of leadership (Fullan 2005, p. 14).

The list is endorsed. A point of departure is the manner in which Fullan has confidence that sustainability can be achieved within 'tri-level' organisation in education: school level, district level, and system level, albeit with a change in role for those who serve. Why not two levels, one at which constitutional powers for education lie, the other the school, with a range of agencies, institutions, organisations and other entities—public and private— providing support? Such a possibility is a reality in some settings and is likely to be more probable, more generally, in the years ahead. For the increasing number of people who choose home schooling, there may be two levels, one 'constitutional', the other 'family'. Some might argue that these are the only two 'levels' under all circumstances! As will be described in several chapters, how and where leadership is exercised may change if the student is considered the key unit of organisation. On the other hand, there must be a starting point, and the current configuration in many countries is the 'tri-level' pattern that Fullan describes. The challenge is to imagine or re-imagine.

Other books provide valuable insights, notably *The Essentials of School Leadership* (Davies 2005), with contributions on leadership that is strategic, transformational, invitational, ethical, learner-centred, constructivist, poetical and political, emotional, entrepreneurial, distributed and sustainable. These contributions, along with those of Hedley Beare, Andy Hargreaves and Dean Fink, David Hargreaves, and Michael Fullan, each cited above, are in broad harmony with what unfolds in the pages that follow, even though the re-imagination of educational leaderships takes a different path in some instances.

This book is different

A book usually begins with a wish by an author to write a book. An outline is prepared and presented to a publisher who then contracts with the author, should there be a more or less assured market. In this instance, the author was commissioned to write three short publications, or pamphlets, for limited circulation among schools affiliated with what is now the Specialist Schools and Academies Trust in England. The commission was part of the author's role in International Networking for Educational Transformation. In each instance the pamphlets were to deal with a leading edge issue, provide accounts of good practice, serve as a resource for others who are searching for such accounts, and be short enough to be read from front to back in less than two hours. It was agreed that the first would provide an opportunity for the author to re-visit and update his work on self-managing schools. Decisions about the second and third were made after the first had been published. The first unveiled such exciting developments that a deeper exploration was warranted. The third followed a decision to go deeper still. It was only after the three limited circulation pamphlets were published that it was decided to bring them together, extending and updating, to provide a book for a wider audience that is the outcome of progressively deeper exploration of a theme of international significance.

In 2004 the author concluded two terms as Dean of Education at the University of Melbourne. In the decade before appointment in 1998, three books had been written on self-managing schools, that is, schools in systems of public education to which there had been decentralised significant authority and responsibility to make decisions while operating within a centrally-determined framework of goals, policies, standards and accountabilities (Caldwell and Spinks 1988; 1992; 1998). These books helped shape policy and practice in several countries, notably Australia, England and New Zealand. It made sense for the first pamphlet to re-visit the concept of the self-managing school and describe what had been accomplished over a decade or more.

Part A is titled 'Re-imagining the Self-Managing School', reflecting the finding that practice has gone far beyond the initial conception of the self-managing school to the point that it was time for the concept to catch up with its best practice. It draws from developments in several countries, notably Australia and especially England, but there is reference to promising developments in countries like Chile. The starting point in Chapter 2 on 'The Need to Re-imagine the Self-managing School' is an account of the models that guided early policy and practice in self-management. These had been honed from discussions in scores of workshops involving thousands of principals, teachers, parents and students over more than a decade. Evidence of the impact of self-management on learning outcomes is summarised. Chapter 3 explores the theme of 'Transformation'. Reference is made to the six scenarios for the future of schools developed in the OECD's Schooling for Tomorrow project. Chapter 4 is about 'Synergy', reflecting the finding that self-managing schools are not the stand-alone independent entities that critics had prematurely predicted. The best of these schools are characterised by an extraordinary capacity to seek support from a range of entities, public and private, and to link their work to other schools, locally, nationally and internationally, as they endeavour to secure high levels of achievement for all students. They were able to do so after being set free from dependence on centralised support services, although these continue to be valued when their primary orientation was service and support. Chapter 5 introduces the concept of 'Sagacity'. It describes how outstanding self-managing schools do not depend on teachers whose preparation is limited to initial teacher education. These schools go beyond the occasional in-service day to ensure that staff are up to date with their knowledge. They are powerful learning communities for their staff as well as their students. They network intensively with other schools to gain knowledge, share resources, and address problems and priorities of concern to all. 'The New Image of the Self-Managing School' emerges in Chapter 6. Ten elements are described and these constitute 'the new enterprise logic of schools', taking up a concept proposed by Zuboff and Maxmin (2004) for a range of organisations in the public and private sectors.

The findings of the review were like a lode of gold in the midst of an unrelenting effort to achieve the transformation of schools. It was decided to devote the second pamphlet to a deeper exploration of 'The New Enterprise Logic of Schools', and this is the theme of Part B. A different methodology was adopted. Nine workshops were conducted over nine weeks in four countries: Australia (1), Chile (2), England (5) and New Zealand (1). Schools that had achieved transformation, or were on their way, were invited to make a short presentation on an element of the new enterprise logic, the centre-piece of which was 'the student is the most important unit of organisation—not the classroom, not the school and not the school system'. Particular attention was given to synergy and sagacity. Except for Chile, these invitations were issued in advance so that presentations were relatively formal. In Chile, examples were volunteered during the workshops. Participants used an interactive technology to ensure that large numbers of responses and ideas were generated and analysed for subsequent reference. Chapter 7 is titled 'The New Enterprise', with enterprise selected as a richer concept than organisation. The new enterprise logic of schools is concerned with an undertaking that is difficult, complicated, and at times risky, often calling for daring activity which is at all times purposeful. The undertaking is coherent in its intent to achieve transformation. The remaining chapters in Part B are clustered around particular themes that invite the re-imagination of roles and responsibilities, with Chapter 8 concerned with 'The New School', Chapter 9 'The New System', Chapter 10 'The New Profession' and Chapter 11 'The New Leader'.

The findings in workshops that shaped Part B had an air of excitement about them, largely generated by leaders who made formal presentations and those that made contributions during the highly interactive discussions. It became apparent that engagement in change on the scale of transformation is an exhilarating experience, and this was selected as the theme for the third pamphlet, as extended and updated in Part C. Chapter 12 on 'Exhilarating Leadership' celebrates the achievements of schools in an era of dramatic change. Their contribution to building a capacity for creativity in the work force of the nation is highlighted. This is the good news. The bad news for school leaders is the heavy workload and high levels of stress.

New methodologies were adopted for Part C. One drew on a series of master classes at the University of Melbourne in late 2004 on 'Leadership for Transformation', a subject in the Master of School Leadership program. Exhilaration was an appropriate word to describe the leader's experience in the seven master classes led by the principals of schools that had been transformed in one way or another. Four were selected for report in Chapter 13 on 'Master Class'. Chapter 14 is based on a decision to listen to 'Leader Voice'. Five workshops were conducted over twelve weeks in two states of Australia in late 2005. Three simple questions were posed to participants, all of whom were principals or other school leaders. 'What aspects of your work are exhilarating?' 'What aspects of your work are boring, depressing, discouraging or dispiriting?' 'What actions by you or others would make your work as leader more exhilarating and less boring, depressing, discouraging or dispiriting?'

The findings in Chapters 13 and 14 are interpreted in Chapter 15 on 'Master Strategy' by three eminent leaders in education who have played an important role in the transformation of schools and school systems: Sir Iain Hall, former Head of Parrs Wood High School in England, now a consultant with the National College for School Leadership and the Specialist Schools and Academies Trust; Steve Marshall, Director of Education and Lifelong Learning in Wales and former Chief Executive, Department of Education and Children's Services in South Australia; and Jim Spinks, former school principal in Tasmania who pioneered the concept of the self-managing school, co-author of the trilogy on self-managing schools (Caldwell and Spinks 1988, 1992, 1998) and now international consultant on resourcing schools in the 21st century. A different meaning of 'master strategy' is also explored, with descriptions of the emerging role of 'system leader'. Chapter 16 on 'Going Global…Going Faster' outlines how schools are now part of a global learning community, in some ways reflecting the description by triple Pulitzer Prize-winning author Thomas Friedman, whose *The World is Flat* made the best-seller lists

(Friedman 2005). There is no possibility that the pace of change will be slower in the years ahead, so the findings on exhilarating leadership need to be taken to heart.

Who benefits?

Just as a new image of the self-managing school emerged at the conclusion of the review of developments around the world reported in Part A, so too did the elements of a new image of the educational leader when the workshops reported in Part C were completed. These elements are summarised in Chapter 17 on 'The New Image of the Educational Leader'. Implications are offered for policy and practice, including for ministers of education, those who work at the central level of a school system, principals of schools, and those who aspire to leadership in education. There are implications for professional bodies that represent the interests or address the needs of school leaders, as well as universities and other providers who seek to offer programs of relevance. There is much of interest to those who lead in private, independent or non-government schools that are non-systemic. The vision that underpins the new image and implications for policy and practice is an end to the air of depression that hangs over school leaders in many settings—to shift the balance to exhilaration and a different approach for those who lead at the system level, who are often battered from pillar to post as they seek to satisfy the often impossible demands of government or other authority, and are seemingly the subject of never-ending criticism from those at the school level. The beneficiaries are students and wider society as well as those who have the privilege to serve as leaders in education.

PART A

Re-imagining the self-managing school

CHAPTER 2

The need to re-imagine the self-managing school

It is time to re-imagine the self-managing school.

This statement may come as a surprise given that self-management has been embraced in so many places that it is now simply 'the way things are done around here'. Despite this acceptance, there are four reasons to re-visit the idea and 're-imagine the self-managing school'.

The first is that there have been two decades of experience in self-managing schools. What has been achieved in some instances goes far beyond the initial conception of the self-managing school to the point that it is time for the concept to catch up with its best practice. The second derives from changes in expectations for schools over these two decades. Nothing short of transformation is now expected, with transformation considered to be change—especially under challenging circumstances—that is significant, systematic and sustained, resulting in high levels of achievement for all students in all settings. It seems that every nation has adopted this expectation for its schools. It is an expectation that has not been met at any time in the history of education.

By themselves these are sufficient reasons to re-visit the concept. There is, however, a third more powerful and enduring reason that derives from change in the nature of the place called school. There are signs everywhere, and in greater number than ever before, that learners and learning have changed at a much faster rate than schools have changed—or could have changed—and that a new conception of school is taking shape. At the heart of the case for re-imagination is that henceforth the unit of organisation is the student—not the classroom, not the school and not the system—and that the 'self' in self-management is the student. The central theme is that self-management as conceived anew is critical to success in schools, whatever form they may take, in the early years of the 21st century. The fourth reason is that the merit of self-management is often challenged on the grounds that there is little evidence of impact, especially on learning. It is worthwhile to update the evidence.

Starting point

Re-imagining the self-managing school is the purpose of Part A, Chapters 2 to 6. The starting point is a description of the initial concept of the self-managing school as set out in a co-authored trilogy spanning a decade of experience in several nations. *The Self-Managing School* (Caldwell and Spinks 1988), *Leading the Self-Managing School* (Caldwell and Spinks 1992) and *Beyond the Self-Managing School* (Caldwell and Spinks 1998). The unifying theme was the self-managing school.

> A self-managing school is a school in a system of education to which there has been decentralised a significant amount of authority and responsibility to make decisions related to the allocation of resources within a centrally determined framework of goals, policies, standards and accountabilities. Resources are defined broadly to include knowledge, technology, power, material, people, time, assessment, information and finance (Caldwell and Spinks 1998, pp. 4–5).

Each book served two purposes. The first was to describe what was occurring in self-managing schools. The books were an account of changing times in the management of schools. The second was to draw from experience to provide guidelines for schools and school systems that sought to decentralise along the lines set out above. Chapter 2 provides a brief summary of the major themes of the three books as they addressed these two purposes. Evidence of impact is examined, especially the link between self-management and learning. It will then be explained how the best practice of self-management, combined with a heightened expectation for the transformation of schools, demands the re-imagination of the concept.

The self-managing school

The Self-Managing School (Caldwell and Spinks 1988) was published as momentum was gathering in several nations for decentralisation of authority and responsibility to the school level. That authority and responsibility could and should be decentralised was considered to be radical at the time. Indeed, the opening lines of the book suggested that the title would most likely be greeted with incredulity because the view that schools in systems of public education could manage themselves would be foreign to most readers. Such practice was to become a reality within months of publication because the Education Reform Act 1988 provided for the local management of schools in the United Kingdom. A very small number of school systems in Canada and the United States had already adopted the practice and New Zealand would follow within a year or so. The foundation had already been laid in some states of Australia, with Victoria embarking on a major initiative in the early 1980s, with further far-reaching change in the early 1990s.

Self-management was as contentious as it was radical, and a number of scholars were critical of the concept and the manner in which it was implemented. It was perceived by some to be a market-oriented reform that reflected a 'new right' or 'neo-conservative' ideology. Some of the steam was taken from this critique when the approach was maintained after a change in government in the nations with early experience in self-management. In Britain, for example, New Labour was elected in 1997 and not only maintained self-management but also extended it. The same was the case in Victoria, Australia when the Bracks Labor Government replaced the Kennett Coalition Government in 1999. A more constrained approach was sustained in New Zealand after a change in government from National to Labour. Decentralisation to the school level is now a major trend in most nations, with evidence from members of the Organisation for Economic Cooperation and Development (OECD) and the Asia Pacific Economic Cooperation (APEC) consortium reported in Chapter 6.

The initial model for self-management was based on the processes of management that should be developed if a school was to be successful in taking on a higher level of authority and responsibility. It was an outcome of a Project of National Significance funded by the Commonwealth Schools Commission in Australia. The Effective Resource Allocation in Schools Project was conducted in two states in 1983. Two sets of schools were identified on the basis of their reputation among knowledgeable people. One set consisted of schools that were deemed to be highly effective in a general sense; the other comprised schools considered to be highly effective in the manner in which they allocated their resources. Schools that were nominated in both sets were selected for detailed study. A model for self-management, derived from experience in one school, but reflecting practice in many, became the centrepiece of a training program from 1984 to 1986 for more than 5000 principals, teachers and parents, and in some cases students, in a three-year project to build capacity for self-management in the state of Victoria. The workshop program was subsequently refined and adapted for use in different settings, including England, Hong Kong and New Zealand, from 1988 to 1992. The model is illustrated in Figure 2.1.

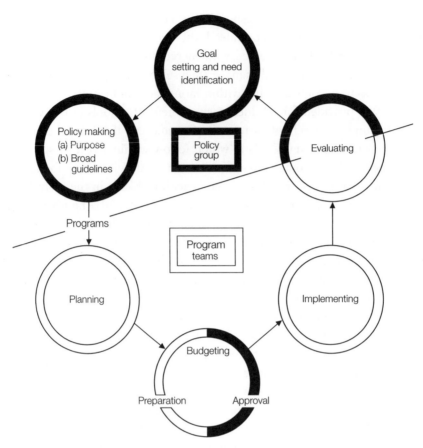

Figure 2.1: The original model for self-management
(Caldwell and Spinks 1988)

In summary, self-management was conceived as a cycle of management that called for schools to determine goals, formulate policies, make annual plans, allocate resources, implement plans of learning and teaching, and evaluate outcomes. Noteworthy features were plans based on programs that were defined by the normal patterns of work in the school, most of which were areas of the curriculum. There were clearly defined roles for different groups. The 'policy group' was normally the governing body, such as a school council, that set goals, formulated policies, approved budgets and shared in the conduct of program evaluations (shaded black in Figure 2.1). 'Program teams', formed mostly of teachers, were also involved in each of these activities, but were mainly responsible for preparing program plans and program budgets. Programs were implemented in the normal day-to-day work of the school. These teams played a major role in the evaluation of programs.

At first sight, some two decades after it was constructed, the model seems a straightforward, sensible approach to management. It was, however, relatively novel at the time of its formulation. It proved a boon when schools were expected to assume a much higher level of responsibility. It is also noteworthy that the model anticipated the now widely embraced concept of 'distributed leadership'. An early Australian version of the book (Caldwell and Spinks 1986) was sub-titled 'A Guide to Collaborative School Management' because the model called for widely dispersed leadership among teams of teachers and others with a stake in the various programs of the school.

Leading the self-managing school

Leading the Self-Managing School (Caldwell and Spinks 1992) drew from experience in several nations after the first book made its appearance in 1988. Particular attention was given to four kinds of leadership: cultural, strategic, educational and responsive. The concept of transformation was introduced, but it was a more constrained view of transformation than is currently in vogue. It was transformation of a system of public education to accommodate and draw on the success of the self-managing school, rather than transformation that was change on a scale that would lead to high levels of achievement for all students in all settings.

By the late 1980s and early 1990s schools were expected to develop plans for improvement. Apart from some changes in wording, the model for self-management was refined to accommodate a more strategic approach, as illustrated in Figure 2.2.

In the refined view of self-management, the initial model was included as the annual management cycle, embedded in a three- to five-year management strategy that included the preparation of a school development/improvement plan. Based on early experience in New Zealand, the concept of a school charter was proposed, this being a document to which a public authority, such as a government, and the governing body of a school, such as a council, gave assent. It contained a summary of the centrally determined framework of goals, policies, curriculum, standards and accountabilities; an outline of the means by which the school addressed this framework, along with any local adaptations; an account of the school's mission, vision, priorities and programs, together with an overview of the strategies to be followed in addressing them; reference to key decision-making processes and approaches to program evaluation—all reflecting the culture of the school and an intended pattern of action in the medium to longer term. Once approved, the charter provided the basis for allocating resources and monitoring outcomes. School charters along these lines became part of the approach to self-managing schools in Victoria.

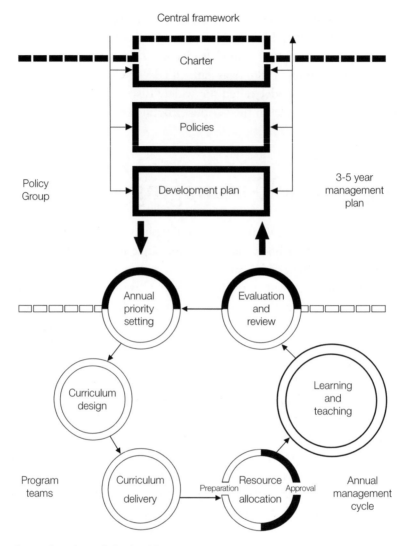

Central framework

Charter

Policies

Development plan

Policy
Group

3-5 year
management
plan

Annual
priority
setting

Evaluation
and
review

Curriculum
design

Learning
and
teaching

Program
teams

Curriculum
delivery

Preparation

Resource
allocation

Approval

Annual
management
cycle

Figure 2.2 The refined model of self-management
(Caldwell and Spinks 1992)

Beyond the self-managing school

Beyond the Self-Managing School (Caldwell and Spinks 1998) described how self-management was one of three tracks for change that were evident at the close of the 20th century. The image of 'track' was selected because there were three kinds of change occurring at the same time, with differences in the distance each school, school system or nation had moved in the direction of change, or how far down each track they had progressed.

Track 1 was 'building systems of self-managing schools', reflecting international developments at the time.

Track 2 was described as an 'unrelenting focus on learning outcomes'. Governments were unrelenting in their concern that all students should learn well, an outcome that called for success in programs in early literacy as well as programs that assisted in the transition from primary to secondary and in the increasingly complex arrangements at senior secondary.

Track 3 was described as 'creating schools for the knowledge society'. At the time of writing, it was not possible to describe in detail what this might entail, although elements were starting to emerge in different places. Instead, a vision was presented and this was illustrated in a *gestalt*—a perceived organised whole that is more than the sum of its parts—as contained in Figure 2.3 and summarised below (Caldwell and Spinks 1998, pp. 13–14).

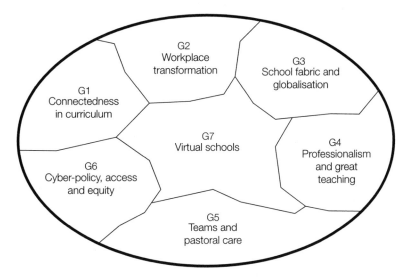

Figure 2.3 A vision for schooling for the knowledge society
(Caldwell and Spinks 1998)

▸ Dramatic change in approaches to learning and teaching is in store as electronic networking allows the 'cutting across' of subject boundaries so 'challenging the very idea' of them, and 'changing the emphasis from impersonal curriculum to excited live exploration' (Papert 1993) (G1 Connectedness in curriculum).

▸ Schools as workplaces are transformed in every dimension, including the scheduling of time for learning, rendering obsolete most approaches that derive from an industrial age (G2 Workplace transformation).

- The fabric of schooling is similarly rendered obsolete. Everything from building design to the size, shape, alignment, and furnishing of space for the 'knowledge worker' in the school is transformed. In one sense the school has no walls, for there are global learning networks, and much of the learning that calls for the student to be located at school is occurring in many places—at home and, at the upper years of secondary schooling and for life-long learning, in the work place. (G3 School fabric and globalisation).

- A wide range of professionals and para-professionals support learning in an educational parallel similar to the diversity of support that may be found in modern health care. The role of teacher is elevated, for it demands wisdom, judgement, and a facility to manage learning in modes more complex and varied than ever. The teacher is freed from the impossible task of designing from their own resources learning experiences to challenge every student: the resources of the world's great teachers will be at hand (G4 Professionalism and great teaching).

- A capacity to work in teams is more evident in approaches to learning, given the primacy of the work team in every formulation of the workplace in the knowledge society. The concept of 'pastoral care' of students is as important as ever for learning in this mode, and in schools that quite literally have no boundaries (G5 Teams and pastoral care).

- Spender's (1995) challenge to formulate 'cyber-policy of the future' is a priority. Issues of access and equity drive public debate until such time as prices fall to make electronic networks as common as the telephone or radio, and that may soon be a reality, given trends in networked computers (G6 Cyber-policy, access and equity).

- The concept of the virtual organisation or the learning network organisation is a reality in the knowledge society. Schools take on many of the characteristics of such organisations, given that learning occurs in so many modes and from so many sources, and is all networked electronically (G7 Virtual schools).

What was described as a vision, and presented in a *gestalt*, has become a reality in many respects. Transformation is an accurate word to describe what has occurred in those schools and schools systems where each of the elements has come to realisation, and where the outcomes include high levels of achievement for all students in all settings. Some self-managing schools have been transformed in a manner that points to the need to re-imagine the concept of the self-managing school.

Much of *Beyond the Self-Managing School* was devoted to illustrations of practice as schools and school systems moved down the three tracks for change. Guidelines were presented in the form of 100 strategic intentions. The following are illustrations of strategic intentions drawn from a set of 10 that were formulated (Caldwell and Spinks 1998, pp. 222–3) as guides for the transformation of learning:

- Approaches to learning and teaching will change to accommodate the reality that every student in every setting will have a laptop or hand-held computer, making the new learning technologies as much a part of the learning scene as books have been since the advent of systems of public education.

- Subject boundaries will be broken and learning will be integrated across the curriculum as the new learning technologies become universal, challenging rigidity in curriculum and standards frameworks, without removing either the need for learning in discrete areas or learning that spans the whole.

- Rigidity in roles, relationships and approaches to school and classroom organisation will be broken down, with multiple but rewarding roles for teachers and other professionals, more flexibility in the use of time, and abandonment of narrow specifications of class size that are rendered meaningless in the new workplace arrangements.

- School buildings designed for the industrial age will be redesigned to suit the needs of the knowledge society.

- Schools will be adept at analysing the relationship between function, form and culture in school design, helping to bring to realisation a design that contributes to making schools exciting and uplifting places of work for staff and students.

Impact of self-management

As far as a description of practice is concerned, 'self-management' is preferred to 'school-based management' or 'site-based management'. This is because school-based or site-based management are the preferred terms in Canada and the United States where the approach has a much narrower connotation. Michael Fullan is critical: 'Local autonomy, whether it is the "let the thousand flowers bloom variety" or site-based management within a framework of external accountability, does not produce results on any scale' (Fullan 2005, p. 13). It is a valid comment if it refers to school-based or site-based management where management is not connected to learning. It is not valid for the self-managing school where a connection to learning is designed assiduously, made effective, and sustained. Providing such a connection is made, it certainly produces results on a large scale, as evidenced in the most comprehensive studies of international student achievement ever conducted, namely, the Program for International Student Assessment (PISA) and Trends in Mathematics and Science Study (TIMSS).

Ludger Woessmann, formerly at the University of Kiel and now Head of the Department of Human Capital and Structural Change at the Ifo Institute for Economics in Munich, undertook a comprehensive study of why students in some countries did better in TIMSS, and found a powerful connection between decentralisation of decision-making at the school level and student achievement (Woessmann 2001). It is a connection that has been affirmed in subsequent results in PISA. Andreas Schleicher, Head of the Indicators and Analysis Division at OECD, identified decentralisation as one of several policy levers for student achievement. He found that, in the best performing countries:

▸ Decentralised decision-making is combined with devices to ensure a fair distribution of substantive educational opportunities.

▸ The provision of standards and curricula at national/sub-national levels is combined with advanced evaluation systems.

▸ Process-oriented assessments and/or centralised final examinations are complemented with individual reports and feedback mechanisms on student learning progress.

▸ Schools and teachers have explicit strategies and approaches for teaching heterogeneous groups of learners.

▸ Students are offered a variety of extra-curricular activities.

▸ Schools offer differentiated support structures for students.

▸ Institutional differentiation is introduced, if at all, at later stages.

▸ Effective support systems are located at individual school level or in specialised support institutions.

▸ Teacher training schemes are selective.

▸ The training of pre-school personnel is closely integrated with the professional development of teachers.

▸ Continuing professional development is a constitutive part of the system.

▸ Special attention is paid to the professional development of school management personnel (Schleicher 2004).

A review of research suggests that there have been three generations of studies and it is only in the third that evidence of the impact of decentralisation on outcomes has emerged, and then only when certain conditions are fulfilled. The first generation was in times when impact on outcomes was not a primary or even secondary purpose. The second generation was when such purposes may have been to the fore but the database was weak. The third, emerging in the late 1990s and gathering momentum in the early 2000s, coincides with a pre-eminent concern for learning outcomes and the development of a strong database. Studies by Woessmann and Schleicher and other research reported by the author (Caldwell and Spinks 1998; Caldwell 2002; Caldwell 2003; Caldwell 2005a) are examples of the third generation of studies.

An important implication is that school leaders should be aware that self-management does not necessarily have an impact on the learning outcomes of students, and they should make every effort to ensure that mechanisms for making the connection are in place in different areas of school operations.

Re-imagining the self-managing school

The initial model of the management process (Figure 2.1) is still a useful guide to capacities that ought to be developed in a self-managing school. The refined model (Figure 2.2) that embedded an annual cycle in a multi-year management strategy is as necessary now as it was in the 1990s. The strategic intentions for schools and school systems as they move down the three tracks of change continue to be relevant. Elements in the vision or *gestalt* (Figure 2.3) have come to realisation. However, there is a need to re-imagine the self-managing school. The reasons were stated in summary form at the start of the chapter and are expanded at this point.

What has been achieved beyond the initial conception of the self-managing school means it is now time for the concept to catch up with its best practice. The initial concept was sharply constrained, even though it was viewed as radical at the time. It referred to the movement of authority and responsibility from one level of a school system (centre) to another level (school) in a vertical line or continuum of the distribution of authority and responsibility. While governing bodies such as school councils were envisaged, there was little to suggest that a more powerful connection of the school to its wider community was desirable let alone necessary. A feature of successful experience and a key element in the re-imagination of the self-managing school is the connections that schools and school systems must make with other organisations and institutions—public and private—in education and non-education settings. Expressed another way, there must be a horizontal network of relationships in addition to a vertical continuum of authority and responsibility.

The second reason derives from changes in expectations for schools. Nothing short of transformation is now expected. The third reason is challenging, if not confronting. The change that is 'significant, systematic and sustained' in the view of transformation presented in these pages may be so dramatic that the school as a place for learners and learning is itself transformed, possibly to the point that its future configuration will be unrecognisable. The work on scenarios in the OECD's Schooling for Tomorrow Project includes such a possibility (OECD 2001). These scenarios are explored in Chapter 3. In the United States the legislated meaning of 'school' now extends beyond a formal organisation of that name to accommodate home schooling, which is one of several approaches to education for young people that respond to the following trend:

In the early twentieth century, public education was a defining characteristic of the new mass order. Primary and secondary education was intended to be a public good, not an object of consumption. But by the end of that century, new individuals had begun seeking approaches to education that reflected their demands for psychological self-determination. These have led to some significant innovations in the public school system . . . but for most of the educational organisations of the old mass order, the new demands have been almost impossible to meet. As a result, individuals have increasingly turned towards new forms of consumption that enable them to take their own (educational) lives in their own hands (Zuboff and Maxmin 2004, p. 150).

The implications for schools and the way they are managed are profound, and self-management takes on a new meaning under these conditions. At the heart of the case for a new image of the self-managing school is the scale of transformation of society. Chapter 3 takes up the story.

CHAPTER 3

Transformation

Transformation is change—especially under challenging circumstances—that is significant, systematic and sustained, resulting in high levels of achievement for all students in all settings. It seems that every nation is signing up to an agenda for change along these lines. It is an agenda that has not been successfully implemented at any time in the history of education as far as outcomes are concerned, hence the choice of the concept of transformation.

The statement that the agenda has not been implemented at any time in the history of education is sobering but it should not be overwhelming. Progress in some schools and schools systems suggests that it is not an impossible dream. Nevertheless, to take up the agenda and succeed will require boldness in design and quality in execution. This is the view of Sir Michael Barber, writing as head of the Prime Minister's Delivery Unit in the United Kingdom (now at McKinsey). According to Barber (2004), a timid reform that is well executed may result in improved outcomes but not transformation. A bold reform that is poorly executed will be controversial but will have little impact. There will be no change at all if the reform is timid and poorly implemented.

The purpose of Chapter 3 is to set the agenda for transformation in schools in the context of expectations for change in society at large, explore a range of scenarios for the future of schools, examine some promising developments in educational policy, and discern the major features of the new image of the self-managing school.

Schools in a time of transformation

Writing in 1993, Peter Drucker declared that 'Every few hundred years in Western history there occurs a sharp transformation…Within a few short decades, society rearranges itself—its world view; its basic values; its social and political structures; its arts; its key institutions. Fifty years later, there is a new world...We are currently living through such a transformation' (Drucker 1993, p. 1).

According to Drucker, the implications for schools are profound: 'As knowledge becomes the resource of post-capitalist society, the social position of the school as "producer" and "distributive channel" of knowledge, and its monopoly, are both bound to be challenged. And some of the competitors are bound to succeed...Indeed, no other institution faces challenges as radical as those that will transform the school' (Drucker 1993, p. 209).

It is fair to say that there is now general acceptance that societal change on the scale of transformation is well under way. There is indeed a global economy. It is a knowledge society. There is much evidence of a 'clash of civilisations and a remaking of the world order' (Huntington 2002). Not all are comfortable with what is occurring.

Writing in 1994, David Hargreaves declared that 'schools are still modelled on a curious mix of the factory, the asylum and the prison' and that 'many of the hitherto taken-for-granted assumptions about schools must now be questioned' (Hargreaves D 1994, pp. 43, 3). Hedley Beare has predicted that 'from what we know already about the twenty-first century, it is clear that the traditional school has no chance of surviving in it, at least not in the developed economies' (Beare 2003, p. 635). A key issue for consideration is the extent to which schools and school systems are responding to Drucker's challenge, Hargreaves's critique and Beare's prediction.

The heart of the matter

The idea that schools should be transformed is now expressed quite freely and there are many claims to achievement of such an outcome. Closer examination reveals that, while some important changes have been made, there are few experiences that can lay claim to the outcome being 'significant, systematic and sustained' and even fewer to having an impact that has resulted in 'high levels of achievement for all students in all settings'. Moreover, and for the most part, schools still look very much like they have for decades, if recent developments in information and communications are taken out of the picture.

The flight from public to private schools and the trend to home schooling suggests that there is a loss of trust in public education. Zuboff and Maxmin paint the scene for the United States: 'The increased popularity of private schools is another sign of the defection from the mass consumption of education. The reasons are fundamentally the same as those for animate home-schoolers. Parents want their children to be recognised and treated as individuals. Private schools promise lower pupil-to-teacher ratios, smaller class size, more access to teachers, more flexibility, and greater opportunity to exercise voice over a child's educational experience...While private schools' fees have never been higher, their waiting lists have never been longer' (Zuboff and Maxmin 2004, p. 152).

There is fragility in Australia's system of public education. In its analysis of findings in surveys conducted for the Fairfax Press, the Australian Council for Educational Research (ACER) found that about one-third of parents whose children attend public schools would prefer to enrol them in private schools. This is serious given that about one-third already attends private schools, with the proportion exceeding 40 per cent and rising at the senior secondary level in Victoria (findings reported in *The Age* and *Sydney Morning Herald* on 10 August 2004). There is a danger that public schools will become safety-net schools of last resort within a decade.

At the heart of the matter is the importance of personalising the learning experience. As noted above: 'parents want their children to be recognised and treated as individuals' (Zuboff and Maxmin 2004, p. 152). Peters's call to re-imagine the school cited in Chapter 1 was based on the view that 'Teachers need enough time and flexibility to get to know kids as individuals. Teaching is about one and only one thing: Getting to know the child' (Peters 2003, p. 284).

The case for transformation through personalisation has been made in the UK in the *Five-Year Strategy for Children and Learners* (DfES 2004a). Charles Clarke, former Secretary of State for Education and Skills, described the scale of the change that has occurred since the landmark reforms of 1944 and what is contemplated in the years ahead.

> Over the last 60 years, a fundamental recasting of industry, employment, technology and society, has transformed the requirement for education and training—not only driving the education system, but introducing new ideas about lifelong learning, personalised education, and self-directed learning. And the story has been of taking a system designed to deliver a basic minimum entitlement and elaborating it to respond to these increasingly sophisticated (and rapidly changing) demands...
>
> The central characteristic of such a new system will be personalisation—so that the system fits the individual rather than the individual having to fit the system. This is not a vague liberal notion of letting people have what they want. It is about having a system which will genuinely give high standards for all—the best possible quality of children's services, which recognises individual needs and circumstances; the most effective teaching at school which builds a detailed picture of what each child already knows and how they learn, to help them go further; and, as young people begin to train for work, a system that recognises individual aptitudes and provides as many tailored paths to employment as there are people and jobs. And the corollary of this is that the system must be freer and more diverse—with more flexibility to help meet individual needs; and more choices between courses and types of providers, so that there really are different and personalised opportunities available (DfES 2004a, p. 4).

The five-year strategy contains a range of approaches to personalising learning, including the use of information and communications technology, individualised assessment for diagnosis, the planning of learning experiences for each student, and the provision of children's services to support the work of teachers as they endeavour to meet the needs of each learner.

New ideas about service and support

The call for personalisation in learning has its counterpart in health and in most other fields of service and support in both public and private sectors. Zuboff and Maxmin (2004) described these developments and proposed a 'new enterprise logic' that has a counterpart in education. The focus on the individual is an outcome of success in an earlier era of enterprise, and individuals are now giving voice to their desire for self-determination. It is an international phenomenon.

> These new voices rise from the United States to the United Kingdom, from Canada to New Zealand, and across Western Europe. They have gathered force in the offices and classrooms of Santiago, Istanbul, and Prague. They form a new society of individuals who share a claim to psychological self-determination—an abiding sense that they are entitled to make themselves (Zuboff and Maxmin 2004, p. 93).

As further illustration in another setting, the former head of the Department of Prime Minister and Cabinet in Australia Michael Keating made the following observation in *Who Rules? How Government Retains Control of a Privatised Economy*:

> The reforms of public administration affecting service delivery stemmed fundamentally from public dissatisfaction with many of the services provided. The major problems were their lack of responsiveness to the particular needs of the individual client or customer…society has become more educated and wealthy and its individual members have developed greater independence and become more individualistic…This individualistic society is both more demanding and more critical of service provision (Keating 2004, p. 77).

This focus on the individual does not mean that concern for the common good is abandoned. It is the proper role of government to be concerned with the common good. As Keating observed: 'there has to be a reinterpretation of the notion of equity as a guiding principle for the delivery of public services', away from uniformity toward the differentiation of services, 'with the assistance provided varying according to each recipient's particular needs' (Keating 2004, p. 78).

Zuboff and Maxmin (2004, p. 94) suggest that the 'old enterprise logic' persists and that its rules are 'woefully inadequate when it comes to responding to the realities of life in the new society of individuals'. Moreover:

The old organisations have become sufficiently insulated and self-congratulatory to ignore the chasm that has formed between their practices, invented for a mass society, and the new society it has spawned. This insularity has afflicted political and civic organisations and is an important explanation for their loss of membership and declining level of active participation…We conclude that the new individuals are being blamed for the problems of the old organisations, when the facts suggest the opposite. It is not the new individuals who have failed the old organisations, but rather the old organisations that have failed the new individuals…When the old clothes no longer fit, make new ones (Zuboff and Maxmin 2004, pp. 116–17).

As noted earlier in the chapter, Zuboff and Maxmin include education in their critique. As far as health care is concerned, they cite increasing 'self-care' over conventional doctor–patient relationships, noting that 52 million Americans or 55 per cent of those with access are using the Internet to gather information about medical matters (Zuboff and Maxmin 2004, p. 154).

Valerie Hannon, director of the Innovation Unit of the Department for Education and Skills in the UK, has applied the argument of Zuboff and Maxmin to needs in the school sector:

Because in recent years people have changed more than the institutions that support them, there is currently enormous dissatisfaction with both private and public service provision. We are just beginning to see a tidal shift in how institutions relate to the people they serve…If consumers are to feel confident that services can deliver what they need, those services must be configured around the needs of the individual, not a supposedly homogenous mass…Service providers will have to ask: 'Who are you, and what do you need?' Then, figure provision based on actual demand…This principle will apply as much to the world of education. We are already seeing public commitments by government to offer more 'choice' in education, particularly to parents, but also to learners in the form of personalised learning (Hannon 2004, p. 304).

Charles Leadbeater explored the possibilities for personalisation of learning in a pamphlet published jointly by the independent think tank Demos, the National College for School Leadership and the Innovation Unit of the Department for Education and Skills (Leadbeater 2004). He invited the reader to consider 'services' as 'scripts'. He believes that 'all public services are delivered according to a script, which directs the parts played by the actors involved' and contends that 'many of the scripts followed by public services—such as schooling—have not changed for decades':

Choose what to study from a pre-defined and delineated set of options; sit with 20–30 other learners; learn from your teacher, who has to deliver set amounts of content often in a particular style; sit some exams; have your learning assessed by an examiner; get your results; move on to the next stage; do it all again…So, if education is a script, how can it be re-written so that the service is more responsive to the user? (Leadbeater 2004, p. 7)

The OECD scenarios

An important issue is the extent to which there has been serious engagement with the scale of transformation and new ideas about service and support. An example of such engagement is the work of the Organisation for Economic Cooperation and Development (OECD) and its Schooling for Tomorrow project that led to the formulation of scenarios for the future of schools (OECD 2001). The starting point was a conference on 'Schooling for Tomorrow' in Rotterdam in November 2000 that involved ministers and senior officers of education systems. Further work with representatives of key stakeholders resulted in six scenarios.

A comprehensive scan of internal and external environments for schools provided the foundation for this work. For the external environment, consideration was given to childhood, generational issues and the ageing society; gender and family; knowledge, technology and work; lifestyles, consumption and inequality; and geo-political dimensions—local, national and international. The internal environment was analysed in terms of existing robust school systems; trends in the development of schools as learning organisations; issues related to evaluation, assessment and certification; and teachers and teacher policies.

The six scenarios described the possible strategic directions for schools over 10–15 years, with two maintaining the status quo, two involving re-schooling, and two resulting in de-schooling. The following is a brief account of the major features of each. It summarises a revised version of the initial formulation (Istance 2003, Chapter 62).

Maintaining the status quo

Of the two scenarios that attempt to maintain the status quo, one was that 'bureaucratic systems continue', with pressure to sustain uniformity and resist radical change, even in the face of critical commentary. Schools remain distinct entities. Efforts to change are countered by claims that equality of opportunity would be threatened and that important roles for schools related to socialisation would be jeopardised. Curriculum and qualifications would remain centralised and student assessment is the key element in accountability frameworks. The classroom and the teacher remain the key units of organisation. There is an emphasis on efficiency, and national and state/provincial departments maintain their roles despite pressures for decentralisation. Teachers are civil servants, and union and professional associations remain strong.

Teachers leaving the profession without replacement characterise the second scenario that endeavours to maintain the status quo. This is the 'meltdown scenario'. Not all school systems or parts of school systems would experience a crisis in this regard. There would be severe teacher shortages in some settings and this would limit capacity to deliver the curriculum. Crisis management would often prevail and a fortress mentality would be evident. The international market for quality teachers would be strengthened. Remuneration for teachers would increase in an effort to sustain the profession.

Many of the characteristics of these scenarios are evident in several nations. There is certainly a sense of crisis and a fortress mentality in some urban settings, especially at the secondary level.

Re-schooling

The re-schooling scenarios see an increase in public support for schools and a new status for the profession. The 'schools as core social centres' scenario would see the school playing an important role in building a sense of community and creating social capital. A range of cooperative arrangements between schools and other agencies, institutions and organisations will be evident. There would be a broadening of the curriculum and more non-formal learning. Management of such enterprises would be more complex and leadership would be widely dispersed. Local decision-making will be important but national and international frameworks of support will be utilised. Additional resources will be secured to upgrade facilities. A core of teachers will enjoy high status but a range of persons from other professions will be involved in different contractual arrangements to support schools.

The second re-schooling scenario sees a strengthening of schools as 'focused learning organisations', with emphasis on a knowledge rather than social agenda. Specialisations and diversity will flourish as will research on different pedagogies. Management involves flatter organisation structures and the building of teams and networks that draw on a range of expertise. There are high levels of investment in infrastructure, especially in disadvantaged settings. There is extensive use of ICT and partnerships with tertiary education and other institutions involved in knowledge creation and dissemination. Teachers enjoy high status as professionals, with substantial engagement in research and development as well as continuous professional learning. Much of the latter is in networks, including international networks. There is diversity and mobility in employment arrangements.

These two scenarios are invariably rated the most desirable among stakeholders. There is strong interest in the schools as 'core social centres' scenario that is consistent with the notion of a 'full-service school'. There is considerable momentum for schools as 'focused learning organisations', especially in the UK, with the shift from comprehensive to specialist secondary schools now well past the tipping point and there are many networks of primary and secondary schools.

De-schooling

Increasing dissatisfaction with the formal institution of the school results in the weakening of schools and school systems and, in varying degrees, leads to the 'de-schooling' scenarios. One is known as 'learning networks and the network society' in which dissatisfaction and demand for more diversified approaches to learning results in a weakening of the formal institution of the school. This scenario is clearly supported by the powerful capacities for learning now possible through ICT. Home schooling flourishes in this scenario. Schools may continue but in networks that together furnish the services that are required. Different governance arrangements prevail but there will be a requirement that certain public obligations are met in the interests of access and equity. There will be a diminution of the teaching profession as it is currently understood but a range of new learning professionals will emerge. There is much in this scenario that resonates with interest in personalising learning, as manifested in the loss of trust in schools as currently constituted that was described earlier in the chapter.

The second de-schooling scenario is described as 'extending the market model'. It is also consistent with the loss of trust described above, as an increasing number of parents see schooling as a private good. The market for different approaches to learning flourishes, with different providers furnishing information on a range of indicators to attract customers. There is a greatly reduced role for public authorities that may be limited to market regulation more than provision. New learning professionals emerge. There is clearly potential for substantial inequities as far as access is concerned.

Global application

These scenarios have application beyond the OECD. The Pacific Circle Consortium (PCC) examined their relevance in the Asia-Pacific region. More than 300 senior education officials and policy-makers in 11 societies were surveyed (Cogan and Baumgart 2003). Respondents were from Australia, China, China Hong Kong, Chinese Taipei, Japan, Korea, Mexico, New Zealand, Thailand, United States of America and Vietnam. They were asked to rank each of the six scenarios on a scale of 1 (high) to 6 (low) for desirability and probability. 'Schools as focused learning organisations' and 'schools as core social centres', in that order, were considered to be the most desirable. However, the most probable were the first of the status quo scenarios—'bureaucratic systems continue' followed by the second of the de-schooling scenarios 'extending the market model'.

There are noteworthy examples of the re-schooling scenarios in settings outside the OECD network. Two schools in Chile warrant particular mention, one as a 'focused learning organisation' and the other as a 'core social centre'. The former is reflected in the work of the Maria Luisa Mombal School located in a high socio-economic setting in the Santiago suburb of Vitacura. It caters for about 520 students from pre-school to upper secondary. It is a public school but is unique in Chile in that teachers manage it. This arrangement followed an invitation from the municipal government for organisations to bid for the right to manage the school. It was a company of teachers at the school that won the bid. In addition to this feature, it is special in another sense because the teachers decided to outsource all services not directly related to teaching and the support of teaching. Teachers have developed the curriculum of the school and priority has been given to personalising learning. Evaluation at the end of primary and secondary has been outsourced. The school networks with other schools in its district, including private schools. There is a high degree of financial flexibility under a special waiver of the municipal government. The principal of the school is Nilda Sotelo Sorribes and she is able to focus her energies almost exclusively on educational leadership, given the outsourcing arrangements described above, but there is a tight connection in her work between financial management and educational leadership. The school has received a Ministry of Education Award for Excellence in Teaching each year since 2000 and is one of the few schools in the country that has been certified by Fundación Chile for the quality of its management.

An example of a school as 'core social centre' is Escuela Básica No. 1577 in the Commune of El Bosque, a highly disadvantaged community in Santiago. The school is a member of the Dagoberto Godoy network of schools that is privately owned but publicly subsidised. There are about 2150 students from pre-school to Grade 8. Its location is unsafe and that explains the building's six metre walls that suggest a prison rather than a school. Once inside the safe environment of the school, the students enjoy a friendly and supportive culture that leads to a high level of engagement in learning. Parents are involved in the School–Family Strategic Alliance that includes a high level of involvement of parents in classroom activities. Other alliances have been forged with the National Council for Narcotics Control, the Peace and Justice Service, and the Centre for Educational Research and Development that has supported a privately funded mathematics and science program entitled Active Minds. Levels of achievement have risen steadily in recent years. The school has the highest number of teachers accredited by the Ministry of Education for pedagogical excellence of any school in Chile and, like the Maria Luisa Bombal School, has been certified by Fundación Chile for the quality of its management. The principal of the school is Claudio Alejandro Barriga Nova who holds the degree of Master of School Management. He attributes the success of the school to a range of factors, including the alignment of educational and management initiatives, as acknowledged in the certification by Fundación Chile.

Next steps

Work continues in the Schooling for Tomorrow project of OECD. Studies in five nations will be utilised to construct a 'toolbox' to assist policy-makers and practitioners at all levels to develop their own scenarios. The National College for School Leadership (NCSL) in England refined the scenarios to a set of four for 2030 (Bentley and Miller 2003). These were labelled 'supply diversity', 'modernising the factory', 'learning benchmark', and 'learning broker'.

There is a clear preference in the different projects for one or other of the re-schooling scenarios. Istance (2003, p. 630) suggests that 'some very powerful obstacles must be over-come' to bring these preferences to realisation. He identified six areas of concern: bureaucracy, resources, public attitudes, teachers, knowledge management, and communities and social capital. His comment about public attitudes is particularly powerful:

> How near is the general consensus so important to re-schooling—that schools are central
> societal institutions warranting high esteem and the end to carping criticism? Or will the
> underlying assumptions of the other scenarios prove to be more realistic—constant
> grumbling and the unwillingness to countenance significant change (status quo) or
> widespread dissatisfaction leading to flight and partial dismantling of school systems
> (de-schooling)? In the context of an ageing society, there is also the open question of how
> an increasingly potent elderly population prioritises education compared with, say, health
> policies (Istance 2003, p. 650).

Promising developments in the UK

The United Kingdom provides the best illustration of a government that has made a commitment to transformation and has made important progress in achieving it. Elements in the strategy include the focus on personalisation, a shift from comprehensive to specialist schools, an expanded role for the private sector, progress in the remodelling of the teaching profession, and leadership development on a scale that has no counterpart. The most significant of these is the involvement of the private sector. This is, at first sight, a paradox given that the aim is to achieve transformation in the public sector.

There are five initiatives in the UK involving the private sector that, with suitable adaptation, would reinvigorate public education in other places. The first was to move in barely a decade from the comprehensive model to a specialist model in the delivery of secondary education. By January 2006, 2502 of about 3170 secondary schools were offering at least one of ten specialisations: arts, technology, languages, sports, business and enterprise, engineering, mathematics and computing, science, humanities and music. An eleventh specialism of special education needs was announced in December 2005. Each school is required to secure cash or in-kind support from the private sector to obtain additional funding from government, and this support is often drawn from industries connected to these specialisations.

The outcome is that specialist schools outperform non-specialist schools on value-added measures in all socio-economic settings, with the highest rate of improvement in schools in challenging circumstances (Jesson 2004). In GCSE results in 2005, 59.4 per cent of students in specialist schools received five good passes compared to 48 per cent of students in non-specialist schools. This is arguably the most significant development in secondary education to be found in any system of public education.

The second initiative lies in re-invigorating secondary schools in urban settings through the creation of what are known in the UK as 'academies'. The government plans to create 200 academies based on successful experience in about 30. The initiative calls for the re-building of schools and the creation of state-of-the-art learning environments. The government established the Academy Sponsors Trust (a role now carried out by the Specialist Schools and Academies Trust) to secure private sponsorship of £2 million for each school, with government providing funds in the range £20–28 million. There is bi-partisan political support.

The experience of the Bexley Business Academy is impressive if not inspirational. Formerly the Thamesmead Community College, there were low levels of achievement, and few teachers were willing to stay or seek appointment to work in sub-standard facilities. The school was re-built with extensive support from the private sector and a substantial injection of funds from the public purse. It is privately managed. Achievement levels have soared and there are waiting lists of students and teachers. Gaps in achievement between boys and girls have narrowed.

The third initiative is the creation of public private partnerships in the refurbishment or replacement of schools. Started by the Thatcher Conservative Government, the scheme has been extended by the Blair Labour Government, with the result that state-of-the-art facilities are making their appearance in some settings years before they would otherwise have been addressed in the seemingly endless waiting list of publicly funded capital works programs. An impressive project in the UK was in Glasgow where virtually all secondary schools have been replaced or refurbished in the last decade.

The fourth area for private engagement is the creation of networks of social entrepreneurs to support the work of public schools. A notable example is the Community Action Network (CAN) that links about 750 agencies, institutions and organisations in the public and private sectors. A CAN Academy Model has been developed to provide support for academies. There are few counterparts in other nations, although there are notable examples of individual schools that have created their own networks along these lines.

Each of these four initiatives is an instance of creating social capital in support of public education. It is interesting to make a comparison with Australia where the social capital of public schools is relatively weak. It is noteworthy that social capital in support of public schools was also weak when the Blair Labour Government came to power in 1997. It is fair to say that the level of support in each setting was comparable in 1997 yet the UK has moved ahead in dramatic fashion.

To a large extent the explanation lies in the level of trust in the private sector for what governments are undertaking in the field of public education. Trust is relatively low in Australia. Expressed simply, the private sector is unwilling to give substantial cash or in-kind support to public schools in Australia because it does not have faith that there will be a major contribution to the public good. The contrast with the UK could not be starker, where a government led by a prime minister whose advocacy has been unrelenting, assembling a coherent, comprehensive and credible program for the transformation of public education.

The final example is related to serious engagement in the UK with an agenda for personalising learning that responds to the aspiration of parents, and with the six scenarios for the future of schools developed by OECD. As noted in previous pages, surveys around the world reveal that most stakeholders prefer the re-schooling scenarios. However, lack of engagement that includes a role for the private sector in public education may lead to a continuation of the status quo that will relegate public schools to a rump as levels of trust decline and parents turn to other providers to achieve their aspirations.

The role of the self-managing school in efforts to achieve transformation

Taking the lead again from developments in the UK, it is clear that there will be an increase in the level of self-management in the implementation of the agenda for transformation. Intentions are clear in the *Five Year Strategy for Children and Young People* (DfES 2004a), the centrepiece of which is personalising learning: 'Tailoring services to meet individual needs means that schools, colleges and children's services must have the freedom to innovate and adapt. So, in the next phase of reform, we will give freedom and autonomy to the front line (DfES 2004a, p. 18)'.

The UK already has a high level of self-management, starting with the Education Reform Act 1988 and accelerating through the years of New Labour. The intention now is to move as far as possible beyond self-management to self-governance especially for specialist secondary schools:

[The aim is] to ensure that every parent can choose an excellent secondary school for their child. At its heart is the development of independent specialist schools in place of the traditional comprehensive—a decisive system-wide advance. We are not creating a new category of schools—rather, giving more independence to all schools within a specialist system. Our best schools already have many of the characteristics we want for every school: autonomy, specialism, freedom of heads and governors to manage and personalise their provision, and an ethos of success and community responsibility...For schools that are failing to reach their full potential, it will encourage greater independence as they are able and willing to take it on. In areas of failure and under-performance, it will equip schools with the leadership capacity essential for successful self-governance, while also opening up provision to a range of new sponsors, through the academies program and the creation of other new schools to meet parental demand (DfES 2004a, p. 44).

The new image takes shape

The new image of the self-managing school now takes shape. It moves beyond self-management toward independence and self-governance, but maintains its place in a system of public education. The most important unit of organisation is the learner rather than the classroom, school or system. This is the first 'essential' in the new image. The self-managing school must achieve new synergies with a range of agencies, institutions and organisations in the public and private sectors. This second 'essential' is explored in Chapter 4. To work and network in this fashion will require the highest levels of knowledge and skill. Indeed capacities beyond knowledge and skill are required—sagacity is a better concept. This third 'essential' is considered in Chapter 5. All of these things must be accomplished in different settings on different continents around the world. Reports of progress and guidelines for further development are contained in Chapter 6 along with a summary of the major features in the new image of the self-managing school.

CHAPTER 4

Synergy

Schools acting alone cannot achieve change on the scale of transformation under conditions that prevail in most societies at the start of the 21st century. They rarely succeed or survive if they endeavour to play a lone hand. A capacity to establish partnerships with a range of organisations and institutions is essential and this is the theme of Chapter 4.

A word like 'partnership' does not capture the complexity of relationships that should be created and the benefits that should accrue to all parties. 'Synergy' best captures the intention. Derived from the Greek *synergos*—working together—Webster's Online Dictionary explains that synergy is 'the phenomenon of two or more discrete influences or agents acting in common to create an effect which is greater than the sum of the effects each is able to create independently'. Synergy has become a buzzword in recent times but an exploration of what has been accomplished in successful self-managing schools points to its power.

Particular attention is given in the first part of the chapter to synergy across public and private sectors. Arguments in support of such arrangements are presented along with illustrations of the benefits that have accrued in selected settings. The second part of the chapter outlines the possibilities for federations or networks of support for schools. Networks are also considered in Chapter 5 in the context of building the intellectual capital of schools.

Synergy across public and private sectors

Until recently, systems of public education tended to 'go it alone'. The private sector was kept at arm's length. At the system level, private sector involvement was limited to capital works or the provision of textbooks and other learning resources. At the school level, parents and other members of the local community were involved in governing bodies and there were limited forms of cash or in-kind support from local business. The self-managing school as initially conceived was expected to operate within such a framework.

There have been dramatic changes in these arrangements, notably in the UK in the manner outlined in the final pages of Chapter 3. Schools and school systems now manage a complex array of partnerships of one kind or another across public and private sectors, and a capacity to succeed in such a synergy is part of the new image of the self-managing school. Such arrangements may involve public private partnerships, networks of social entrepreneurs, and philanthropy.

The case for a new synergy

Five arguments for a new synergy across public and private sectors emerge from a study of recent developments: the failure of a public authority to meet expectations, securing higher levels of funding, a 'third way' in the delivery of services to the public, the building of social capital, and the transformation of public sector services in a knowledge society.

One argument derives from the perceived failure of a public authority to deliver education at a standard acceptable to citizens. Successive efforts to improve the situation have been unsuccessful and, often as a last resort, government has turned to a non-public entity in an effort to remedy the situation. These are the conditions that led to the privatisation of educational services in support of schools in the London borough of Islington, or the privatisation of the management of certain schools in the UK that continue to be owned and funded by a public authority. These actions are based on the assumption that the services provided by the non-public entity will be delivered more efficiently and effectively. This assumption is challenged by those committed to an exclusive role for the public authority and the merits of the argument often turn on evidence of impact.

Another argument is concerned with the availability of funds. Funding from the public purse may be insufficient to provide an educational service at the desired level and one or more mechanisms may be employed to secure support from a private entity. An example is the growing number of arrangements under the Private Finance Initiative in the United Kingdom that calls for a private investor to build, or substantially re-furbish, and then manage school facilities over a longer term, under a leasing arrangement with the public authority. Payments from the public purse are spread over time. The alternative may be a significant increase in taxation or major change in budget priorities among different kinds of public services. Objections are based on the long-term costs to the public authority or a failure to fulfil the contract, for example, when demographic shifts or perceived school performance lead to closure of the school, resulting in financial penalty for breach of contract.

A third line of argument calls for a shift in the concepts of public and public good. In educational terms, the concept of public good may be reflected in an unwavering commitment to achieve the highest level of attainment for every student regardless of circumstance, but who owns the school, or who delivers the service, or even who provides the resources may be the subject of a more pragmatic outlook, depending on what it takes to deliver this outcome. Such approaches are often framed by the concept of a 'third way' in terms of absolute adherence to basic values but, in respect to how to get there, to cite Tony Blair: 'We should be infinitely adaptable and imaginative in the means of applying those values. There are no ideological pre-conditions, [and there is] no pre-determined veto on means. What counts is what works' (Blair cited by Midgley 1998, p. 44).

Invoking the power of the community leads to the fourth line of argument that is, in many respects, the most substantive and persuasive. It suggests that partnership with a non-public entity draws on and enhances the social capital of the school or school system.

Interest in the concept of social capital has waxed and waned. The concept dates from 1916 and its first use, according to Putnam (2000), was in the context of school education: 'The term social capital itself turns out to have been independently invented at least six times over the twentieth century, each time to call attention to the ways in which our lives are made more productive by social ties. The first known use of the concept was not by some cloistered theoretician, but by a practical reformer in the Progressive Era—L. J. Hanifan, state supervisor of rural schools in West Virginia. Writing in 1916, to urge the importance of community involvement for successful schools, Hanifan invoked the idea of 'social capital' to explain why it was needed (Putnam 2000, p. 19).

Hanifan considered social capital to be 'those intangible substances [that] count for most in the daily lives of people: namely good will, fellowship, sympathy and social intercourse among the individuals and families that make up a social unit'. Hanifan believed that 'the community as a whole will benefit by the cooperation of its parts' (cited by Putnam 2000, p. 19).

Fukuyama defined social capital as 'the ability of people to work together for common purposes in groups and organisations' (Fukuyama 1995, p. 10) (see Adler and Kwon 2000 for a range of definitions). Fukuyama (1995) and Putnam (2000) have written of the loss or absence of social capital, especially in western democracies.

In one sense, the interest of a non-public profit entity would be considered as a more limited kind of capital—in the form of money, in expectation of a benefit—in the form of profit. In the line of argument presented here, however, such arrangements may be seen as part of a larger movement to secure a wider and deeper base of support for schools. Expressed simply, the provision of capital that delivers additional financial resources to schools can be viewed as a contribution to social capital when there is a commitment to 'work together for common purposes' in support of those schools. Similarly there is a contribution when individuals in profit or non-profit entities provide expertise in support of schools or school systems on a pro bono basis. The form of capital provided here is intellectual capital.

The social capital line is evident in the involvement of non-public non-profit entities in the support of schools. An example is the Community Action Network (CAN) in the UK that describes its work in the following terms:

Community Action Network (CAN) and its partners are creating a model that will assist both in the transformation of education and community regeneration through networking, collaboration and innovation. Our focus is on improving education attainment through a new integrated approach to public service delivery. Through our work in some of the most deprived areas in the UK, CAN is able to deliver practical help and advice aimed at establishing creative and sustainable partnerships across all sectors (CAN 2003, p. 1).

Established about twenty years ago CAN has, in partnership with Rural Net, built the largest network of voluntary organisations in the UK, with over 750 members connecting the social, business and public sectors. It works in some of the most deprived areas in the country. CAN employs the image of the 'social entrepreneur', citing Prime Minister Blair's view that 'the combination of strong social purpose and energetic, entrepreneurial drive can deliver genuine results. But if the UK is to benefit fully then I believe it is important that the Government seeks to do all it can to help the future development of social enterprise' (CAN 2003, p. 1). The CAN model is an interesting one, given its non-profit orientation and its extensive involvement in 'the transformation of education and community regeneration'.

There is a line of argument that suggests that maintaining a view of public as synonymous with government ['owned, funded and operated by government'] has served to deny or limit access to social capital, and that to continue to do so will lead inevitably to the decline of the public school. Under this 'residualisation' scenario, the public school is merely a 'safety net' for those who cannot afford to attend a private school where, in addition to other forms of capital, social capital is perceived to be relatively strong. The need for greater involvement of the private sector and for the building of social capital appears to be particularly strong in countries that are multi-cultural in character, and where there are gross disparities in levels of achievement, fears of 'residualisation' are high, and social capital is perceived to be weak. These countries include Australia, United Kingdom and the United States, especially in large urban school systems. In contrast, social capital is already strong in countries like Finland, Korea, Japan, Norway and Sweden. In Finland, for example, the impressive performance of its 15-year-old students in PISA has been explained by many factors, but noteworthy is the strong level of support for schools throughout the community.

The final argument for a new synergy of public and private sectors lies in the analysis of trends in the transformation of public sector services. The Centre for Research and Innovation (CERI) of OECD provides such an analysis:

Education is being transformed, albeit unevenly and at varying pace, from a producer-led, planned system to one more guided by its multiple stakeholders, as are many other public services. It is called upon increasingly to be more responsive to the needs of the knowledge society and partnerships offer one way in which the new demands can be met. Required competencies change, more advanced, specialised skills are called for, and learning programs 'tailor-made' to individuals or groups are in demand. New opportunities and competition are tending to open up in the conventionally public sector, a further driving force for public-private partnerships, and cutbacks in expenditure are also pushing the public sector to search for new (including private) partners (Istance and Kobayashi 2003, p. 12).

Innovation is a noble pursuit, as made clear in the mission of UNESCO and the five functions that this organisation of 188 nations has chosen to carry out that mission. The mission of UNESCO includes an intention to 'stimulate experimentation, innovation and policy dialogue'. Its functions include service as a 'laboratory of ideas' so that it 'identifies emerging problems, seeks strategies to solve them, creates space for dialogue, and tests innovative solutions' (UNESCO, n.d.). It is evident that public education faces a range of problems as efforts are made to promote education as a fundamental right and to improve its quality. The creation and testing of innovative arrangements, including new synergies of public and private sectors, is consistent with these intentions.

Illustrations of the new synergy

Several approaches to achieving a new synergy have been identified in earlier sections, notably the specialist schools initiative in the UK (described at the end of Chapter 3) and the work of the Community Action Network that is an example of social entrepreneurs in action and the building of social capital (earlier in Chapter 4).

Another approach to the involvement of the private sector in public education is in the management of schools. The transformation at Bexley Business Academy was described at the end of Chapter 3. The school is managed by a private firm known as the 3E's (derived from the slogan of 'education, education, education' used by New Labour in a statement of its three top priorities in the lead-up to its election in 1997). The 3E's is just one of a number of private companies now managing schools in the UK. The oldest and largest is CfBT, founded in 1965 as the Centre for British Teachers. Based in Reading, it employs over 1300 full-time members of staff and currently operates in 20 countries. Its turnover in 2001 was £70 million. It is a non-profit entity, registered as a charity, and donates over £1 million annually to education projects and research endeavours around the world. Another large firm is Cambridge Education Associates (CEA) founded in the late 1980s by a small group of successful school principals and education officers from Cambridgeshire, a pioneering authority in the local financial management of schools.

Initial concern about private management largely dissipated once it was realised that the key personnel were highly successful if not eminent educators in their own right. Concern was particularly high when it was announced that a school in Guildford was to be the first under private management in England. This is the school now known as the Kings College for the Arts and Technology, managed by the 3E's.

There had been three efforts over a decade to establish a successful school on the site in Guildford. The original Park Barn School was re-named Kings Manor under a new principal in 1993. It was closed on 31 August 2000 and re-opened on 1 September 2000 under its new name of the Kings College for the Arts and Technology. There were, however, 18 months of preparation by 3E's, with another headteacher David Crossley appointed after six months, taking up the post and then making new staff appointments and establishing the senior team five months before re-opening. Enrolments grew from about 280 to about 750 in three years. Local primary schools would previously not recommend the school but it is now the destination of choice for those completing Key Stage 2 (upper primary). Indeed, enrolments at these schools have grown with the success of Kings.

An interesting model of another kind of partnership can be found in Australia with the development of the Brookside Learning Centre in Caroline Springs, on the western boundary of Melbourne in Victoria. Delfin Lend Lease was the developer of this new residential community that included an education precinct in the design. Three schools from the government and non-government sectors are located on site, including Brookside School (government primary), Mowbray College (independent), and Christ the Priest Catholic Primary, with co-location of a kindergarten, municipal health and community services, and a private childcare facility. Gabrielle Leigh, principal of the Brookside School (now extended to become the Caroline Springs College), describes the approach as a 'Multiple Ownership Design Model' (Leigh 2002).

Private philanthropy is another example of the involvement of the private sector in public education. The United States provides the benchmark. Large philanthropies include the Bill and Melinda Gates Foundation, the Pew Charitable Trust and the Annenberg Challenge. The Annenberg Challenge is focused on the needs of disadvantaged schools in urban settings, with impressive gains in educational outcomes in most instances.

Developments in the UK warrant closer attention because a culture of engagement has emerged over the last ten years, gathering momentum in the first and second terms of the Blair Government. Prime Minister Blair cited the following examples in his address at the opening of the Bexley Business Academy (Blair 2003). Each is a specialist school in London and he highlighted the leadership of the principal, the support of sponsors, and the increase in the percentage of five good passes in the GCSE (the standard measure of school achievement in the UK).

▸ The Harris City Technology College has improved its five GCSE success rate from just 11 per cent in 1990 to 92 per cent this year. Much of this success is due to its outstanding headteacher Carol Bates and its inspired sponsors Philip and Pauline Harris.

▸ Sir John Cass Language College in Tower Hamlets has transformed its results from just 8 per cent in 1995 to 80 per cent this year. It was the most improved school in the country (in 2002). It is one of the few secondary schools in Europe that teaches Mandarin Chinese. Again, its success is due to the outstanding leadership of its headteacher, Haydon Evans, and the marvellous support of its sponsors HSBC and the Sir John Cass Foundation.

▸ The St Marylebone School of the Performing Arts in Westminster has improved its results from 33 per cent in 1994 to 93 per cent this summer under the outstanding leadership of Elizabeth Phillips with strong support from its sponsor British Airways.

As far as philanthropy is concerned, public schools in Australia draw little support compared to their counterparts in the UK. An outstanding example by international standards is the substantial support of the private sector for the Port Phillip Specialist School in Port Melbourne that serves about 140 students with moderate to severe disabilities. It brings together on the one site a range of education and health services and is a model of a 'full service school'. Successive state governments have helped fund the extensive refurbishment of a formerly derelict site. The current government has provided $1 million and the Pratt Foundation $300 000 to help establish a Centre for Performing Arts at the school. The social capital at Port Phillip Specialist School is therefore impressive by any standard. There are counterparts in other states but overall the scale is minimal compared to what has occurred in the UK, where it is striking that most of the support of philanthropists, trusts and foundations and the additional support of government is directed at schools in challenging circumstances.

The Port Phillip Specialist School is noteworthy for another reason and that is the manner in which it personalises learning. It may be that all schools that seek to personalise the learning of their students should look to the approaches used in outstanding special schools like Port Phillip for a template for the design of a program of activities to support their efforts. Each Wednesday morning from 8.15 to 10.00, a teacher discusses the work of each of her students in a meeting attended by the principal Bella Irlicht and others, including several psychologists, a social worker, an assistant principal and a member of staff. These meetings are held with different teachers every second Wednesday so it is possible to plan for and monitor the work of each student on a regular basis. Meetings on the alternate Wednesday are devoted to follow-up of actions taken in earlier meetings. The approach at Port Phillip can be adapted to any school no matter the size. Another feature at Port Phillip is the manner in which it networks the support of its teachers, with several experts in the private and public sectors on call to assist on any matter.

Federations of support

Another kind of synergy is emerging in practices that call for the creation of federations. There are two types: one involves a small number of schools sharing the same structure for governance while the other seeks synergies through federations of support. An example of the former is in the UK, where regulations now allow the creation of federations of schools. The following excerpts from the School Governance (Federations) Regulations illustrate how this may be accomplished and why:

> The policy objective is to allow up to five maintained [fully publicly funded] schools to federate under one governing body if they wish to do so. A range of collaborative working is possible between schools, and these provisions remove an impediment to very close collaboration short of amalgamation into one school. It makes easier economies of scale in human and other resources...The constitution of federated governing bodies is based upon the same principles of stake-holder representation as that of individual governing bodies, and parents, staff and other groups that would have been represented on an individual governing body are represented on a federated governing body...Schools in federations remain separate schools, and retain their individual admission arrangements and delegated budgets (although these may be pooled by the schools if they wish)... Schools wishing to federate must consult parents, staff, and other interested parties, including other schools and the local education authority (DfES 2004a).

The second kind of federation is focused on support rather than governance. An example was offered earlier in the work of the Community Action Network in the UK. The idea is extended here by drawing on the work of Zuboff and Maxmin (2004) who asserted in *The Support Economy* that the structures of the industrial age corporation are ill suited to the needs of the modern consumer. They propose federations that bring together different companies that then collaborate in combining their capacities to create new services that respond to these needs. Zuboff and Maxmin argue that health and education share the same dislocation of services and needs as far as current provision is concerned.

Support for schools has traditionally come from 'the system'—from locations that are variously named, depending on governance and administrative arrangements in different places: the education department, the regional office, the district office, the local education authority and so on. Sometimes schools acquire support through universities, either through formal study or from consultancy services provided by academics. More recently, schools have sought the services of individuals, agencies, organisations and institutions across the public and private sectors. For the most part, support outside 'the system' was viewed as an aberration or a breakdown in service. People who used services outside 'the system' were often regarded as mavericks.

A different view is now emerging and it is likely that the traditional view of support and service will become the exception for the simple reason that other arrangements are more effective. The self-managing school should be adept in utilising these new arrangements.

What is described here is not unique to schools. Indeed, schools are late starters compared to what is emerging in the corporate sector and, more significantly, what is unfolding for individuals who, consistent with themes already explored, are seeking personalisation in everything from health care to selection of music.

Zuboff and Maxmin select the idea of a federation to describe the new arrangements for support of an enterprise. A federation may involve one or more networks. Writing in a general sense they state that: 'Federations are not defined by what they make, what they sell, or what services they perform. Federations are defined by the constituencies that select them for support and by the ways they invent to provide that support. Some federations may specialise in supporting certain constituencies, others may specialise in providing only levels of deep support, and still others might specialise in their ability to aggregate support through various levels' (Zuboff and Maxmin 2004, p. 338).

Zuboff and Maxmin describe federations in a variety of ways including 'flexible, agile and operationally excellent', distinguished by 'style, creativity, imagination, authenticity, and consistency'. They are likely to be mobilised by a leading enterprise or alliance of enterprises that have recognised a particular domain in which value for all can be realised (Zuboff and Maxmin 2004, pp. 338–9).

The forms that federations may take in the support of schools are readily apparent. A group of schools in a particular geographical area or offering a particular specialisation may form an alliance and seek the support of a range of individuals, agencies, organisations and institutions in public and private sectors. The focus may be a problem that schools in the alliance may be facing, such as changing demography or falling enrolments; or a development in pedagogy or curriculum for which capacity must be built among their staff. A school may elect to create a federation of support for its own purposes, outside any alliance that may be formed or already exist. When acting together, however, it is evident that high levels of trust are required if the federation is to succeed. Moreover, these things do not just happen by themselves. There will need to be agreements on resource arrangements to ensure that people are available to create and energise the federation.

Roles and responsibilities in creating community and building social capital

The benefits that have been achieved by new synergies of the public and private sectors, and the promise of more through the creation of federations, do not happen by themselves. These outcomes cannot be secured by an education department or school acting alone in a system of public education. It is a proper role of government to make a contribution to the creation of community and the building of social capital. This has been the case in the UK in the various initiatives outlined thus far. The importance of such a role is also recognised in Australia. Michael Keating, former head of the Australian Public Service and the Department of Prime Minister and Cabinet stated that 'the goal of government should be to build stronger communities, not bigger bureaucracies' (Keating 2004, p. 5). Consistent with the analysis of Zuboff and Maxmin (2004), he contends that 'too often the critics ignore the pressure from a more individualistic society for services that are more responsive to individual needs, and the way in which markets can assist in meeting those needs' (Keating 2004, p. 9). Helping to build a stronger community, with its federations of support from the private as well as the public sector, is the responsibility of many institutions, and government is one of these.

Principals and other leaders in schools clearly have a critical role for they must identify, and then make connections with, the range of individuals, agencies, institutions and organisations in the public and private sectors that can provide services in support of their schools. There is reciprocal responsibility because the heads of these other entities must also be actively engaged in making connections to schools. There are similar responsibilities for leaders in business and industry whose good sense of corporate citizenship should ensure that they are actively seeking schools to which they can give cash or in-kind support. That this can be achieved is evident in recent experience in the UK. These synergies can be strengthened with unrelenting advocacy and support by government, especially at the senior level. Many observers consider Tony Blair to be an exemplar.

What has been explored in these pages as far as synergies are concerned is itself a kind of transformation, from public education as a closed system, with schools revolving around and being supported by 'the centre', to new arrangements where 'the centre' is just one possible source of support, as federations are created to add value as schools seek what may no longer be the impossible dream—high levels of achievement for all students in all settings with the student the key unit of organisation in the system. Zuboff and Maxmin (2004, pp. 318–19) consider the transformation of enterprise in a general sense to be no less a transformation than the shift in a view of the universe held by Ptolemy, with the Earth as centre, to the breakthrough of Copernicus, with the Sun as centre.

CHAPTER 5

Sagacity

Success in the education profession calls for a substantial body of knowledge and a comprehensive array of skills. Initial teacher education lays the foundation, and ongoing professional development is essential. However, words like 'knowledge', 'skill' and 'values' are inadequate to describe the capacities that are demonstrated in successful self-managing schools and required to achieve transformation. 'Sagacity' seems a better word, but it is important to recover its meaning for it is rarely used in the profession. The Merriam-Webster Online dictionary defines sagacity as 'the intelligent application of knowledge acquired from years of learning and experience'. Webster's Online Dictionary includes the following as words that are related to sagacity: acumen, astuteness, cogency, comprehension, contemplation, discernment, experience, farsightedness, grasp, incisiveness, judiciousness, looking ahead, past experience, penetration, perception, perspicacity, practical knowledge, practice, prediction, preparation, providence, provision, prudence, readiness, sensibility, sensitivity, sophistication, understanding, wisdom. These capacities are included in the new image of the self-managing school. How they have been demonstrated in the best practice of self-management and how they may be acquired as a driving force for transformation are of central concern in Chapter 5.

Informed professionalism

Some may contend that there is nothing new in this view of requirements for the transformation of schools. A different position is taken here, consistent with the insights of McKinsey's Sir Michael Barber, former head of the Prime Minister's Delivery Unit in the UK, who played a key role in shaping education reform after the election of New Labour in 1997. Barber reviewed four decades of efforts to achieve change in education. He considered the 1970s to be a decade of 'uninformed professionalism', the 1980s to be a time of 'uninformed prescription', the 1990s to be shaped by 'informed prescription', and the 2000s would unfold as an era of 'informed professionalism' (Barber 2002). In respect to the last of these, his assessment was a combination of description, prediction and advocacy. It is descriptive in the sense that the knowledge base for guiding significant change in schooling is better than it has ever been. It is predictive in the sense that the knowledge base will become stronger, making it possible for schools and school systems to move beyond two decades of prescription. It is advocacy because these developments do not occur by themselves, and it will require a sense of discipline and a high level of commitment to achieve a new level of professionalism in schools.

Evidence of 'informed professionalism' may be found in nations that embarked on efforts to raise levels of literacy in schools. These have been largely successful, as indicated by higher levels of achievement by all or most students in many schools, even those in challenging circumstances. Moreover, these levels of achievement have been sustained over several years, thus providing a case for this element of reform being an instance of transformation. It should not be claimed that the outcomes are evidence of transformation of the school except when the change has been significant, systematic and sustained across all or most programs. A feature of these efforts has been the large investment of resources in building the capacity of teachers to adopt a different approach to the teaching of literacy. It is fair to say that 'informed professionalism' has been achieved in many schools in the case of programs in literacy.

Two important issues are raised. The first concerns the nature of pedagogical and curriculum change; the second is how a state of 'informed professionalism' can be achieved. The focus of the chapter is on the latter.

The starting point is acknowledgement of the limitations of traditional approaches to building the capacity of the profession through pre-service education in universities and in-service education through a combination of in-service training provided by a school system and graduate education offered by universities. These approaches may have enabled the profession to get by in the past but it is inadequate if the intention is to achieve transformation. There is general agreement that new approaches are required and a consensus is building around the networking of knowledge.

The networking of knowledge

There is a high level of interest in knowledge-based networks, often with a focus on innovation (OECD 2003). It is important to stress that these do not replace traditional approaches:

> Knowledge-based networks are not the alternative to existing forms of public provision: they are an essential complement. Rather than being represented by an organisational

structure or single policy lever, transformation becomes [a feature] of the whole system as it learns to generate, incorporate and adapt to the best of the specific new ideas and practices that get thrown up around it (Hargreaves, D 2003, pp. 12–13).

Expressed simply, there are important roles for governments and other systemic authorities in providing the frameworks for transformation, and self-management is essential if schools are to have the capacity to respond to the unique mix of student needs that exist in the local setting. However, significant, systematic and sustained change can only reach every classroom and achieve outstanding outcomes for all students in all settings if there are effective mechanisms for the lateral transfer of knowledge through networking.

There is interest in several nations in creating and supporting networks of schools. Some of the most extensive systems may be found in England. The Specialist Schools and Academies Trust has established three kinds of networks that have been identified as an important factor (Prime Minister's Delivery Unit, 2004) in explaining why specialist secondary schools, now numbering about 80 per cent of all secondary schools in England (2502 out of 3170 by January 2006), are outperforming non-specialist schools in terms of value-added and rate of improvement, especially under challenging circumstances. These are (1) networks of schools that offer the same specialism, (2) networks of specialist schools in the same region, and (3) networks of secondary schools with their neighbouring primary schools. In another important initiative, the National College for School Leadership (NCSL) has established more than 100 Networked Learning Communities (NLC).

Traditional approaches to achieving change by top-down mandate or support from a central location may be helpful, if not necessary, but outcomes have generally fallen short of expectations if there is exclusive reliance on these arrangements. The Blair Government is now satisfied that networking is a key factor in achieving transformation, as evidenced by proposals in its five-year strategy for each level of schooling, including pre-school, primary and secondary:

> Networks are an emerging feature of the landscape—networks of schools working together to solve shared problems, networks of schools and care agencies sharing information about vulnerable children, networks of schools, colleges and universities developing and sharing materials. Community learning, for families and adults wishing to upgrade their skills offers another form of network, linked by ICT to education hubs such as schools and colleges (DfES 2004a, p. 108).

Of particular note are intentions in England for the networking of primary schools to support each other in raising standards, offer children a wider range of opportunities by sharing resources including staff, provide more comprehensive services to their communities, and support leadership and management through the sharing of bursars, or federating their governing bodies, or appointing a single executive principal to lead several schools. It was acknowledged that:

It may not be right for the same networks to perform all these different functions. But supporting effective learning networks of primary schools will be the single most important way in which we can build the capacity of primary schools to continue to develop and improve, and in particular to offer better teaching and learning and a wider range of opportunities to pupils and their communities (DfES 2004a, p. 42).

An example of a broadly based network in the UK is the Community Action Network (CAN), described briefly in Chapter 4. Established in the mid 1980s, CAN has, in partnership with Rural Net, built the largest network of voluntary organisations in the country, with over 750 members connecting the social, business and public sectors. It works in some of the most deprived areas. Examples include its work with CISCO in 'wiring up' more than 5000 homes in Tower Hamlets to the educational and community facilities at the Bromley by Bow Centre.

The network has developed a CAN Academy Model for application in secondary schools at the local, regional and national levels. The aims of the model (adapting CAN 2003, pp. 6–7) are to:

- Improve the quality of educational achievement in schools by developing partnerships beyond the classroom with local social entrepreneurs, voluntary groups, health and social services, further and higher education, business, crime prevention and others.

- Tackle the causes and effects of poverty by integrating education, health, welfare and employment opportunities.

- Integrate schools with their communities by building on these partnerships to tackle disadvantage.

- Support schools to become a visible and positive force in the local community and develop the infrastructure they need to manage community links and programs.

- Connect failing schools with a support network of both successful, enterprising schools and less successful schools beyond the local boundaries.

- Develop strong school leadership teams who are committed social entrepreneurs.

- Establish in all schools an 'enterprise culture' that creates a flexible workforce ready to respond to a changing job market.

- Create a pathfinder model that can be replicated across the country and share best practice between partnership schools.

The network has the strong and active support of the Innovation Unit of the Department for Education and Skills (DfES) and the Policy Unit at 10 Downing Street.

Governments now realise that the creation of networks is important if transformation is to be achieved. Australia, for example, has run into difficulties with the education of boys, whose performance at all levels of schooling falls behind that of girls, with relatively high levels of alienation in the middle years. There are parallels in some other countries. The Australian Government took the initiative to address the problem and made substantial funds available. Rather than follow the traditional route of establishing a unit within its bureaucracy or channelling funds through the eight State and Territory Governments, or through central agencies in systems of non-government schools, it put the project out to tender with a requirement that the successful bidder create networks of 350 schools and 34 school systems to achieve particular outcomes.

Another initiative of the Australian Government derives from an important review of teaching and teacher education concerned with the teaching of science, mathematics and technology in schools, with a focus on innovation. Grants of $39 million support a range of projects over seven years, with most of the funding going to 500 initiatives 'to build school clusters, achieve better coordination of the teaching of science, technology and mathematics between primary and secondary schools, help connect learning across disciplines and promote innovative approaches and cultures in schools' (Harmer 2004).

The findings of a Queensland project on the sharing of knowledge within the profession are noteworthy. The Queensland Consortium for Professional Development in Education (2004) explored the contribution to professional growth of 71 professional associations and networks. The findings confirmed an earlier report of the Board of Teacher Registration (2002, p. 45) that concluded that 'networks appear to provide optimum environments within which understandings of, and insights into, knowledge of learners (including the teachers themselves) and knowledge of educational contexts (including the networks themselves) can be developed, examined and integrated'.

The report acknowledged that 'the traditional roles, responsibilities and structural arrangements of professional associations are under challenge' and proposed that they 'take stock and reappraise both the role they play in the broader educational context and the services they provide to members and the profession' (Queensland Consortium for Professional Development in Education 2004, p. 1). The report drew attention to a range of issues for leaders of professional associations and networks and highlighted the guiding principles of communities of practice (Wenger, McDermott, and Snyder 2002).

The possibilities of networking are also evident in the work of the Schooling for Tomorrow project of the Organisation for Economic Cooperation and Development (OECD) that published a book under the title of *Networks for Innovation: Towards New Models for Managing Schools and Systems* (OECD 2003). The following excerpts illustrate the case for networks:

> School autonomy goes hand-in-hand with being connected to community, other educators, and the broader society. Hence, the key roles of networks and partnerships. Too much educational practice in OECD countries is characterised by isolation: schools

from parents and the community and from each other; teachers and learners in isolated classrooms (Ylva Johansson, of the Swedish E-Learning Organisation, in Johansson 2003, p. 149).

The challenge of reforming public education systems is therefore acute. Those responsible are in no position to deal with uncertainties. What they can do is manage and transfer knowledge about what works effectively, intervene in cases of under-performance, create the capacity for change in the system and ensure that it is flexible and adaptable enough to learn constantly and implement effectively (Michael Barber, former Head of the Prime Minister's Delivery Unit in the UK in Barber 2003, p. 115).

Another project of the Schooling for Tomorrow initiative of OECD is the formulation of six scenarios for the future of schools (OECD 2001). These were described in Chapter 3. Of particular note is the place of networks in the preferred scenarios:

▸ **Scenario 3** 'Schools as core social centres' [are] characterised by high levels of public trust and funding; ...centres of community and social capital formation; and greater organisational and professional diversity as well as greater social equity (OECD 2001, p. 85).

▸ **Networks in Scenario 3** Community interests—linguistic, cultural, professional, geographical—find very strong expression in this scenario, using the school as the focal point. Schools would be allowed a great deal of room to respond to, and promote, these interests. Networking and cooperation would therefore flourish... (OECD 2003, p. 25).

▸ **Scenario 4** 'Schools as focused learning organisations' [are] characterised by high levels of public trust and funding; schools and teachers networking widely in learning organisations; and strong quality and equity features (OECD 2001, p. 89).

▸ **Networks in Scenario 4** Networks of expertise, including among teachers, would be an essential feature of this scenario. Bureaucratic and hierarchical models would give way to flatter, collaborative arrangements of networks, and there would be numerous partnerships involving the different stakeholders. The very management and governance of schooling arrangements would come to rely heavily on networks, with all the positive features of professionalism and dynamism this implies, but also the potential problems of instability and patchiness (OECD 2003, p. 26).

The OECD is continuing its work on scenarios, with several countries conducting case studies that will be published in a 'tool kit' to guide others. Catholic Education Office Melbourne (2003) is taking the lead in Australia, with several primary schools engaged in its Schools as Core Social Centres Project. The project is funded by the Victorian Health Promotion Foundation, initially for 2002–03 but extended to 2004–05. Networking is evident in the creation of a 'research circle...to disseminate research findings, promote a learning community in the field and to share good practice related to the model' (Tobin

2004). The project is intended to construct a model 'to inform the development of collaborative school community partnerships, [and] to facilitate the promotion of wellbeing and the development of social capital. Importantly the project acknowledges the links between the promotion of wellbeing, inclusivity and learning outcomes, and effectively explores the interface between health and education practice' (Tobin 2004).

It is apparent that there are important developments under way in the manner in which a school system approaches the challenge of change on the scale of transformation. Barber's observation about the traditional approach to change in education is sobering: 'The era of the large, slow moving, steady, respected, bureaucratic public services, however good by earlier standards, is over. In the new era, public services will need to be capable of rapid change, involved in partnerships with the business sector, publicly accountable for the services they deliver, open to diversity, seeking out world class benchmarks, and constantly learning' (Barber 2003, p. 115).

While there is now a high degree of interest in networks and networking, it is fair to ask what the outcomes have been and how networks can be designed to achieve the high expectations that have been set. Before reviewing the evidence, it is helpful to summarise the different kinds of networks and approaches to networking.

Typology of networks and networking

Van Aalst's definition of networking is a helpful starting point in describing the forms that networks may take. 'The term "networking" refers to the systematic establishment and use (management) of internal and external links (communication, interaction and coordination) between people, teams or organisations ("nodes") in order to improve performance' (van Aalst 2003, p. 33).

According to van Aalst (2003, pp. 36–7) there are three types of networks that may operate alone or in combination:

▸ A 'community of practice' that involves the relatively informal sharing of knowledge within a network of professionals. The knowledge may or may not be codified and much of the activity within the network involves the identification of who has the knowledge to address a particular issue.

▸ A 'networked organisation' that involves a more or less formal relationship between autonomous organisations with the intention of adding value to each, the chief advantage being that each partner can remain autonomous yet build its capacity to achieve its mission through synergies achieved with other partners.

▸ A 'virtual community' may take many forms, with the common element being the medium of ICT.

Smith and Wohlstetter (2001, p. 501) described four types of networks in education: (1) professional networks of educators operating largely on an informal and voluntary basis, (2) policy issue networks that pursue a single issue or a small set of issues on a related theme, (3) networks that link different schools to an external partner in the expectation that benefits will flow to participating schools, and (4) affiliation networks where schools are related to one another because of their membership of the same organisation. The more formal of these is the affiliation network described by Smith and Wohlstetter in the following terms:

> In this type of network, people representing different organisations can work together to solve a problem or issue of mutual concern that is too large for any one organisation to handle on its own. The norms associated with professional networks serve as the foundation on which network structures are built, but the focus is on inter-organisational collaboration rather than on professional advancement (Smith and Wohlstetter 2001, p. 501).

Problems and issues that suggest a benefit to schools through participation in affiliation networks (within a system or across systems in national and international settings) include the identification and sharing of good practice in different pedagogies or different aspects of curriculum; approaches to supporting students with special education needs, defined broadly, or more specifically, such as students from families who are refugees; or initiatives in professional practice such as efforts to reduce the administrative workload of teachers.

Research about networks

There has been surprisingly little research on the processes and outcomes of networking in education. Stimulated by the creation of the Networked Learning Communities of the National College for School Leadership (NCSL) in the UK, Kerr et al. (2003) concluded in a report to the National Foundation for Educational Research (NFER) that:

> The research and evaluation base is very fragmented and there is a diversity of opinion …Much of the evidence available is dependent on the beliefs of researchers and interested parties and the approaches and interests they represent. The literature is sparse and contradictory about the benefits, key lessons and challenges arising from building and how best to sustain professional learning communities…There is a lack of research that captures the messy and complex nature of network processes. This is because of the difficulty of evaluating and monitoring multi-faceted network processes. It is also the case that network coordinators and facilitators often manage their networks in informal and

implicit ways, often with limited recording procedures because of pressures of time and limited resource.

The NCSL has commissioned research on the impact of its Networked Learning Communities and publishes the findings from time to time. While cause-and-effect is not attributed, it was found, for example, that schools in Networked Learning Communities in Cornwall consistently outperformed those that were not, on value-added measures at Key Stage 2 (upper primary) (National College for School Leadership 2005, p. 15) (see also Earl and Katz 2005).

Smith and Wohlstetter (2001) reported an extended study of large-scale networking (see also Wohlstetter, Malloy, Chau and Polhemus 2003). It focused on the Los Angeles Annenberg Metropolitan Project (LAAMP) funded by the Annenberg Challenge in the amount of $53 million over five years in the mid-1990s. A total of 250 schools were distributed in 21 networks termed 'school families'. Smith and Wohlstetter found evidence of benefits that included community-based collaboration, the transformation of school leadership, cost sharing, knowledge sharing, and the involvement of external partners. Challenges included the development of group process skills and the generation of quality information. They concluded that:

> The Annenberg approach to school improvement emphasised building capacity for innovation among an integrated set of schools. Through joint network activities, problems could be conceptualised in a more integrated holistic fashion, and technical competencies and other resources from a network of mutually supportive schools could be shared to respond rapidly to changing environmental conditions…Although networks cannot change a turbulent policy climate, preliminary findings suggest they can moderate the negative impact of turbulence on member schools (Smith and Wohlstetter 2001, pp. 516–17).

An Australian study considered the processes and outcomes of 16 pilot projects funded as communities of practice in the Vocational Education and Training (VET) sector (Mitchell, 2002). Communities of practice were defined as 'groups of people who share a concern, a set of problems, or a passion about a topic, and who deepen their knowledge and expertise in this area by interacting on an ongoing basis' (Mitchell 2002, p. 6 based on Wenger, McDermott and Snyder 2002, p. 4). A number of benefits were reported including the fostering of communication and the sharing of new knowledge, improvements in productivity, encouragement of innovation and reinforcement of strategic direction. Challenges included perceptions that the communities were marginal or lacked legitimacy, reluctance of some members to adopt new conventions for networking, and absence of documentation (based on Mitchell 2002, p. 7).

Knowledge management

The successful transformation of schools calls for a 'new professionalism' in which teachers' work is increasingly research-based, outcomes-oriented, data-driven, and team-focused, with lifelong professional learning as important in education as it is in medicine. This suggests that the capacity of a successful school will be determined as much by its intellectual assets or its intellectual capital as its financial and physical capital. Stewart (1997, 2002) has energised the recent interest in intellectual capital. He considers intellectual assets to be 'talent, skills, know-how, know-what, and relationships—and machines and networks that embody them—that can be used to create wealth' (Stewart 2002, p. 11) or, in educational terms, 'to ensure learning'. Intellectual assets are intangible and are comprised of human capital (the knowledge and skills of students and staff), structural capital (patents, processes, databases, networks) and customer capital (relationships with customers and suppliers) (adapted from Stewart 2002, p. 13). This raises an issue for schools and school systems of what account is taken of intellectual assets, and what strategies are in place or are planned to enhance them. One of these strategies is knowledge management.

Knowledge management in education refers to the creation, dissemination and utilisation of knowledge for the purpose of improving learning and teaching and to guide decision making in every domain of professional practice. According to Bukowitz and Williams (1999, p. 2), 'knowledge management is the process by which the organisation generates wealth from its intellectual or knowledge-based assets'. In the case of school education 'knowledge management is the process by which a school achieves the highest levels of student learning that are possible from its intellectual or knowledge-based assets'. Successful knowledge management is consistent with the image of 'the intelligent school' (MacGilchrist, Myers and Reed 2004).

School systems and schools thus face the challenge of creating and sustaining a powerful capacity for knowledge management if the vision of transformation is to be realised, that is, outstanding outcomes are to be achieved for all students in all settings. This is not simply an enhanced capacity for in-service training. It means ensuring that all teachers are at all times at the forefront of knowledge in professional practice. There are many implications for governments, school systems and schools but also for those engaged in the preparation and ongoing development of teachers and other professionals. There are also powerful implications for ICT that is now an essential medium in knowledge management. Hislop made the link between networks and knowledge management in the following terms:

> Increasingly, organisations are supporting and developing CoPs [Communities of Practice] as part of their Knowledge Management (KM) initiatives, due to the benefits they provide in facilitating knowledge processes. Almost universally, the knowledge literature considers CoPs advantageous for both individuals and organisations. Thus, they are argued to

provide workers with a collective sense of identity and a social context in which they can develop and utilise their knowledge. For organisations, they can provide a vital source of innovation (Hislop 2004, p. 38).

There is a powerful connection between the themes of Chapter 4—Synergy and Chapter 5—Sagacity. In terms of capital formation, this is the connection between social capital and intellectual capital. Fukuyama's definition of social capital, cited in Chapter 4, helps explain the association. He wrote that social capital is 'the ability of people to work together for common purposes in groups and organisations' (Fukuyama 1995, p. 10). Eric Lesser, who is a consultant at the IBM Institute for Knowledge Management, described the importance of social capital in these terms: 'Knowledge in organisations is typically thought of as being either explicit (relatively easy to capture while maintaining its value) or tacit (difficult to articulate and document without losing its value). Social capital is necessary to enable the effective management of both explicit and tacit knowledge' (Lesser 2000, p. 9).

He illustrated by noting that 'the extent to which documents are shared with others is based on issues around trust, obligation and the perceived value of the intellect of others. If individuals feel that they do not trust others with the knowledge, or believe that others will not be forthcoming with their knowledge, it is unlikely that they will take the time or energy to contribute' (Lesser 2000, p. 9).

Networks will be ineffective if there is a weak connection between social capital and intellectual capital. This connection may be difficult to achieve if schools in the same community are competing for students. They may not trust each other or be forthcoming in the sharing of knowledge. The challenge here is to settle on a common purpose, the achievement of which will add value to each member of the network; for example, to acquire additional resources that can be shared among all, or to increase the attractiveness of schools in the network by the adoption of strategies to raise levels of student achievement.

Implications for the self-managing school

An important implication of these developments is that the self-managing school cannot remain aloof from efforts to build the capacities of all schools through the creation of effective networks. It will be a member of one or more networks in a changing pattern according to the gains it expects to achieve and the contributions it can reasonably make. It is concerned with the management of knowledge for itself and for the networks in which it participates. Engagement in these matters is an important feature in the new image of the self-managing school.

There is at first sight a paradox in re-imagining the self-managing school along these lines. Some may contend that there is a loss of capacity for self-management when the school becomes a contributing member of networks along the lines explored in these pages. An alternative view is preferred, that it is an organisational counterpart to three individual needs that were described by Zuboff and Maxmin in the following terms:

> The first is what we call the *claim of sanctuary*; the second is the *demand for voice*. These expressions of independence, self-control, and self-definition also lead people, paradoxically, to reach out toward new interdependencies in what we call the *quest for connection*. This quest frequently takes the form of seeking trusted others who can provide the support necessary to fulfil the needs associated with sanctuary and voice (Zuboff and Maxmin 2004, p. 143).

The new image of the self-managing school includes its engagement in a 'quest for connection'. This engagement calls for leaders in successful self-managing schools to share their knowledge—their sagacity—with others. They may do this in many ways, including contributions to formal programs of study in universities, in-service education organised by a school system or an institution such as the National College for School Leadership in the UK or its counterpart in other places, and increasingly through networked arrangements of the kind described in this chapter. In respect to the first of these, it is sobering to note the relatively small numbers of people who prepare for leadership or extend their capacities for leadership through a university program. There is a need for universities to respond to the challenge of transformation and draw more extensively on the sagacity of successful school leaders through a master class approach, along the lines reported in Chapter 13.

CHAPTER 6

The new image of the self-managing school

The notion that there is a 'tipping point' in social change has been popularised by Malcolm Gladwell (2000). He suggests there are certain 'rules' to explain the phenomenon that 'ideas and products and messages and behaviours spread just like viruses do' (p. 7), and the tipping point is 'that one dramatic moment in an epidemic when everything can change all at once' (p. 9). David Hargreaves (2003) employs the same imagery in *Education Epidemic* to explain how change on the scale of an epidemic may be created in schools. His advocacy of knowledge-based networks as a mechanism to encourage change on this scale was cited in Chapter 5.

There are several examples of change in education that have the characteristics of an epidemic and for which a tipping point can be identified, or a time can be pinpointed when there is realisation that the change is irreversible. One is the shift from comprehensive to specialist schools in the UK. Specialist schools had been around for some time in the form of technology colleges but not in sufficient number and diversity that they formed a critical mass from which there was no turning back. A tipping point was reached in 2004 by which time nearly two-thirds of schools had became specialist schools and commentators were acknowledging the end of the comprehensive era, contemplating 'what next' when all schools were specialist schools. It is likely that the word 'specialist' will cease to be used in naming a particular category of schools.

The self-managing school reached a tipping point in the UK in the late 1980s after several years of experience in a handful of local education authorities. The same was achieved in Edmonton in Canada in the late 1970s and in Victoria, Australia in the early 1990s. The term self-managing school or its local variant is rarely employed in these settings to describe the way in which schools are managed in these places—it is just accepted as the way things are done. The models of self-management illustrated in Figures 2.1 and 2.2 in Chapter 2 were novel at the time of publication of *The Self-Managing School* (Caldwell and Spinks 1988) and *Leading the Self-Managing School* (Caldwell and Spinks 1992), but were not particularly noteworthy once the tipping point was reached.

There is a wave of curriculum change in nations around the world and pedagogies are changing rapidly, shaped in particular by developments in information and communications technology. The latter, along with social changes of a kind described in earlier chapters, are helping to personalise learning. The ubiquity of the cellular phone and its capacities to access information of all kinds and from many sources tell us that the time for this is near. Another indicator is the take-up of technology that enables personalisation in the downloading of music. Indeed, the notion of personalisation is embraced more widely in this context than it is in education. These technologies make classroom learning in the traditional mode seem slow and cumbersome. The tipping point that consigns such learning to history may be close at hand. The argument that traditional approaches to learning are necessary for social development may carry little weight, given that learning that employs the new technologies is arguably more interactive than in many classrooms, even if it is conducted in cyber space. In any event, different providers in different school or non-school settings may ensure that the full range of learning objectives are addressed in an approach that comes close to one of the de-schooling scenarios in the set of six formulated in the OECD Schooling for Tomorrow project ('learning networks and the network society') as described in Chapter 3.

These developments are likely to come together in some nations before the end of the decade. Networking of schools and other providers, aided by a range of mutually supporting services in the public and private sectors, with the vision of personalisation of learning a reality, securing high levels of achievement for all students in all settings, will mean that there has indeed been a transformation of schools. Schools will of necessity be self-managing, but the image of the self-managing school will be rather different to the one that was formulated nearly two decades ago.

While different tipping points can be identified or anticipated for each of these changes, it is likely that they will come together in rapid fashion at some point in the near future and irreversible change on the scale of transformation will have been achieved. There will be one large tipping point that marks this event. This is the kind of transformation for schools that responds to the challenge of Peter Drucker and is described in the opening lines of Chapter 3 ('no other institution faces challenges as radical as those that will transform the school').

Charles Taylor (2004) has employed the concept of a 'social imaginary' to describe the constellation of values, beliefs and practices that come together in a particular society for a period of time to form its institutions and define its culture. David Hargreaves (2004) has employed the same concept to describe how these come together in an 'educational imaginary'. He believes that transformation occurs when a new 'social imaginary' or a new 'educational imaginary' has taken shape. Hedley Beare (2006) has taken up the same theme in describing what the new 'imaginary' will be like in schools of the 21st century. Taylor considers that Western modernity has three characteristics—the market economy, the public sphere, and self-governance—but that this is just one social imaginary. He explores the idea that there are multiple modernities. This suggests a need for caution in advocating for all societies a transformation of schools along the lines taking shape in the West.

While recognising the need for caution, it is noteworthy that decentralisation and the emergence of the self-managing school are features of important changes in the management of education in non-Western settings. There is also a framework for governance that transcends international borders. Brief explanations and illustrations are set out in the following pages, suggesting that the new image of the self-managing school may, in time and in different ways, have wider application.

Worldwide trends in decentralisation and self-management

It is timely to re-imagine the self-managing school given the worldwide trend to decentralise authority and responsibility to the school level. Nations that are decentralising are also adopting a transformation agenda. Their chances of achieving success will be enhanced if experience that has led to this re-imagination is brought to bear.

It is worthwhile to document the scale of change on the international stage. What follows is drawn from surveys conducted by the OECD and published in an annual report on indicators of performance under the title *Education at a Glance*. The 2004 report (OECD 2004a) included information on the extent of decentralisation among participating nations.

OECD has 30 members that provide information for *Education at a Glance*. These are: Australia, Austria, Belgium, Canada, Czech Republic, Denmark, Finland, France, Germany, Greece, Hungary, Iceland, Ireland, Italy, Japan, Korea, Luxembourg, Mexico, Netherlands, New Zealand, Norway, Poland, Portugal, Slovak Republic, Spain, Sweden, Switzerland, Turkey, United Kingdom and United States. In addition, there are 20 partner nations participating in the project: Argentina, Brazil, Chile, China, Egypt, India, Indonesia, Israel (classified as an observer), Jamaica, Jordan, Malaysia, Paraguay, Peru, Philippines, Russian Federation, Sri Lanka, Thailand, Tunisia, Uruguay and Zimbabwe. Not all nations (members and partners) contribute information on each of the indicators.

The report provides evidence that a higher priority is being given to education as a factor in ensuring success from the standpoint of the individual and the nation. There is a belief that benefits should extend to all and should be life long. In this respect, the report provides support for the view that the transformation agenda is broadly international and not limited to a relatively small number of countries. The following excerpts illustrate this contention.

> Changing social and economic conditions have given education an increasing central role in the success of individuals and nations. Human capital has long been identified as a key factor in combating unemployment and low pay, but there is now also robust evidence that it is associated with a wide range of non-economic benefits, including improvements in health and a greater sense of well-being…The benefits of education have driven increased participation in a widening range of learning activities—by people of all ages, from earliest childhood to advanced adulthood. As the demand for learning grows and becomes more diverse, the challenge for governments is to ensure that the learning opportunities provided respond to real, dynamic needs in a cost-effective manner (OECD 2004a, p. 11).

The report provided an analysis of patterns in centralisation and decentralisation. It considered the locus and mode of decision making in four domains. Locus referred to the six levels where decisions were made: national, state, regional, municipal, local, or school. Mode referred to the four ways decisions were made: full autonomy at the level concerned, consultation with other bodies at that level, independently but within a framework set by a higher authority, or other. The four domains were: organisation of instruction, personnel management, planning and structures, and resources.

As far as trends in centralisation and decentralisation are concerned, the report compared patterns in 1998 and 2003. It found that 'in 14 out of 19 countries decisions are taken at a more decentralised level in 2003 than in 1998. This is most noticeable in the Czech Republic, Korea and Turkey where more than 30 per cent of decisions are taken at a more decentralised level in 2003 than five years earlier. Focusing on the school level, over 20 per cent more decisions are made by schools in the UK, Korea, the Netherlands and Norway over the same period. But at the same time, in the French Community of Belgium and Greece, there have been shifts towards more centralised decision-making' (OECD 2004a, p. 428).

The following summarise the major findings:

▸ Overall, based on data for 2003, decision-making is most centralised (taken at the central and/or state level of government) in Australia, Austria, Greece, Luxembourg, Mexico, Portugal, Spain and Turkey, with central government particularly dominant in Greece.

▸ Decisions are more often taken at the school level in the Czech Republic, UK, Hungary, New Zealand and the Slovak Republic and in particular in the Netherlands where all decisions are taken at the school level.

- Decisions on the organisation of instruction are predominantly taken by schools in all OECD countries, while decisions on planning and structures are mostly the domain of centralised tiers of government. The picture is more mixed for decisions on personnel management and allocation and use of resources.

- Just less than half of decisions taken by schools are taken in full autonomy, about the same proportion as those taken within a framework set by a higher authority. Decisions taken by schools in consultation with others are relatively rare. Schools are less likely to make autonomous decisions related to planning and structures than related to other domains (OECD 2004a, pp. 21–2).

Report summary

The report summarises trends in the following manner:

An important factor in educational policy is the division of responsibilities among national, regional and local authorities, as well as schools. Placing more decision-making authority at lower levels of the educational system has been a key aim in educational restructuring and systemic reform in many countries since the early 1980s. Yet, simultaneously, there have been frequent examples of strengthening the influence of central authorities in some areas. For example, a freeing of 'process' and financial regulations may be accompanied by an increase in the control of output from the centre, and by national curriculum frameworks (OECD 2004a, p. 34).

Care should be taken in interpreting some of the patterns, as there are important differences within countries. This is particularly the case in Australia, which is reported as being one of the most centralised. In Australia, like Canada and the United States, constitutional powers for making laws in relation to education lie with the states (provinces in Canada) with the Australian Government able to influence arrangements through its powers to make grants available to the states. The statement that the country is highly centralised is a generalisation that cannot be applied to all of the states. It does not apply to states that have shifted significant authority and responsibility to the school level in recent times. In Victoria, for example, 94 per cent of the state's recurrent budget is decentralised to the school level for local decision-making, albeit within a centrally determined framework, and this level exceeds that in the UK and New Zealand that are reported as being highly decentralised.

Earlier work on self-management may be helpful in achieving success in decentralisation to the school level in those nations that are embarking on such a course. More specifically, the model of the annual cycle in Figure 2.1 is likely to have universal application. The same may be the case for the refined model in Figure 2.2 that embeds the annual cycle in a three to five year management strategy that includes the preparation of a school development/improvement plan. The concept of a school charter may also be helpful. The vision or *gestalt* in Figure 2.3 may also assist, along with the various strategic intentions that were offered as a guide to practice on the three 'tracks for change'— building systems of self-managing schools, an unrelenting focus on learning outcomes, and creating schools for the knowledge society. The extent of utilisation may be constrained by values in particular settings as far as participation in decision-making is concerned, and also by the level of resources, particularly in respect to the adoption of information and communication technologies. The new image of the self-managing school, as summarised at the end of the chapter, may serve to accelerate success to the extent that it is based on the best of practice in nations with experience in this domain, and that are on the track to success in the transformation of their schools.

The new 'teaching imaginary'

David Hargreaves's adaptation of 'social imaginary' to 'educational imaginary' is also relevant in non-Western settings. The work of Hong Kong's Cheng Yin Cheong provides an illustration. Cheng is Director of the Centre for Research and International Collaboration at the Hong Kong Institute of Education. He proposed that every enterprise in education, including schools, school systems and universities, needs a new paradigm or framework to shape its operations. There are three dimensions in this paradigm: globalisation, localisation and individualisation. He has coined the concept of 'triplisation' to give it coherence. The case for a new paradigm ('educational imaginary') is based on different kinds of intelligence that are necessary in the 21st century. These are learning intelligence, technological intelligence, economic intelligence, social intelligence, political intelligence, and cultural intelligence. He describes these as 'contextualised multiple intelligences' (Cheng 2001, p. 39). Cheng contrasts the new paradigm of teaching ('teaching imaginary') with the traditional site-based paradigm, as illustrated in Table 6.1. The differences are significant.

Networking has an important place in the new paradigm, with Cheng referring to 'multiple local and global sources of teaching and knowledge', 'networked teaching', 'teacher with local and international outlook' and 'a world class and networked teacher'.

Table 6.1: THE NEW TEACHING PARADIGM
(Cheng 2001)

NEW PARADIGM	TRADITIONAL SITE-BOUND PARADIGM
Individual teacher and teaching:	Reproduced teacher and teaching:
‣ teacher is the facilitator to support students' learning	‣ teacher is the centre of education
‣ multiple intelligence teacher	‣ partially competent teacher
‣ individualised teaching style	‣ standard teaching style
‣ teaching is to arouse curiosity	‣ teaching is to transfer knowledge
‣ teaching is a process to initiate, facilitate, and sustain students' self-learning and self-actualisation	‣ teaching is a disciplinary, delivering, training, and socialising process
‣ sharing joy with students	‣ achieving standards in examinations
‣ teaching is a life-long learning process	‣ teaching is a transfer and application process
Localised and globalised teacher and teaching:	School-bounded teacher and teaching:
‣ multiple local and global sources of teaching and knowledge	‣ teacher as the sole source of teaching and knowledge
‣ networked teaching	‣ separated teaching
‣ world-class teaching	‣ site-bounded teaching
‣ unlimited opportunities for teaching	‣ limited opportunities for teaching
‣ teacher with local and international outlook	‣ teacher with only school experiences
‣ as a world class and networked teacher	‣ as a school-bounded and separated teacher

International framework for governance in education

The concept of governance was not employed in the first model of self-management (Caldwell and Spinks 1988) as illustrated in Figure 2.1. The notion of a 'policy group' rather than 'governing body' was used, with the principal functions of the former being goal-setting, policy-making, planning, budgeting and evaluation. Governance is now more widely used in education, at the level of government and also in schools. It is particularly relevant in the new image of the self-managing school as the trend toward autonomy gathers pace and the range of connections and interactions in the various networked arrangements become more complex. A definition of governance and a framework for assessment of practice is set out below. It is drawn from a project of the Human Resource Development Working Group of Asia Pacific Economic Cooperation (APEC) on *Best Practice Governance: Education Policy and Service Delivery* (Department of Education, Science and Training, 2005).

The Governance Working Group of the International Institute of Administrative Sciences (1996) provided a helpful definition of governance, adapted as follows:

▸ Governance refers to the process whereby elements in a society wield power and authority, and influence and enact policies and decisions concerning public life, and economic and social development.

▸ Governance is a broader notion than government. Government's principal elements include the constitution, legislature, executive and judiciary, whereas governance involves interaction between these formal institutions and those of civil society.

▸ Governance has no automatic normative connotation. However, typical criteria for assessing governance in a particular context might include the degree of legitimacy, representativeness, accountability and efficiency with which policies are developed and implemented, and services delivered.

This definition suggests that descriptions of governance arrangements should go beyond accounts of how policies are determined and decisions are made, and by which institutions. The notion that governance is concerned with the interaction between these and civil society suggests a broader approach. Civil society is considered here to be the network of mutually supporting relationships between government, business and industry, education and other public and private sector services, community, home, and voluntary agencies and institutions.

The World Bank Group (2001) has proposed a range of indicators for governance. While not taking an official position, it noted that 'new global standards of governance are emerging' and that 'citizens...are demanding better performance on the part of their governments'. It described several approaches to assessing the quality of governance, distinguishing between performance measures and process measures. Indicators can be classified in terms of aspects of governance assessed, specificity, demonstrated links to outcomes, data coverage, method of data generation, transparency, capacity for replication, ownership, data quality and accuracy, correspondence with related measures, financial incentives for accuracy, and the use of data in published studies.

The Appendix contains a framework for the description and assessment of governance, drawing on the work of the International Institute of Administrative Sciences (1996) and the World Bank Group (2001) as set out above. Broad indicators are provided in four domains (purpose, process, policy, standards). There are several elements in each domain.

The framework may be helpful in assessing the quality of governance in a school system and in a self-managing school because engagement with civil society is far more extensive in the new image and there are higher expectations than ever before as far as the performance of schools is concerned.

The adaptive state

The new image of the self-managing school is most readily observed in, or proposed for, systems of public education that already have considerable experience in the decentralisation of authority, responsibility and accountability to the school level, and are committed to an agenda for transformation. Such systems of education may be found in the United Kingdom, New Zealand and parts of Australia, Canada, Europe, Scandinavia and the United States. With appropriate adaptation it may be helpful in other settings where there is a commitment to decentralisation and an agenda for transformation is taking shape, as is the case in the APEC economies, illustrated in the examples from Chile in Chapter 3.

It is clear there is no single approach to self-management that will suit all settings. Moreover, whatever approach suits a particular setting at a particular time is likely to change with the passage of time. The one constant seems to be the passing of highly centralised approaches to governance in education that dominated the 20th century. Michael Barber noted the passing of the era of the bureaucratic public services and the beginning of a new era of public services 'capable of rapid change' (Barber 2003, p. 115). Flexibility of a kind that Barber has in mind is illustrated by Bentley and Wilsdon (2004) who suggest an 'adaptive state' is required if the best approaches to service delivery are to be achieved at a particular point in time.

> We need new systems capable of continuously reconfiguring themselves to create new sources of public value. This means interactively linking the different layers and functions of governance, not searching for a static blueprint that predefines their relative weight. The central question is not how we can achieve precisely the right balance between different layers—central, regional and local—or between different sectors—public, private and voluntary. Instead, we need to ask *How can the system as a whole become more than the sum of its parts?*' (Bentley and Wilsdon 2004, p. 16).

The image of the self-managing school is likely to change from time to time and from setting to setting in a manner that is consistent with the notion of the 'adaptive state'. What follows are the key elements in this image as they appear in the middle of the first decade of the 21st century.

Elements in the new image of the self-managing school

The original image of the self-managing school, when it took shape nearly two decades ago, was of a school that had the capacity to take on new authorities, responsibilities and accountabilities through decentralisation from the centre of a school system to the school level. It was essentially a movement in a vertical line or a shift in the balance of centralisation and decentralisation. It was expected that this capacity would become a routine approach to management, embedded in a centrally determined framework of policies, priorities, curriculum and standards. Leaders and managers in schools were expected to be adept in budgeting, curriculum, human resources, pedagogy, program evaluation and strategy. Expectations for links beyond the immediate educational community were not high at any level in the school system. Schools were expected or required to have a consultative or governing body that included parents and other members of the school community. This image of the self-managing school was contentious at the time but has been broadly accepted in many nations.

The image is incomplete if account is taken of best practice in self-management in the 2000s, and if expectations for the transformation of schools are to be achieved. The following are the key elements in the new image of the self-managing school as they emerged from a review of practice and an exploration of expectations, as set out in Chapters 3, 4 and 5. Adopting the terminology of Zuboff and Maxmin (2004) this is the 'new enterprise logic' of the self-managing school.

1. The student is the most important unit of organisation—not the classroom, not the school, and not the school system—and there are consequent changes in approaches to learning and teaching and the support of learning and teaching.
2. Schools cannot achieve expectations for transformation by acting alone or operating in a line of support from the centre of a school system to the level of the school, classroom or student. Horizontal approaches are more important than vertical approaches although the latter will continue to have an important role to play. The success of a school depends on its capacity to join networks or federations to share knowledge, address problems and pool resources.
3. Leadership is distributed across schools in networks and federations as well as within schools, across programs of learning and teaching and the support of learning and teaching.
4. Networks and federations involve a range of individuals, agencies, institutions and organisations across public and private sectors in educational and non-educational settings. Leaders and managers in these sectors and settings share a responsibility to identify, and then effectively and efficiently deploy the kinds of support that are

needed in schools. Synergies do not just happen of their own accord. Personnel and other resources are allocated to energise and sustain them.

5. New approaches to resource allocation are required under these conditions. A simple formula allocation to schools based on the size and nature of the school, with sub-allocations based on equity considerations, is not sufficient. New allocations take account of developments in the personalising of learning and the networking of expertise and support.

6. Knowledge management takes its place beside traditional management functions related to curriculum, facilities, pedagogy, personnel, and technology.

7. Intellectual capital and social capital are as important as other forms of capital related to facilities and finance.

8. New standards of governance are expected of schools and the various networks and federations in which they participate. These standards are important in the likely shift from dependence and self-management to autonomy and self-government.

9. Each of these capacities requires further adaptation as more learning occurs outside the school, which is one of several major places for learning in a network of educational provision. The image of the self-managing school continues to change in different settings.

10. The sagacity of leaders and managers in successful self-managing schools is likely to be the chief resource in preparing others if transformation in a short time and on a large scale is the goal.

The metaphor of an epidemic has been invoked to describe the scale of the transformation that is within the reach of schools and school systems in some nations. 'What must underlie successful epidemics, in the end, is a bedrock belief that change is possible, that people can radically transform their behaviour or beliefs in the face of the right kind of impetus' (Gladwell 2004, p. 258). Re-imagining the self-managing school can make a contribution to this endeavour.

PART B

The new enterprise logic of schools

CHAPTER 7

The new enterprise

There must be fundamental change in the operation of schools that are organised along traditional lines if they are to survive for more than a few years in the 21st century. This change must be so pervasive and so deep that it amounts to the operation of 'a new enterprise logic'. Identifying its major features and illustrating its practice are the major purposes of Part B, as set out in Chapters 7 to 11.

The concept of 'new enterprise logic' is moving into the mainstream of organisational thought through the work of Shoshanna Zuboff and Jim Maxmin and their book *The Support Economy* (Zuboff and Maxmin 2004). In their view, the need for a new 'logic' arises from realisation that henceforth the way the organisation works must be turned on its head, so that the starting point of organisational form and function is the needs and aspirations of clients, customers and consumers or, in the case of schools, students and parents. This contrasts with the traditional approach where these people are seen as the end points in a delivery chain, and operations from start to finish are configured accordingly.

The notion of the 'logic' of the organisation is preferred to 'philosophy' or 'process'. While it encompasses each of these aspects of life in the organisation, it is intended to convey a sense of coherence and intent. It is related to the notion of 'culture' or 'the way things are done around here'.

The use by Zuboff and Maxmin of 'enterprise' includes, but enriches, the concept of 'organisation'. While the latter conveys all of the activities that arise from common purpose, 'enterprise' has a meaning that captures much of what is intended and has been achieved in schools that have set themselves for success in the 21st century.

The Merriam-Webster Online Dictionary defines enterprise—derived from the Old French word *entreprendre* ('to undertake')—in several ways. First, it is a project or undertaking that is especially difficult, complicated or risky. This seems entirely appropriate to describe the work of schools where expectations are high and where transformation is intended. As noted in previous chapters, transformation is considered to be significant, systematic and sustained change that results in high levels of achievement for all students in all settings. Second, it means readiness to engage in daring action. This certainly characterises the way school leaders have gone about their work when transformation has been achieved. The third meaning has two parts. One is a unit of economic organisation or activity; the other is a systematic purposeful activity. Educators usually resist the view that the school is an 'economic organisation' or that their work is 'economic activity'. We need not engage in debate along these lines. The other meaning describes a normal expectation for a well-run organisation.

Setting aside the economic connotation, which can also lead to consideration of concepts like 'free enterprise' or 'private enterprise'—contestable in the school setting—it is helpful to reflect on the main shades of meaning: an undertaking that is difficult, complicated or risky; readiness to engage in daring action; and systematic purposeful activity. Roget's *New Millennium Thesaurus* offers the following synonyms for enterprise or resourcefulness: activity, adventurousness, alertness, ambition, audacity, boldness, courage, daring, dash, drive, eagerness, energy, enthusiasm, force, foresight, get-up-and-go, gumption, hustle, industry, initiative, inventiveness, pluck, push, readiness, resource, self-reliance, spirit, venturesomeness, vigour, and zeal.

The new enterprise logic of schools is thus concerned with an undertaking that is difficult, complicated and at times risky, often calling for daring activity which is at all times purposeful. It is an undertaking that is coherent in its intent to achieve transformation. It is an undertaking that is thrilling in its execution when one contemplates the kinds of change that are illustrated in the pages that follow.

The old enterprise logic

The words of some of the most influential writers in education can be employed to characterise the 'old enterprise logic' and to build the case for change. They were cited in Chapter 3. David Hargreaves declared in 1994 that 'schools are still modelled on a curious mix of the factory, the asylum and the prison' and that 'many of the hitherto taken-for-granted assumptions about schools must now be questioned' (Hargreaves D 1994, p. 43 and p. 3, respectively). While we have come a long way in a decade, these images still come to mind in many settings.

The state of school buildings in the public sector is a symbol of the old enterprise logic of schools. There was remarkable expansion in the third quarter of the 20th century. In Australia, for example, thousands of schools were built in the years of the baby boom, accentuated by the effects of large-scale immigration. The public works programs of state and territory governments were commendable, given the size of the challenge. Thirty to fifty years later, there is a challenge of a similar proportion, and that is the replacement of most of these schools as well as the smaller number of still-standing older schools. However, a second public works program on a scale that matches the first seems beyond the capacity of government if approaches to funding are limited to the traditional.

There are two main reasons for the emergence of a challenge on this scale. One is that the physical condition of many schools demands urgent action. Most were built up to 50 years ago with a limited life span. There was acknowledgement that they would need to be replaced. The most important reason for replacement or rebuilding is educational. It has become a cliché that most schools were built on an industrial model that is now ill-suited to needs in the 21st century. Closer examination reveals just how much is at stake if large-scale change does not occur. Consider, for example, the typical primary school built between the late 1950s and the mid-1990s. It consisted of a series of classrooms each designed for 30–40 students. There was an office for the principal and secretary, and also a staff room. There may be a small library and a sick bay. There will be some space for playing fields. There may be a multi-purpose hall, often built with the support of locally-raised funds. There will have been little variation on the model even though the physical appearance may differ from setting to setting. It was assumed that students would move from room to room as they progressed through the school, in assembly-line fashion. The same model applied to the construction of secondary schools, with variations reflecting a subject approach to school organisation, including the provision of specialist facilities for science, technology and the arts.

A visit to schools that were built in this era and earlier reveals the mismatch between the physical design of the school and professional and pedagogical needs in the 21st century. Classes must now be smaller, given generally uncontested evidence that the class sizes in the low 20s, at least in the early years, are needed. Unless the school was located in a community where enrolments were declining, this meant the addition of classrooms, which for many schools came in the form of portable or demountable units, which have limited capacity for heating in winter and cooling in summer.

Increasing concern that many students left the primary school with low literacy and numeracy skills has meant a change in approaches to teaching and learning that often requires the withdrawal of some students from the regular classroom to receive one-to-one or small group instruction. Where does this occur? New areas have had to be created out of the already limited classroom space, and in some cases the corridors of the school have had to suffice.

There have, of course, been profound social, cultural and demographic changes that have had a major impact on the programs of schools, with serious consequences on the use and availability of space for those built several decades ago. There are many single parent families and, where families are intact, both parents often work. While the effects of post-war immigration were already being felt at the time of construction, schools were still relatively homogeneous in terms of their cultural mix. Now, schools in urban areas often have dozens of cultures in their make-up. Change of this breadth and scale means that a range of support services is required. These may include staff who can arrive early and leave late, often providing breakfast for students, and parent drop-in centres that have made their appearance in some settings. Links that were never needed in the past must now be made between education, health, welfare and law enforcement. The outcomes have included greater diversity among professional staff and different kinds of working space.

In the past, teachers either used their classrooms as personal professional space, or had a desk in a staff room, or had both. They did not have personal computers. They may have had a few books, largely textbooks related to their areas of teaching. Now, teachers are expected to have laptops and their professional learning needs are constantly changing so that personal libraries are expanding. New and different kinds of space are required. More recent building design at the secondary level, in particular, often provides rooms for teachers, either individual or in small groups according to year level or subject area, but space in the majority of schools is insufficient or inappropriate. Developments in technology have also meant a change in design. Classrooms have been converted to computer laboratories in most schools. The integration of technology in day-to-day learning and teaching is inconsistent with the standard size and shape of classrooms and the traditional alignments of desks.

A visit to almost any school built before the early to mid-1990s will reveal the combined effect of these changes. The following is a worst case account of what might be found. Regardless of the physical condition of the buildings, there is little flexibility in the use of space, classrooms are frequently overflowing with different technologies, corridors are being used for learning and teaching in small groups, teachers are hidden behind a mountain of books in overcrowded staffrooms or are working in isolated fashion in their classrooms; meetings of, and with, parents occur in makeshift facilities, and there are few fit-for-purpose working spaces for professionals other than teachers. Portable or demountable classrooms have become permanent fixtures, providing crowded and unhealthy spaces for teachers and students in seasonal extremes.

The effects go beyond those described. An increasing proportion of teachers are leaving the profession within a few years of graduation. Apart from the demands of teaching under conditions more challenging and complex than in the past, their physical working conditions compare poorly with those in most private schools, or their peers who work in other professions. Indeed, they are inferior to those found in almost any business.

The drift to private schools can be explained in part by school design and the facilities suffered by students and staff. Many private schools have the resources to create schools to a 21st century design, leaving behind the industrial model of the last century. Such a comparison is readily made by parents who will exercise choice when they can afford the fees, as an increasing proportion of parents can, given the continuing strength of the economy. Some observers may find it puzzling that schools built on factory lines can still be found in many communities when the factories upon which they were modelled have long departed the scene.

The good news is that the old enterprise logic, as symbolised in the design of school buildings, best summarised in Hargreaves's memorable 'curious mix of the factory, the asylum and the prison', is giving way to a new enterprise logic and a step change to transformation.

The new enterprise logic

A number of generalisations emerged from the review of changes under way in self-managing schools, as described in Part A. Examples were drawn from Australia, Chile and the UK, but developments in two major networks of nations were also described. These were the Organisation for Economic Cooperation and Development (OECD) in respect to scenarios for the future of schools, as constructed in the Schooling for Tomorrow project, and to findings in its Program for International Student Assessment (PISA). Reference was also made to tests of student achievement in the Trends in Mathematics and Science Study (TIMSS). Information was also drawn from a project of Asia Pacific Economic Cooperation (APEC) on Best Practice Governance in Policy Formation and Service Delivery.

The new image of the self-managing school was described in Chapter 6. The main themes are as follows:

1. The student is the most important unit of organisation—not the classroom, not the school, and not the school system.
2. Schools cannot achieve expectations for transformation by acting alone or operating in a line of support from the centre of a school system to the level of the school, classroom or student. The success of a school depends on its capacity to join networks to share knowledge, address problems and pool resources.
3. Leadership is distributed across schools in networks as well as within schools.
4. Networks involve a range of individuals, agencies, institutions and organisations across public and private sectors in educational and non-educational settings. Personnel and other resources are allocated to energise and sustain them.
5. New approaches to resource allocation are required under these conditions. These take account of developments in personalising learning and the networking of expertise and support.
6. Intellectual capital and social capital are as important as other forms of capital.

It is the first of these that lies at the heart of the need for a new enterprise logic, and it is the response of an increasing number of school systems. In the UK, for example, that response is captured in the priority for personalising learning (DfES 2004a).

Exploring the new enterprise logic

Part B provides an opportunity to look more closely at the new enterprise logic of schools. The first step in this exploration is to examine what lies at its heart, namely, the voices of customers or consumers, or in the case of schools, students and parents. Some will contest the view that change on the scale of transformation should be based on the voice of the individual. This issue is taken up in the next section of the chapter, along with some general principles of new enterprise logic as outlined by its proponents (Zuboff and Maxmin 2004).

Many of the policies and practices described in Part B were presented in workshops on three continents. Their purpose was to gather information about how the new enterprise logic was shaping their work, and to challenge participants to 're-imagine the school' in the face of expectations for transformation. One workshop was conducted in Australia in Melbourne in mid-February 2005. Five workshops were conducted in England in late February and early March. These were organised by the Specialist Schools and Academies Trust on a regional basis in Cambridge, Derby, Ilminster, Leeds and London. One workshop was conducted in New Zealand in early April. It was presented in Christchurch by Core Education, formerly Ultralab South. Finally, two workshops were conducted in Chile in early May as part of a leadership festival sponsored by International Networking for Educational Transformation. Partners in these events, conducted in Santiago and Viña del Mar, were Fundación Chile, Fundación Minera Escondida, the Latin American Heads Conference, and Australian Education Internacional.

Each session featured a short presentation by a leader from a school regarded as an exemplar in the area under consideration, and discussions among participants on two key questions designed to elicit accounts of current practice and proposals for work in the future. Each group of participants was able to record its deliberations by keyboard entry, with responses from all groups displayed on a large screen for subsequent synthesis. A document with all responses, along with syntheses of strategies, was available for participants at the conclusion of the day. The technology was developed by Sydney educator John Findlay and is known as Zing. It has a range of applications in educational and non-educational settings, including use by students in the classroom. It has wireless and Internet capability.

Examples of the new enterprise logic in action, as shared and constructed by participants in each workshop, are included in Chapters 8, 9 and 10. Chapter 8 (The New School) contains an extensive selection to illustrate the major propositions in the new enterprise logic. Chapter 9 (The New System) is concerned with how a system of schools can provide direction and support for the effort. Elements of a new enterprise logic of a school system are evident. Chapter 10 (The New Profession) draws on a range of approaches to illustrate how the work of teachers and other professionals is changing. Chapter 11 (The New Leader) provides a framework to guide the efforts of those who lead in a school that seeks to achieve change on the scale of transformation. Issues related to the attractiveness of leadership are canvassed. Illustrations in each chapter come from several nations, providing international evidence of the new enterprise logic.

Tensions in transformation

The notion of new enterprise logic was drawn from *The Support Economy* (Zuboff and Maxmin 2004). The case for a new logic is based on the need to respond to the needs of clients, consumers and customers, and in the case of schools, students and parents. Zuboff and Maxmin (2004) suggested that this is an international phenomenon:

> These new voices rise from the United States to the United Kingdom, from Canada to New Zealand, and across Western Europe. They have gathered force in the offices and classrooms of Santiago, Istanbul, and Prague. They form a new society of individuals who share a claim to psychological self-determination—an abiding sense that they are entitled to make themselves (Zuboff and Maxmin 2004, p. 9).

The examples that illustrate the new enterprise logic of schools in the chapters that follow are drawn from most of these settings.

According to Zuboff and Maxmin, 'psychological self-determination describes the ability to exert control over the most important aspects of one's life, especially personal identity, which has become the source of meaning and purpose in a life no longer dictated by blood lines and tradition' (Zuboff and Maxmin 2004, p. 135). The personal freedom that is implied here does not mean that community is unimportant or that the individual may not act with high moral purpose. In his final book Pope John Paul II referred to the 'proper use of freedom'—'If I am free, I can make good or bad use of that freedom' (Pope John Paul II 2005, p. 37). Moral purpose and social responsibility are important matters to be addressed in schools.

Characteristics of new pedagogies that rise from the voices of students include a capacity to work in teams, even though the individual is the most important unit of organisation. A capacity for schools to operate in networks to share knowledge, address problems and pool resources is important in the new enterprise logic. Schools should not be isolated silos. Similarly in respect to the importance of social capital: schools should be part of a network of individuals, agencies, organisations and institutions that provide mutual support to their different endeavours. In summary, self-determination and its articulation in the voices of students and parents is not inconsistent with—indeed it is supported by—a sense of community and the building of strong social capital.

Leadership

Peter Hyman wrote about the relationship between policy-makers and professionals in *1 out of 10: From Downing Street Vision to Classroom Reality* (Hyman 2005). Hyman was speechwriter and policy advisor to Tony Blair for 10 years before leaving Number 10 and taking up an appointment as a classroom assistant at Islington Green School. The book is remarkable for its insights into the leadership style of the Prime Minister and headteacher (Trevor Averre-Beeson), referred to throughout as simply Tony and Trevor.

Hyman has great admiration for the role of the head. 'There isn't a more important role than trying to educate, stimulate, [and] inspire teenagers as they teeter on the tightrope from childhood to adulthood…The power and responsibility of a headteacher over the 1000 students in his school seems to me much more immediate than the power of a Prime Minister' (Hyman 2005, p. 379). [Hyman refers to Winston Churchill's opinion that 'Headmasters have powers at their disposal with which Prime Ministers have never been invested'.] This view suggests that, without abandoning a commitment to 'distributed leadership', we ought to give even greater recognition to headship or executive leadership in the school.

Hyman is very clear in his belief, now that he has worked in both worlds, that policy-makers and professionals hold rather different beliefs about what ought to be done and how. He makes several recommendations. While it is beyond the scope of this short account to offer a commentary, one recommendation is pertinent in addressing an agenda for transformation. He suggests that policy-makers ought to have greater confidence in professionals and be less prescriptive. 'For lasting change to occur in public services, politicians need to show more humility and bring on board the professionals' (Hyman 2005, p. 390). 'Governments must take the need to let go more seriously, and to empower the frontline. It must produce a climate where frontline public servants do not become risk-averse. This means less dictating, less putting up pots of money to be bid for—ambitious targets yes, accountability yes, but also back creativity and imagination' (Hyman 2005, p. 385). This is consistent with the meaning of 'enterprise' as it was outlined at the start of this chapter.

Hyman's conclusion is also consistent with the view of Malcolm Gladwell, who coined the concept of 'the tipping point' ('that one dramatic moment in an epidemic when everything can change all at once'). He concluded that 'What must underlie successful epidemics, in the end, is a bedrock belief that change is possible, that people can radically transform their behaviour or beliefs in the face of the right kind of impetus' (Gladwell 2004, p. 258). This 'bedrock belief' must exist at all levels, including governments and schools, among policy-makers and professionals at the front line. For governments to hold such a belief, they must be assured that schools have the capacity to deliver. For practitioners to believe, they must be confident in their capacities and be assured the cause is a good one and that the policy settings are the right ones.

CHAPTER 8

The new school

How is the new enterprise logic shaping the form and function of schools in the early years of the 21st century? This chapter provides illustrations from Australia, Chile, England and New Zealand. They were provided by principals, headteachers and other leaders who contributed to nine workshops from February to May in 2005 on the theme 'Re-imagine the School'. Some contributions were formal presentations, others were examples shared in discussions among participants that were then summarised and synthesised using the interactive technology described in Chapter 7.

Transformation

Transformation was defined in Chapter 1 as significant, systematic and sustained change that results in high levels of achievement for all students in all settings. The agenda for transformation underpins much of the school reform effort around the world. There is realisation that the outcome cannot be achieved unless learning is personalised. This was made explicit, for example, in *The Five-Year Strategy for Children and Learners* in the UK (DfES 2004a). It is this intention, more than any other, which requires a change from the old to the new enterprise logic. Some believe it cannot be achieved, so powerful is the traditional way of organising a school for learning and teaching. While transformation on this scale will take time, impressive progress is being made in schools where there are enterprising leaders.

The Leigh City Technology College in England, under the leadership of Frank Green, combines many elements of the new enterprise logic. Synergies have been created with several organisations with global reach, illustrated by its status as a Cisco Systems Networking Academy, an Oracle Networking Academy, and a Microsoft Academy. It is an Investors in People, an international program for the certification of human resource management. Noteworthy is the move to a vertical 13–19 curriculum that enables the learning program for each student to be a personal one. As described by deputy head Bill Watkin: 'all tutor groups are composed of students from each of years 7 to 14, and teaching groups, at least in years 9 to 14, will be made up of students of differing ages. Students will begin and end courses, and be entered for exams, when they are ready, irrespective of age'. Other features include a condensed Key Stage 3, vertical tutoring, a remodelled workforce, a vocational curriculum that enjoys high esteem, and links with other educational providers. The difficulties of implementing the approach are acknowledged and are being worked through. As Watkin describes it: 'there will be a need for some constraints, in the form of timetable blocks. The main shift here will be that the blocks will not be formed with reference to year groups, but rather to the stage of the course. Furthermore, effective communication, detailed tracking and monitoring, and a cooperative home-school partnership will be essential. Students will need a sophisticated level of curriculum guidance and advice, which will be the responsibility of the new "vertical-learning tutors"'.

David Carter is head at John Cabot City Technology College in Bristol. He has played a leading role in a national project to remodel the workforce in England, described in more detail in Chapter 10. David describes the challenge of preparing an Individual Learning Plan (ILP) for every student: 'creating the time and scope for a pupil to be mentored and coached on a regular basis requires a different look at the school day, the timetable and the curriculum structure. The role of the mentor to work on learning targets, helping children to understand their learning styles, and to look at the information the data are providing and to advise on a future pathway, requires cultural as well as systemic change across the school'. This has been achieved at John Cabot.

Shifting the focus to the student can be achieved in a relatively short time if the process is right. Karen Cain built on her successful experience at Traralgon Secondary College in rural Victoria in Australia to get a flying start in her new appointment as principal at Lowanna College, which undertook a review of its operations in late 2004 when Karen took up her appointment. Building on an already strong base in ICT, a vision entitled 'Learning Anywhere Anytime' was created. International research, partnerships with the ICT industry, future visioning, creation of a concept for a 'future' learning space, and building an interactive portal linked knowledge to action within 12 months. An architect was engaged to create such a space. Teachers are engaged in addressing critical questions of curriculum and pedagogy.

More examples of transformation and the personalising of learning are contained in subsequent pages, since they have been accomplished through synergy, sagacity and new approaches to school design. Further illustrations are contained in a series of publications by David Hargreaves (for example, Hargreaves D 2004). He conducted seminars and workshops with more than 250 school leaders in 2004 and formed the view that there are nine interconnected 'gateways' to personalising learning: curriculum, workforce development, school organisation and design, student voice, mentoring, learning to learn, assessment for learning, new technologies and advice and guidance. Readers will recognise that the 'new enterprise logic' is giving shape to the '21st century imaginary' that lies at the heart of transformation in schools (see Hargreaves D 2004, pp. 30–2 for a description of 19th and 21st century imaginaries).

Synergy

The concept of synergy is captured in the realisation that schools cannot achieve expectations for transformation by acting alone or operating in a line of support from the centre of a school system to the level of the school, classroom or student. The success of a school depends on its capacity to join networks to share knowledge, address problems and pool resources. This is not to deny the importance of a line of direction and support from the centre of a school system (government, local education authority) to the school in a system of public education. What changes is that this is not the only line of support for schools, as evidenced by those that have achieved change on the scale of transformation or are on the way to achieving it. In some instances, however, schools are doing so well in their networking that reliance on traditional sources of support is minimal. The work of leaders who have energised these new arrangements is enterprising in the sense outlined in Chapter 7: it is 'concerned with an undertaking that is difficult, complicated and at times risky, often calling for daring activity'. The new enterprise logic is embedded in their action.

One of the most impressive examples of synergy to achieve transformation can be found at Ringwood Secondary College (RSC) in the eastern suburbs of Melbourne. During 2004 the Australian Government funded a Local Community Partnership (LCP) to help establish a training centre to address the skill shortfall in the automotive, engineering and manufacturing sectors. This funding was the catalyst for the establishment of the Automotive and Manufacturing Technology Centre (AMTC) at Ringwood Secondary College. The committee of management includes leaders from industry. Industry partners have helped design the programs. Networks of schools in the region and other providers in educational and non-educational settings have been critical to early success. For the first time, boundaries between public and private schools have been spanned. The principal at Ringwood is Michael Phillips, who is Co-Chair of the Principals Reference Group of International Networking for Educational Transformation—Australia. He plays a vital role in establishing and maintaining the partnerships that are creating the synergy for success. The mapping of these partnerships yields a complex pattern that illustrates the demanding role of 'the new leader' as modelled in Chapter 11. The linkages between the various stakeholders and developments in curriculum are illustrated in Figure 8.1.

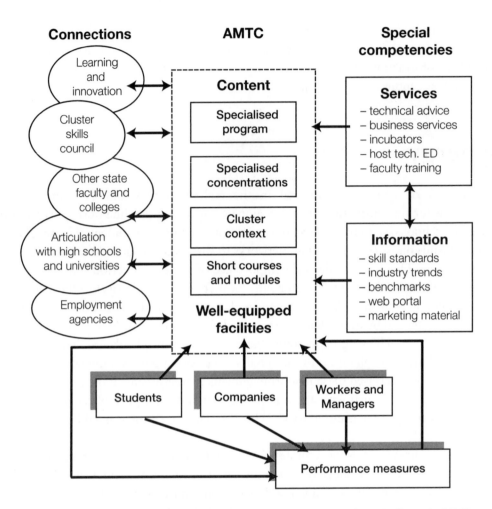

Figure 8.1: Achieving synergy for success at Ringwood Secondary College in Melbourne

Ron Richards, head of Priory Community School, is a leader in the powerful Weston Education Partnership (WEP), comprised of four secondary schools and two special schools in Weston-Super-Mare in North Somerset. The heads of these schools worked together in recent years in a 'Family of Schools', and this led to WEP, one of the first federations to be approved and funded by the Department for Education and Skills (DfES). It was launched in January 2004 at an event that brought together in one building the 600 staff from each of the six schools. It was the first time that many had ever met colleagues from other schools.

A Director, who also takes responsibility for the Excellence Cluster, leads the Partnership. An Assistant Director and two administrative staff support her. The initial planning was carried out by a committee of the heads and some governors from each of the schools. This has been formally constituted, with the heads meeting as the Strategic

Leadership Team and the heads and governors meeting as the Strategic Management Board. The Local Education Authority (LEA) is represented on both by the Senior Secondary Adviser. The Federation works through a number of Strand Groups, each coordinated by a Strand Leader, who is a member of the senior leadership team of one of the schools. The Strand Groups are Learning and Teaching, Organisation, Continuing Professional Development (CPD), initial teacher training, and ICT. The Excellence Cluster program, which also involves some primary schools, is similarly organised on a Strand Group basis (Learning Support Units, Learning Mentors, Gifted and Talented, Tailored Strand). Similar structures also exist for the Aim Higher program, which also takes in Weston College (a sixth form college) and higher education institutions.

The third proposition in the new enterprise logic is that leadership is distributed across schools in networks as well as within schools. This is illustrated in each of the examples set out above. The old enterprise logic meant that principals, headteachers and other school leaders were constrained to work in their own school, and sometimes with their local communities of parents, under the direction and with the limited support of central authorities and agencies in the school system. Compare this with the vibrant and dynamic role of Michael Phillips at Ringwood Secondary College (RSC) and with the work of Ron Richards and his colleagues in the Weston Education Partnership (WEP). The fourth proposition is that networks involve a range of individuals, agencies, institutions and organisations across public and private sectors in educational and non-educational settings. Personnel and other resources are allocated to energise and sustain them. This proposition is illustrated at RSC and WEP, and in other examples in Chapter 9, where networks and federations are considered in the context of 'The New School System'.

The fifth proposition is that new approaches to resource allocation are required under these conditions. Such approaches take account of developments in personalising learning and the networking of expertise and support. In most instances, additional funds must be secured under different government schemes or from private sources. An unresolved issue, however, is the manner in which funds are allocated to schools under the new enterprise logic, once it is embedded in schools and school systems. Traditional single-school-focused, needs-oriented and formula-based approaches do not take account of the necessary costs of networking. Schools are dealing with this by pooling their funds to make additional appointments to support the networks. Brian Caldwell and Jim Spinks have written two pamphlets for the Specialist Schools and Academies Trust that explore the possibilities (Caldwell 2006b; Spinks 2006).

Sagacity

Sagacity as explained in Chapter 5 is 'the intelligent application of knowledge acquired from years of learning and experience' (Merriam-Webster Online Dictionary). The challenge for schools that are striving to achieve transformation is that every teacher and other professional, and those who support them, must be at the forefront of knowledge and skill in their areas of expertise, and must remain so. The new enterprise logic calls for this challenge to be met. The old enterprise logic was based on initial teacher education and occasional professional development. Continuing Professional Development (CPD) that does not engage every member of staff, or which lacks coherence and relevance to the agenda for transformation, offers little advance on the old enterprise logic.

The sixth theme in the new enterprise logic is that intellectual capital and social capital are as important as other forms of capital. Sagacity is required to build them. The Comberton Village College near Cambridge has developed a coherent and comprehensive program of professional learning that was praised in a recent Office for Standards in Education (OFSTED) report: 'the majority of teachers are actively involved in developing their work, some by undertaking research, some by leading innovation...and some by contributing to departmental developments [that are] effective in developing students'

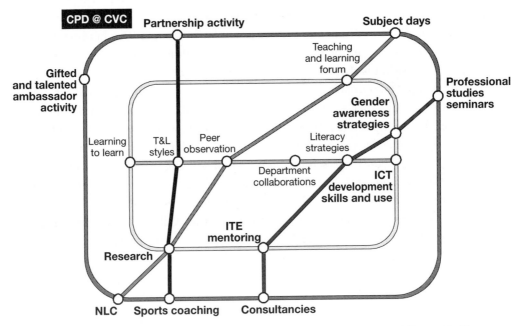

Figure 8.2: The professional learning program at Comberton Village College near Cambridge

(Illustration created by Mary Martin and Leigh McClelland)

learning and achievement [and develop] a culture and atmosphere where innovation and experiment are the norm.' Mary Martin and Leigh McClelland are leaders in the program. They adapted the map of the London Underground in Figure 8.2 to illustrate the range of activities and the various connections that make them so effective. There were 12 discrete action research projects under way at Comberton at the time of presentation.

John King is head of Gable Hall School in England. His school has embarked on a journey through the nine gateways to personalising learning as proposed by David Hargreaves. Student voice is heard because students serve as associate governors. Noteworthy among the changes at Gable Hall is the redesignation of positions among senior staff to reflect the view that the student is at the centre and the importance of embedding the new enterprise logic in the school. The headteacher is the lead learner (research and development). One deputy headteacher has responsibility for curriculum design; the other for pedagogy, sagacity and workforce reform. One of three assistant headteachers is responsible for advice, guidance, mentoring and coaching; another for school organisation and design as well as technology; and the third for synergy.

The Fendalton Open-Air School in Christchurch on the South Island of New Zealand has built a powerful capacity for professional learning. Four Quality Learning Circles (QLCs) have been formed and each member of staff joins one according to personal preference. These circles are concerned with Literacy, Numeracy, Diverse Learners, and Our Way. Our Way is a future-oriented group that deals with the way in which professional learning should support the strategic plan of the school. Each QLC has an external mentor from the Christchurch College of Education (teacher education), the University of Canterbury, or the Ministry of Education. The program has an overall mentor (known at the school as the 'extreme mentor') in the person of Joan Dalton, who is a highly valued consultant to schools in Australia and New Zealand. There is synergy with other schools in building professional capacity. The principal, for example, is a member of the Future Focus Principals Group, established to encourage innovation and share ideas about the future of schools. Mentor to this group is Julia Atkin, who also has a reputation as an outstanding consultant to schools in Australia and New Zealand.

A superb example of synergy and sagacity in combination may be found in the Doveton-Endeavour Hills cluster of government (public) schools in south-east metropolitan Melbourne. Consisting of five primary and two secondary schools, it serves communities that are culturally and linguistically diverse, with 38 per cent of the population born overseas. While there is substantial industry in this part of Melbourne, only 14 per cent of adults are in full-time employment, and 14 per cent receive disability pensions.

Michael Polack is Cluster Educator for the network. He mapped the work of the cluster against a key element of the new enterprise logic of schools: 'the success of a school depends on its capacity to join networks, to share knowledge, address problems and pool resources' (Figure 8.3). The schools work together to address problems in numeracy, literacy, transition to secondary and welfare. Knowledge is shared, with a rich data base, including outcomes of system-wide testing in the Achievement Improvement Monitor (AIM) and the mapping of activities that reflect Principles of Learning and Teaching (PoLT). There is a shared professional development program that addresses the Victorian Essential Learning Standards (VELS). Resources are shared in several ways, including the pooling of cluster funds for Casual Relief Teaching (CRT).

Several elements in Figure 8.3 can be mapped at another level. For example, the common welfare problem is addressed through a program that resulted from a memorandum of understanding with the Centre for Adolescent Health at the University of Melbourne. The program involves the Brotherhood of St Laurence, Anglicare and the Leath Foundation. Another program is connected to an employment opportunity project supported by the City of Casey, Adult Multicultural Education Services (AMES) and the Education Foundation. The traditional line of support through the Department of Education and Training is still evident, but it is one of many. Several cross-network committees have been formed to guide the development and implementation of a complex array of projects. These are known as the Belonging, Engaging and Succeeding Together (BEST) Committees.

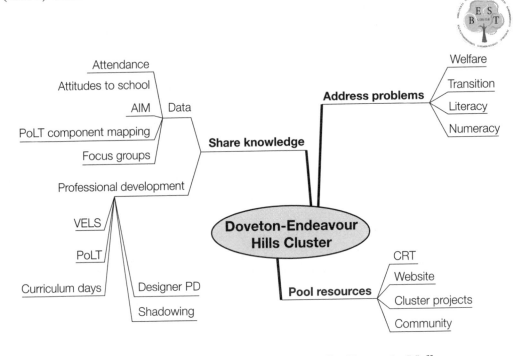

Figure 8.3: Networking in the Doveton-Endeavour Hills Cluster in Melbourne (Mapping by Michael Polack)

An even more complex picture emerges when the 'sharing knowledge' aspect of networking is mapped. The result is contained in Figure 8.4. Activities are organised around six Principles of Learning and Teaching (PoLT). A striking feature of Figure 8.4 is how traditional professional development activity finds its place among a rich menu that includes classroom visits, home visits, twilight forums, breakfast clubs and shadowing. It is noteworthy that learning in BEST involves teachers and the wider community as much as it involves teachers alone.

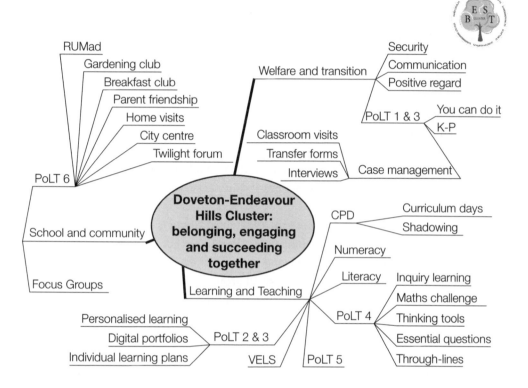

Figure 8.4: Synergy and sagacity in the Doveton-Endeavour Hills Cluster
(Mapping by Michael Polack)

The author visited Doveton North Primary School where Michael Polack is based. Much of the ground-breaking work for networking with the community was undertaken by its principal Murray Geddes, including the building of the Family Resource Centre on the school's site to serve and support the community. It was an inspiration to see how so much could be achieved at a school that, in structural terms, had long passed its 'use by' date. For example, the school undertook a comprehensive review of its curriculum in 2005 led by Pauline Canfield, the school's Curriculum Coordinator, and shared with the cluster in the light of the new Victorian Essential Learning Standards (VELS). The process and the product are fine examples of sagacity, with implementation taking account of the importance of the network and the synergies it enjoys with the wider community. The school and the wider network demonstrate that intellectual and social capital are as important as other forms of capital in the new enterprise logic of schools.

Design

It is important that there is coherence among the different themes that comprise the new enterprise logic. This coherence is evident in the nine gateways to personalising learning, with the notion of design in the broadest sense included in one gateway ('school organisation and design') (Hargreaves D 2004).

Kings College in Guildford, Surrey is an 11–18 state school that opened in September 2000. It is based on the site of a previously failing school with very low student achievement levels. Five years later Kings College was fully subscribed and highly praised by inspectors. How this transformation was achieved is described elsewhere (Crossley 2003) and was introduced in Chapter 4. A range of strategies has been adopted and these come together in a coherent 'school design'. Changes have been made to the physical layout of the school and to the ways its various facilities are used. The focus is on the student. The concept of 'anytime anywhere learning' has been adopted to enable students to study 'free from the tyranny of the timetable'. As Crossley describes it:

> the aim is to create a situation where the timetabled lesson is one of a number of ways where a particular course can be completed. We also sought to break the paradigm of the class of up to 30 led by one teacher being the normal day-in day-out mode of learning. Plans included fostering individual and small group tutorials, distance/on line learning, videoconference or e-mail links to teachers and other 'guides on the side'. Technology is the servant enabling this transformation to occur. Even after four years we were in my view still at the beginning of the journey (Crossley 2003).

It is inevitable that design should include the physical design of the school, and how its space is used. It is difficult to embed the new enterprise logic if school buildings are hostile. There is an unprecedented opportunity in England and Scotland to build or re-furbish schools that are friendly. Developments along these lines are discussed in more detail in Chapter 9. The following are brief accounts of how two schools are dealing with the possibilities.

The tensions between innovation and practicability in school design are illustrated in plans for new buildings for the City of London Academy. The school was in fact the first City Academy in England, opening in 2003 but occupying a succession of temporary facilities until shifting to its permanent site in Bermondsey, South London in September 2005. Martyn Coles is its headteacher, taking up his appointment in April 2002. He therefore had the opportunity to help shape the design. He served his previous headship in Tower Hamlets for eight years. He is a member of the Director-General's Headteacher Reference Group at the Department for Education and Skills. The City of London Academy is sponsored by the Corporation of London and is a Business and Enterprise College.

Coles describes the tensions in progressing the design that had to provide 'a learning environment that is infectious', outstanding sports facilities and ICT, and facilities consistent with the needs of specialisation in business and enterprise. The architects' wish for a dramatic building and teacher trepidation about open plan classrooms had to be addressed. The outcome is a balance 'combining the traditional classroom design with the opportunity to experiment in a potentially exciting teamwork approach to learning and professional development for staff in "cluster areas"'. The six-hour day is divided into three two-hour sessions, providing a flexible framework for creative work.

Dave Baker is the head of Bradley Stoke Community School in a new town of 22 000 in South Gloucestershire. The school opened in September 2005 and so Baker and his assistants had a rare opportunity to prepare a school design, in the broadest sense of that term, to establish a school to suit the 21st century learner. Every element of the new enterprise logic is evident in the design. Baker points out that 'the vision is for a school which will be both in the community and for the community'. He acknowledges the tensions: 'at one end of the spectrum is the pressure to conform to what is perceived as the reliable and robust "script" by anxious parents who are worried about their children being guinea pigs; whilst at the other end is the pressure to be radically different from all that has gone before, because the opportunity is there to be innovative and pioneering and write a new "script"'. Baker and his colleagues are networking widely to capture ideas and complete the design.

The way forward

Participants in the nine workshops in Australia, Chile, England and New Zealand were invited to share their experiences on each of the topics around which this chapter is organised and to devise strategies for the future. Most schools had made a start on a transformation agenda and proposals for the future invariably involved entry through one or more of the gateways to personalising learning.

Participants gave a rating from 1 (low) to 10 (high) of the strength of synergy their schools had achieved. The range of responses was 2 to 9 with a mean of about 5. They had no difficulty identifying ways in which their schools could make progress in this area. It was clear that networks and networking are embraced, if progress and intention are taken as a guide, especially in England through the different networks of the Specialist Schools and Academies Trust and the Networked Learning Communities of the National College for School Leadership. The challenge is to make them effective through the allocation of time, personnel and other resources.

A similar range of responses was received for ratings of intellectual capital. In this instance, participants were asked to give a criterion-based rating, so that a score of 10 was given in a situation where it was judged that all staff are at the forefront of knowledge and skill that would enable the school to achieve transformation. No participant gave their school a score of 10. There was no shortage of ideas on how the intellectual capital of schools could be strengthened, and most of these were variations of approaches illustrated in this chapter.

The topic of design proved particularly challenging. Responses generally affirmed the priority that should be given to building or refurbishing schools to accommodate the new enterprise logic. It is in this respect that the matter of a new enterprise logic for a school system should be addressed, and this is done in Chapter 9.

CHAPTER 9

The new system

An important issue for all stakeholders is whether the new enterprise logic is consistent with a sense of system in a nation that values public education. The same issue arose with the trend to self-managing schools, especially when these moved toward autonomy. Concerns about equity and a commitment to the common good were raised. This chapter explores the implications for school systems of the new enterprise logic of schools, drawing on developments in several nations.

In a broader sense, the issue has been explored in a number of publications that deal with the role of the state and the provision of public services. Several were cited in Chapter 6, especially in respect to the need for a more responsive, adaptable public service ('the adaptive state'). What Barber and Bentley and Wilsdon proposed has happened on a small scale, but momentum is building and a new enterprise logic of a system is emerging.

How many levels?

In the old enterprise logic there were three levels of a school system: the state, the district or other local or regional authority, and the school. This arrangement is assumed in commentaries on educational reform. Michael Fullan refers to a 'tri-level model' in describing the shift from whole school reform to whole system reform (Fullan 2004, 2005). While his proposals for development at each level are consistent with the new enterprise logic and of practices illustrated in these pages, it may be helpful to re-cast our thinking about the number of levels, if form and function are to follow the proposition that the student is the most important unit of organisation.

As far as authority, responsibility and accountability are concerned, it may be best to conceive of a national system of public education as comprising two levels: the state and the school. The state is the level of government at which constitutional powers for education reside. In most nations this is the national government (in some nations such as Australia, Canada and the United States, these constitutional powers lie at the level of state or province). Other levels of government, or agencies of other levels of government, are defined in legislation and these include districts and other authorities at the local or regional levels. While those subsidiary authorities have power to direct and provide support to schools, it is evident that they are rapidly becoming just one of many sources of support and the authorities concerned are providing a 'light touch' when it comes to direction. It is noteworthy that in England, in the five regional workshops that furnished evidence of the new enterprise logic, local education authorities (LEAs) were rarely mentioned, and participants described a range of ways in which they were networking to share knowledge, address problems and pool resources. These arrangements were facilitated in some instances by a local authority. This does not mean that these layers of government or agencies of government do not have critically important roles to play in some circumstances. These are addressed in another section of the chapter.

The other level of authority, responsibility and accountability is the school. There is recognition that the school is but one provider of services in some settings, and the challenge for leaders at the school level is to link these services to the best advantage of the student. It is evident in the examples of networks and networking in Chapter 8, and others to be shared in Chapter 9, that there is no one best way to configure these arrangements, and this underscores the concept of 'the adaptive state'.

More about networks and networking

The workshops that gave shape to Chapter 8 provided more examples of how networks and federations are part of the new configuration of support for schools, and four are described in the following pages. These are helpful in illustrating how particular issues that have been raised about networking can be resolved. Does it work when schools are in competition? How can networks be maintained when government priorities change? How do networks function when schools are small and geographically isolated? How can networks be sustained over time? Three examples are from England and one from Australia.

The question often arises as to whether networks or federations can be established under conditions of competition among schools. The Waverley Educational Federation in England is an example where this can be accomplished with benefits to all. Four secondary schools, a special school and a sixth form college are now working together after agreement among headteachers on common issues. In September 2001 a joint project was set up between the schools for the purpose of working with a group of disaffected and disengaged students to raise self-esteem and keep them within a learning environment that would help avoid permanent exclusion of students who are at risk. The project supports between

12–24 students at any one time. Students are referred by the schools and are mainly Year 11. This proved to be a successful collaboration. Funding of £75 000 was secured from the local education authority (LEA) to employ a coordinator, administration support and funding to enable students to access courses beyond the schools. According to Chris Lee, head of Broadwater School and chair of the Waverley Federation Steering Group, issues of time, resources, and ownership are of concern, but several new projects are in the planning stage, suggesting that value is being added through the work of the federation.

An interesting example of how one government initiative leads to another is illustrated in the creation of the Saffron Walden and Stansted Mountfitchet Federation of Schools in England. The majority of the partner schools have been involved in a number of collaborations in recent years. These included the South East England Virtual Education Action Zone and a Leading Edge partnership. A proposal to form a federation was submitted to the DfES Innovation Unit in March 2004. According to John Hartley, Head of Saffron Walden County High School, 'the federation's mission and aims were received enthusiastically, but unfortunately it was not possible for the DfES to fund the activities of the federation at the level that the bid initially envisaged. At this stage, however, it was suggested that the Business Development Unit at the DfES should become involved, with the objective of engaging private sector partners to provide financial and practical support'. The federation came into formal existence in September 2004.

The management structure consists of the Governors' Forum, comprised of one governor from each school. It will meet twice yearly to provide support and accountability. The Headteacher Steering Group/Executive Board has headteachers from each school, meeting approximately twice each term to set the overall direction of the federation and oversee the monitoring of the program. The Federation Consultant Coordinator (one day per week) is responsible to the Steering Group, providing day-to-day drive and coordination of activities. The Steering Group has established these aims: (1) to address the dip in attainment when young people move through key stages; (2) to develop a voluntary, innovative learning network in a local federation of schools to maximise the use of best practice; (3) to develop leadership training that is 'fit for purpose'; and (4) improve student interaction within the schools, across the key stages and in the community.

Schools do not have to be in geographic vicinity to create networks or federations to achieve synergy for transformation. Clive Peaple, headteacher at Cartmel Priory Church of England School, outlined the work of the Rural Academy of Cumbria that has nine small rural specialist secondary schools in its membership. The furthest distance between two schools involves about 2.5 hours of driving. Commencing in 2003, each of the secondary schools works closely with neighbouring primary and special schools, which means that the Academy extends to about 60 sites. These schools are small by English standards (150–520 students). According to Peaple, they were 'united by the concept of rural entitlement and, quite frankly, a sense of alienation from funding sources and educational opportunity commonly available to other secondary schools'. Heads, deputies and leaders in key departments meet regularly, with heads meeting each month and once each term on a residential basis. There is shared professional development for all schools on matters of importance, for example Assessment for Learning in January 2005. These events are organised by Rural Academy Research and Development (RARD), consisting of deputy heads and professional development officers. A RARD self-evaluation group of heads visit each other's schools to monitor developments.

There is a need to identify examples of networks and networking that have proved successful over time. One example where sustainability has been achieved is the Lanyon Cluster of schools in the Australian Capital Territory (ACT). There are six schools in the cluster: one high school, four primary schools and one outdoor school. It is located in one of three regions of the ACT. A director of the Department of Education and Training has oversight of about thirty schools in the region and therefore plays an important role in the support of the cluster. She also has several system-wide responsibilities including literacy and numeracy, and school excellence.

The oldest and smallest school in the cluster is Tharwa Primary established in 1899, currently enrolling just 28 students in a rural setting and enjoying strong community support. Not far from Tharwa is the Birrigai Outdoor School that provides a residential facility for schools in the ACT, offering school and non-school camps in a rural setting. Three primary schools have been established in the last fifteen years, reflecting the strong suburban growth in and around Lanyon. Two of these were designed so that they could be converted in the longer term to units in a retirement village. Lanyon High opened in 1995, with current enrolments around 730. The primary schools, that had begun networking in 1993, were involved in aspects of the design of Lanyon High.

A cluster executive was formed in 1996 and an initial conference in a retreat setting laid the foundation for a strategic plan, mobility across the cluster, continuity of curriculum, information and communications technology, specialist programs, and a literacy centre. Starting in 1997, the executive has held an annual two-day strategic planning conference to set goals, determine priorities and devise strategies for work in the cluster. Meetings of staff in all schools commenced in 2004 and these are now an important part of the program, as described below. A major literacy and numeracy project commenced in 2003 and in 2004 a cluster deputy principal was appointed.

There has been a change of principal at most of the schools in the cluster in recent years. Continuity in approach and philosophy is maintained through the involvement of the director in principal appointments. Other principals are also involved. This has been an important factor in achieving sustainability in the network. The following strategies are currently in place:

1. All staff in each of the six schools meet together in the sixth week of each term to consider matters of priority as identified in the plan for the year, as determined by the cluster executive.

2. A cluster deputy principal was appointed in 2004. This person is based at Lanyon High but schools in the cluster share costs of the position, with support from the Professional Learning Fund of the Department of Education and Training. The appointee is recognised as a deputy principal of each of these schools (she has six name badges that are worn according to the school where she is working at a particular time). Her primary role is capacity building across the cluster.

3. An executive teacher specialising in mathematics is also based at Lanyon High and provides services to each school, with sharing of costs along the same lines as for the deputy principal.

4. Technical support in ICT is also shared across schools.

5. An integrated curriculum designed at Charles Conder Primary was readily shared among all primary schools in the cluster.

6. A number of primary teachers 'followed' their Year 6 students to Lanyon High as part of a transition strategy. A particular benefit to Lanyon High is the understanding it has built of needs and programs in primary school and issues to be addressed in the years of transition.

7. Lanyon High is part of a network of five schools in the Tuggeranong Valley. An important aspect of these networked activities is vocational education and training (VET).

8. A recently retired principal from a school outside the cluster was employed on a contract basis to help schools in the cluster develop a strategy to deal with bullying.

9. There are particular benefits of the networking arrangements for teachers in the very small school at Tharwa. They meet their colleagues on a regular basis and are kept in touch with developments such as the integrated curriculum.

10. There are also benefits for the staff at Birrigai Outdoor School, who are not permanently placed at the school: they will return to the 'system' at the conclusion of their current placements. Being part of the cluster ensures that they keep in touch with developments.

Foundations are part of the 'new system'

The richness and complexity of arrangements at the school level, consistent with the concept of synergy and building the intellectual capital of the school, are illustrated in the opportunities schools are taking up to work with foundations with an educational focus. Examples were provided in Chapter 4, with several from the UK and brief reference to the scene in the United States. However, Chile warrants particular mention because it is an exemplar on the Latin American scene. More than 87 000 institutions fall into the category of non-profit social organisations. Two examples from Chile are of interest because they illustrate the concept of the 'new system' but also the 'new profession', considered in more detail in Chapter 10. Fundación Gabriel and Mary Mustakis was created in 1996 by a family from Greece. The foundation supports INTER@CTIVA, a network which in 2005 was helping 92 schools in highly disadvantaged settings, involving some 60 000 students through seven targeted technology-based programs aimed at achieving high standards of deep learning for all children in the context of the national curriculum.

Fundación Minera Escondida was created in 1996 by a large copper mining company operating mainly around Antofagasta in Northern Chile. Minera Escondida Limitada is owned by BHP Billiton (57.5 per cent), Rio Tinto (30 per cent), Japan Escondida (10 per cent) and the International Finance Corporation of the World Bank (2.5 per cent). The charter of the foundation (Fundación Minera Escondida, 2003, p. 5) refers to its aspiration to be a 'proven and respected model of the practice of the social responsibilities of business'. Its purpose is to 'invest in the development of human and social capabilities, as an expression of the social responsibility of Minera Escondida Limitada, which constitutes a valuable legacy that transcends the mining activity'. Its support covers education, health and social development, especially among youth and indigenous people in the Antofagasta region. Executive Director of the foundation is José Miguel Ojeda F, who has written an eloquent treatise on the social responsibilities of companies in the mining industry (Ojeda 2002). He describes how 'we have come to know many fragile social organisations that are maintained on the basis of volunteers whose spirit of giving doesn't seek any other compensation than the relief of the profound pain and frustration that accompanies the scourge of poverty'. It is a well-resourced foundation that provides substantial support but 'with time we have had to assume a good dosage of modesty and humbleness, and ensure we are not in competition with the state social programs which can lead to a duplication of efforts and the waste of precious resources' (Ojeda in Fundación Minera Escondida 2003, pp. 12–13). Its programs in education include 'Active Minds: Applied Mathematics' for those in Grades 7 and 8, and an Education Improvement Fund to support municipal and subsidised semi-private schools. It supports the Regional Educational Quality Improvement Network. In May 2005 it formalised arrangements for 17 schools to affiliate with International Networking for Educational Transformation.

Developments of note at the national level

Governments and their departments or ministries of education have important roles to play in setting goals, formulating policies, establishing standards, building frameworks for accountability, and providing resources. Two particular developments are selected for comment at this point: the building or refurbishment of schools, and providing support for networks and federation.

It was noted in Chapter 8 that much of the new enterprise logic of schools and the potential for transformation is constrained by the design of schools. It is evident that many schools (most schools in some systems) need to be replaced. Developments in England and Scotland illustrate how governments can take the lead to provide an environment in which transformation can occur.

The aim of the Building Schools for the Future (BSF) initiative in the UK is to rebuild or renew every secondary school over a 10–15 year period. A 50:35:15 formula has been adopted: 'new building' for 50 per cent of floor area, 'major refurbishment / remodelling' for 35 per cent, and 'minor refurbishment' for 15 per cent. Public private partnerships (PPP) constitute the major strategy for achieving this outcome in a relatively short time. Construction shall be state-of-the-art and shall take account of curriculum and pedagogy that will lie at the heart of school education for the decades ahead, with due consideration of developments or requirements in underperforming schools, extended or full service schools, specialist schools, academies, ICT and workforce reform.

The budget announced by the Chancellor of the Exchequer on 16 March 2005 also included provision for a £9.2 billion rebuilding program for up to 9200 primary schools to enable them to provide the new services expected of 'extended schools', which are to be open from 8 am to 6 pm. Secretary of State for Education and Skills Ruth Kelly described these plans as 'the most significant building and refurbishment program since the Victorian era' (cited in Smithers 2005).

There are similar intentions in Scotland, as set out in the Partnership for a Better Scotland Agreement (Scotland 2003). 'We will develop the largest school building program in Scotland's history, renewing 200 more schools by 2006, rising to 300 by 2009...New schools should demonstrate commitment to the highest design and environmental standards. We will make sure that by 2007 every school is an integrated community school'.

The intention to make every school an integrated community school is based on a favourable evaluation (Scotland 2005) of a pilot program of New Community Schools (NCS). This engaged over 170 schools in 37 projects, with most schools working in clusters. The aim was to achieve a higher level of integration between education, health and other services for young people in disadvantaged settings.

There are some interesting developments in Singapore, where the government is pursuing a major reform that moves the system away from standardisation. The Minister for Education summarised intentions in words that harmonise with the notion of personalising learning:

We are providing many more opportunities for students to discover their strengths and follow their passions. New pathways in secondary school education; more talents being recognised for progression in the system, new subjects being introduced for those with special interests and elective modules that allow students to engage in applied, hands-on learning; more schools offering niches of excellence in the performing arts or sports or specific fields of intellectual endeavour; more fluidity between our different streams of education; and even more flexibility within a subject, like how you study the mother tongue language (Shanmugaratnam 2005).

The Minister for Education in Singapore stressed the importance of 'customising space in schools to maximise learning and interaction' when he announced a new program to enhance the infrastructure of schools. He referred to 'top down support for ground up initiative':

> We will now take this to a new plane, by introducing a framework for schools to exercise greater autonomy in the design of learning spaces. The Flexible School Infrastructure—"FlexSI" for short—will give greater autonomy to the school to decide how its spaces and facilities can support a variety of teaching approaches and new ways of engaging students in learning. It will allow schools to use their collective imagination to give teachers more leeway, and give our students more opportunities for interaction or for independent and hands-on learning.
>
> With FlexSI, schools will be able to customise their environment to a greater extent than they currently can. School specifications will be more flexible and a new process of identifying schools' educational and operational needs will be introduced. Schools can rethink what the classroom of tomorrow should look like, to better engage their students. They can ask questions like—must learning take place within four walls with specified boundaries, and with a fixed number of students in a class? What if the walls were not fixed structures? How can learning be done differently if furniture and fittings could move from place to place? (Shanmugaratnam 2005).

The Governor of California recently announced a new issue of bonds to build 40 000 new classrooms and modernise 140 000 existing classrooms. Re-building California's infrastructure across all sectors in the public domain will cost an estimated US$222 billion over 10 years, with US$68 billion to be raised through bonds (reported in Broder 2006).

The synergies evident in the Scottish initiative are consistent with the new enterprise logic and demonstrate how governments can support the creation of networks and federations. The approach is well established in England through the support of Networked Learning Communities of the National College for School Leadership and those of the Specialist Schools and Academies Trust. Each of the examples of synergy in Chapter 8 at Ringwood Secondary College and the Priory Community School has support from government. Another example is Raising Achievement Transforming Learning, an initiative of the Department for Education and Skills, supported by the Specialist Schools and Academies Trust through its Achievement Networks. 'The Project seeks to embed innovative and energising ways of schools working and learning together. Its core aim is for improvement to be delivered by schools and for schools' (Crossley 2005). Mentor schools support the more than 200 schools from across England that made a commitment to raise levels of student achievement.

New Zealand is another nation that has recognised the importance of networking in pursuing an agenda for transformation. Secretary for Education Howard Fancy has written a comprehensive account of the reform effort over the last 15 years and plans for the immediate future (Fancy 2005). He noted that 'policy is now more explicitly focused on raising achievement. Central to this is the emphasis on the effective teaching of diverse students' (p. 15) and 'schooling means a move away from the traditional bricks and mortar approach to education, towards one that thinks much more about how students can access the best possible sources of learning. It implies that a more collaborative and networked system will be characterised by strong relationships that increase the educational opportunities and access available to students' (p. 16). He highlighted the importance of building professional capability and refers to the development of professional clusters of teachers. 'Experiences since 1989 have provided deeper insights into the nature of the focus, capabilities, attitudes, supports, information and relationships that are required within a system, if it is to perform very well and on a sustainable basis [that is, achieve transformation]. We have learned that schools cannot be "isolated islands" in themselves, but need to be seen as archipelagos, with a mix of both independence and interdependence (p. 17)'.

It is noteworthy that New Zealand is one of a handful of nations engaged in the exploration of scenarios that have emerged from the Schooling for Tomorrow project of OECD. The focus in New Zealand is on the future of secondary schools over the next 20 years. A novel arrangement 'to avoid it becoming a battleground between deeply entrenched groups' is the appointment of four 'guardians', each a prominent New Zealander, who have the task of 'developing rules of engagement, and with overseeing processes of engagement that ensure that no party can take control of the debate' (p. 17).

More about the adaptive state

These developments at the national level are nurturing the new enterprise logic in schools to the extent that they are energising networks that cut across the boundaries of other levels of government and link agencies and providers across different sectors. There is still an important role for local, district or regional authorities. It is at this level that the 'adaptive state' is most evident. It was noted at the outset that a light touch is all that is needed in some settings. In others, much direction and support may be required to get things started and to build commitment to a shared vision of transformation. Examples from Australia and England are offered as illustration.

Steve Munby became Chief Executive of the National College for School Leadership in England in April 2005. He served previously as Director of Education and Lifelong

Learning in Knowsley where many schools are in challenging circumstances. He worked with key stakeholders to develop a mission statement on 'Achievement and Learning for All'. He conducted an annual 'visioning conference', the first of which was held in March 2001. Within three years there had been significant gains in student achievement on a range of measures. His role was critical in securing these gains and building a shared commitment across the local education authority. This did not preclude the engagement of schools in a range of networks.

Wayne Craig became Director of the Northern Metropolitan Region of the Department of Education and Training in Victoria at about the same time. He was previously principal of Box Hill Secondary College, which offered a specialism in sport. Many of the schools in the region are in challenging circumstances, mostly from demographic changes over which they had little control. His first task is to get to know the schools and their circumstances and to then, like Munby, build commitment to a shared vision that takes account of likely and preferred futures for schools. Networks and networking will be important elements in a strategy for transformation.

Adaptability is important in matters of management at these levels. A contentious development in England was the placing of the management of some local education authorities in private hands. There is now evidence that these measures have had a positive impact on educational outcomes.

The Confederation of British Industry (CBI) has prepared a report entitled *The Business of Education Improvement* (CBI 2005). CBI is the UK's leading employers' organisation, representing over 250 000 public and private sector employers. Digby Jones, Director-General of CBI, described the interest of his organisation in education by noting a 2004 survey that revealed that one in three companies offered remedial training 'to compensate for failures in the education system' (cited in CBI 2005, p. 3).

The Business of Education Improvement reported independent research that found that the nine local education authorities (LEAs) out of a total of 150 that had outsourced their management services to the private sector had improved their performance on key educational indicators at a greater rate than the national average across all LEAs, and in comparison to LEAs with previously comparable performance that had not gone down this route. Islington was the first of the privatised LEAs and it was the most improved among all authorities across England. The report attributes these outcomes to 'a combination of political will, decisive leadership, improved governance, effective contracting and performance management' (CBI 2005, p. 5). It is important to note that the private companies involved, such as Cambridge Education Associates (CEA) in the case of Islington, bring together a range of experienced leaders and managers from the education and business sectors. One leader in Islington described success in the following terms:

> There is no doubt that the partnership between Islington Council and CEA@Islington over the last five years has transformed education in Islington. The combination of

strategic political and community leadership and high quality school support services has created a shared vision and supported schools in raising attainment for pupils. The partnership has worked by putting the needs of pupils and schools at the heart of what we do and ensured that the contractual framework has been an enabling factor (James Kempton, Executive Member for Children, Islington Council cited in Quinn 2005).

Despite these successes, the CBI report raises serious concerns about the capacity of government to successfully implement further reforms, including the Building Schools for the Future (BSF) initiative described earlier. It contends that 'commercial capacity within the DfES [Department for Education and Skills] needs to be strengthened through the creation of a dedicated commercial team with the skills, competencies and authority to understand and make interventions in the management of the public sector education market' (CBI 2005, p. 6). It is noteworthy that the BSF team at the DfES has been expanded to include such a capacity.

CHAPTER 10

The new profession

The new enterprise logic of schools has the potential to enhance the status of the teaching profession. This chapter provides a brief overview of how such an outcome is unfolding. Attention is given first to the professional aspects of the preferred scenarios for the future of schools, as identified in the OECD Schooling for Tomorrow project (OECD 2001) and described in Chapter 3. Then follows a short account of efforts to remodel the profession, exemplified in recent work in England. It is acknowledged that change on the scale of transformation will take time. Reference is made to another OECD report entitled *Teachers Matter* (OECD 2004b) that suggests professional development in the 25 participating countries is still set in a status quo scenario. Examples in the nine workshops that furnished illustrations for Part B are more consistent with the creation of powerful professional learning communities, as described in the preferred 're-schooling' scenarios.

Preferred scenarios

Chapter 3 contained an overview of the six scenarios in OECD's Schooling for Tomorrow project. The preferred 're-schooling' scenarios call for an increase in public support for schools and a new status for the profession. 'Schools as core social centres' calls for a range of cooperative arrangements between schools and other agencies, with services often co-located. Teachers work closely with professionals in other fields. 'Schools as focused learning organisations' emphasise a knowledge rather than social agenda. Teachers have high status as professionals, with extensive engagement in research and development, participation in knowledge-based networks, and a high level of mobility.

Remodelling the profession

England is leading the way in remodelling the profession. Dame Patricia Collarbone, Director of Leadership Programs at the National College for School Leadership and of the National Remodelling Team, provided an account of progress to date (Collarbone 2004). A major report for the government by PriceWaterhouseCoopers concluded that teachers were overworked and that much of what they did was unproductive. This led to an agreement between the government, employers and union under the title of Raising Standards and Tackling Workload. Key elements in the agreement provided for a phased introduction of new arrangements: no more routine clerical and administrative tasks (September 2003), a maximum of 38 hours per year in the amount of cover ('extras') to be carried out by teachers (September 2004), and guaranteed planning and leadership time (from September 2005). The intention was to help change the culture and build capacity so that teachers could tackle such challenges as personalising learning, assessment for learning, ICT in the classroom, leadership, observation and reflective practice, and performance management. Surveys in 200 'early starter' schools provided evidence of improvements in the following: opportunities for learning, work/life balance of teachers, pupil attendance, job satisfaction of support staff, and time and energy for teaching.

Gathering momentum

Dr Patrick Hazlewood is head of St John's School and Community College in England. He described the change in culture of professional learning and the challenges now being addressed:

> Over the past three years the focus on every teacher becoming an 'extended professional', taking risks with learning and challenging each other to go further, became the norm. The school has now reached a position where certain fundamental questions for the future management of the organisation arise. Do we need heads of department any longer? What will a school structure look like when teams of extended professionals work across the curriculum to lead in learning? If all classrooms are to have a global dimension, how do we create meaningful teams across schools/learning organisations? Are schools reaching a point where real and sustainable transformation must involve both students and teachers in networks of learning communities?

> George Spencer Foundation School and Technology College in Nottinghamshire is an 11–18 co-educational comprehensive school with 1300 learners. It is a Leading Edge

school, a Training School, part of the Investors in People program as well as being a Microsoft and Cisco Academy. It places a high priority on personalising learning, realised through its curriculum and L2L (Learning to Learn). It draws extensively on the work of Guy Claxton in the design of its curriculum and pedagogy. In Year 7, for example, the focus is on L2L, meaning that Key Stage 3, normally three years, is delivered in two years in Years 8 and 9. There are three modules in L2L in Year 7: The Positive Learner, The Responsible Learner and the Resourceful Learner. Each of these modules has three components that capture clusters of particular attributes: resilient-confident-positive-persistent; resourceful-effective-independent-social; and reflective-individual-purposeful-aware.

New roles have been created to support the learner. These involve a shift from Form Tutor to Learning Manager, and the appointment of Information Managers and a Director of Learning and Teaching. Heads of Years have become Directors of the rPhase (readiness for learning in the condensed Key Stage 3) and the iPhase at 6th Form where the focus is on independent learning. Headteacher Susan Jowatt reports that staff are 'secure, confident and skilled for L2L' and that 'visitors comment on how much the language of learning is evident in the lessons and through visual display'. There has been favourable feedback from parents. There is 'cautious optimism' that the already high levels of student achievement will be even higher.

The student has become the most important unit of organisation at Eltham College of Education. This is a privately owned publicly subsidised school in an outer suburb of Melbourne. Principal David Warner has documented its experiences in *Schooling for the Knowledge Era* (Warner 2006). He stresses that the structure of the school was based on the developmental stages of learners. Teachers are expected to select a group of students with whom to work. Career development for teachers follows success in such arrangements. As Warner observes: 'we will help you gain the experiences you need for your career, but the school is about what is best for young people'. This illustrates how a new enterprise logic that recognises the student as the most important unit of organisation has consequences for career advancement in the profession.

There are also implications for how leadership is exercised in a school. Mt Waverley Secondary College in the eastern suburbs of Melbourne is an outstanding example of a school that distributes its leadership. The Distributed Staff Leadership Model was created over the last decade to the point that 95 of the current teaching staff of 140 have leadership responsibilities. Glenn Proctor is principal at Mt Waverley. He faced a particular challenge in recent years, with a major fire destroying many of the facilities. The new design supports the agenda for transformation. Ongoing professional learning is deeply embedded among teachers, with the school now serving as one campus for post-graduate programs of the Faculty of Education at the University of Melbourne. In 2006, 22 early career teachers are involved in a 'young leader' project.

An example of the preferences of teachers when they have the power to make change is afforded by experience in Chile at the Maria Luisa Mombal School, located in a high socio-economic setting in the Santiago suburb of Vitacura. It caters for about 520 students from pre-school to upper secondary. It is a public school but is unique in Chile in that teachers manage it (see Chapter 3 for more information about the Maria Luisa Mombal School).

A remarkable example of the 'new profession' in action, combining two elements in the new enterprise logic of schools, has emerged in Northern Chile in the copper mining region of Antofagasta. It combines synergy and sagacity, and utilises a powerful capacity for networking, including the online conferences organised by International Networking for Educational Transformation. The school is a private school from Grade 1 to 12 named Colegio Antonio Rendic. Marcia Villanueva Orrego is a former principal of the school. Transformation is evident in several aspects of the school's operation. In discussing her leadership with the author, Orrego stressed three qualities: fight, give and listen. 'Fight' refers to what is required if there is to be an unrelenting focus on high levels of achievement for all students. 'Give' refers to the attitude that she must adopt, along with members of her leadership team and other members of staff. 'Listen' refers to the means by which the school responds to the needs and aspirations of students and parents. It is a fine example of 'servant leadership'. She describes experiences at the school in 2005 in the following terms.

The first iNet online conference reinforced our belief in the importance of 'student voice'. So in April we had a 'student conversation' led by 58 12th graders on the theme 'the school we dream about', with all classes from 5th to 11th grade organised randomly in groups. The following week, we had the same experience with the 1st to 4th grade students, led by teachers and parents. From these meetings, we got several proposals to improve our school. One of them was the painting of the benches in the playground by the students. In the third iNet online conference on 'learning to learn', we translated into Spanish the focus paper 'Theory to practice' that described an experience at the George Spencer Foundation School and Technology College in Nottingham [described earlier in this section] including one hour a week of learning in the 'Philosophy for Children' subject. We downloaded the papers from three online conferences and created a student translator team with 11th and 12th graders, who translated these papers and gave them to non-English speaking teachers, as a way of sharing experiences.

Also in April, 20 teachers from our school attended the Santiago College in Santiago for the Expotaller, organised by the Association of British Schools in Chile (Santiago is 1300 kilometres from Antofagasta). The aim was to learn what these teachers are doing in their classes. Our next project was to organise a similar experience, an Expotaller, here in Antofagasta in the last week of June, with all the schools, public and private, to share classes and create synergy. Seven students travelled abroad on exchange programs. On return in August, they will serve as teachers' helpers in English classes.

It is experiences such as these that give cause for confidence that an 'education epidemic' (to use the imagery of David Hargreaves) can be created. In less than six months, ideas have been collected from one setting (England) in an online conference, modelled in a school in a mining community in Northern Chile ('student voice' and 'learning to learn'), with further networking in another part of Chile, and modelled yet again in the local setting in a cross-sectoral partnership of public and private schools. Further impetus is given through international exchange programs of students. It is a remarkable story.

The 'new profession' is characterised by schools working with other-than-traditional agencies of support. Noteworthy are the opportunities for support from foundations that now need to be considered part of the 'new system', as suggested in Chapter 9. Fundación Gabriel and Mary Mustakis supports 92 schools in highly disadvantaged settings. One program is Pitagoras 1, 2 and 3, offered in Grades 1 to 8. It seeks to stimulate love of mathematics while developing creativity, language and spatial imagination, as well as an understanding of the relationship between arithmetic and geometry. The program 'Think, think, Tholomeus' offered from Grades 1 to 4 enhances problem-solving capacity in daily life, along with independent learning skills and the integration of mathematics with science. In language, some 34 'Socratic classrooms' focus on improving reading, analytical, cognitive, verbal skills, and oral expression that in turn contribute to raising self-esteem and leadership capacity. For 7th graders, the study of Greek mythology is used to introduce children to classical values and to help understand Western culture. A Youth Science Fair is organised every year, with linkages to the scientific community. The impact of these initiatives on learning has been high. The foundation consolidates these gains by providing professional learning opportunities and supervision and by disseminating information about new research and technological developments.

Building capacity in the profession

Building the capacity of the profession to adopt the roles illustrated should be a high priority in schools and school systems. The old enterprise logic suggested that this could be accomplished through professional development. In a provocative paper on the topic, Australian education consultant Peter Cole suggested that 'millions of teacher hours and education dollars are wasted on teacher professional development—the form of professional development in which most teachers indulge, and the least effective for promoting changed teacher behaviour in the classroom'. He concluded that 'teacher professional development, as it is generally conceived and practised, has had little impact on improved student learning' (Cole 2004, p. 3).

Cole contends that 'professional learning, rather than professional development, seems a more helpful construct to drive teacher improvement' (Cole 2004, p. 4). Such a construct is evident in the range of practices illustrated in this and preceding chapters. Notable examples include the approach at Comberton Village College near Cambridge, described in Chapter 8 and illustrated in Figure 8.2; the sustained approach to professional learning in the Lanyon Cluster of Schools in the Australian Capital Territory described in Chapter 9; and the change in culture at St John's School and Community College in England, described above. Much of this learning occurs in networks. A nation-wide networking project is exemplified in the Raising Achievement Transforming Learning initiative of the Department for Education and Skills in the UK, supported by the Specialist Schools and Academies Trust through its Achievement Networks, as described in Chapter 9.

Several non-government (private subsidised independent) schools in Australia are building a powerful capacity for professional learning through the creation of an institute. Wesley College in Melbourne, the largest non-government school in Australia, has established such an entity. Launched in 2005 with eminent scientist Sir Gustav Nossal as its patron, the Wesley Institute aims to 'gather the best minds, encourage the best talent, promote the best research and explore the best ideas to further the cause of education and to lead to the best possible outcomes for teaching and learning'. In carrying out its work, the institute will be a laboratory of innovation where ideas are generated, translated, evaluated and implemented; an observatory of excellence, monitoring world's best practice for implementation; and a conservatory of ideas embodying the memory, heritage and identity of the College as a leader in educational innovation. It is intended to build a capacity to impact on classroom learning outcomes within the school; contribute to the wider educational community, nationally and internationally; and influence the broader development of society. It will conduct seminars, conferences, publish a professional journal and develop partnerships with other institutions and educational and philanthropic organisations. It is intended that there be substantial external funding to support the enterprise.

Deep professional learning through a combination of ministerial leadership, tailored programs at the graduate levels, and local and international networking is illustrated in the Young Leaders Program of the Department of Education and Training in Victoria. The program is based to a substantial extent on the developing leaders program of the Specialist Schools and Academies Trust in England. Each year the Department selects on the basis of application 20 middle level leaders in schools with between five and ten years' experience. Successful applicants undertake the purpose-designed Master of School Leadership at the University of Melbourne and participate in local and international conferences, including the Annual Conference of the Specialist Schools and Academies Trust. Associated with the latter are a series of school visits. Participants are mentored throughout the two-year program. Some participants undertake additional projects. For example, Wayne Samuels from Dallas Primary School and Naomi Stewart from Corio West Primary School accompanied the author on a weeklong series of seminars and workshops as part of a leadership festival in Chile. Samuels and Stewart participated in some of these events but spent the majority of time visiting schools in similar settings to their own in Victoria. They met with senior policy-makers and were briefed on major developments in education in Chile. A feature of the program was the opportunity for them to make presentations on several occasions about practice in their schools and in the system of public education in Victoria. These were made to large audiences of academics and practitioners, with simultaneous translation to Spanish, and to small groups of senior officials. Experiences such as these are exhilarating for those who have the opportunity to be involved. An important issue is whether such a sense of adventure can spread throughout the 'new profession'.

Teachers Matter

Teachers Matter (OECD 2004b) is almost certainly the most comprehensive report on initial teacher education and professional development ever compiled. It draws on surveys and case studies from around the OECD. Twenty-nine systems in 25 countries participated in the project from 2002 to 2004. It provides dependable knowledge on current concerns, practices across the range of countries, and promising approaches in teacher preparation and professional development, in addition to policies and practices for attracting and retaining teachers.

Teachers Matter is about policy and practice in schools and school systems that continue under status quo scenarios, although some approaches are consistent with limited development along the lines of the re-schooling scenarios. One scenario for professional development is that all of the approaches identified as good practice in *Teachers Matter* are implemented. This section of the chapter briefly summarises the features of such a scenario.

The focus of training programs for teachers has been overwhelmingly on initial teacher education, which includes training on pedagogy, the subject matter that the pre-service teacher aims to teach and, often, subject-specific pedagogy. This report suggests that pre-service education needs to be more focused on the things teachers will be expected to know and do once in the classroom. This shift in focus requires changes to be made to pre-service education in order to provide teachers with an understanding of reflective practice and research skills as a basis for lifelong learning and the continuous development of their teaching practices. David Hargreaves has stated that, for schools to become 'learning organisations' teachers will be required to have the '*motivation* to create new professional knowledge; the *opportunity* to engage actively in innovation; the *skills* of testing the validity of innovations; and the *mechanisms* for transferring the validated innovations rapidly within their school and into other schools' (cited on p. 130). *Teachers Matter* states that, for a teacher, ongoing learning is paramount as 'it is unrealistic to expect that any initial teacher education program, no matter how high quality, will be able to fully develop student teachers in all of these regards' (p. 134).

Teacher professional development programs vary dramatically between the OECD countries. In many countries there is no minimum requirement for teachers to participate in in-service training. The average, in countries where such minimum requirements are set, is approximately five days per year, although this varies from 15 hours in Austria to 169 hours in the Netherlands (10 per cent of annual workload).

While all countries involved in the study agreed that participation in professional development activities is considered 'beneficial in career progression' (p. 123), completion of in-service training is only required for promotion or recertification of teachers in approximately 25 per cent of OECD countries. These countries provide an example of the incentive-based system for professional development that is one of three strategies described in this report. The other two strategies described are entitlement-based training, which means that a certain level of training is required by teachers' employment contracts, and school-based professional development, which links in-service training with the needs of the school. The study found that these professional development strategies do not have to function independently from one another and that 'a comprehensive approach to professional development would encompass all three strategies' (p. 136).

Teachers Matter states that there is 'very little knowledge about the nature and extent of professional development as an activity' (p. 127) and that evidence of the effect that teacher training has on the outcomes of students is scarce. It goes on to indicate that professional development activities which have clear focus, are based on both content, pedagogy and the management of students, enable teachers to observe others and learn from an 'apprenticeship' model and provide ongoing support to teachers within the school, appear to be the most effective forms of training.

The International Centre for Classroom Research (ICCR) in the Faculty of Education at the University of Melbourne is using advanced computer storage and longitudinal analysis of lessons in mathematics, videotaped in 14 countries. Knowledge of approaches to teacher development will be enhanced with the dissemination of the findings. The Learners' Perspective Study at ICCR is exploring how the findings can be relayed to classrooms to improve practice. Work at ICCR includes studies of classrooms in Japan and China, as summarised below.

There is an approach in Japan that illustrates a form of professional development that is so deeply embedded in teaching practice that the two are indistinguishable. It might be considered an 'ideal form' of teacher development within a status quo scenario. With its origins in the early 1900s most primary (elementary) and many middle school teachers participate in 'lesson study'. In 'lesson study', small groups of about four to six teachers collaborate, and are assisted by a teacher or member of staff from the ministry of education who is expert in content, pedagogical or curricular knowledge, or the research aspects of teaching. Some teachers are involved in more than one 'lesson study' at a time. The teachers set a goal that they would like to address and they collaboratively design a detailed lesson plan. One of the teachers then carries out this plan in a classroom while being observed by the others. Within a week of the lesson being carried out, the group reconvenes to discuss the outcomes. A revised lesson plan may then be used, with another member of the group giving the lesson. The work on the shared goals of the group may continue for a few years. The lesson studies are written up and published, so that others may learn from these experiences. Teachers are thus participating in active research in the classroom, reflective practice and in the dissemination of their findings.

An approach in China is 'keli', or 'exemplary lesson development'. It is a new model of in-service teacher education developed since 2003. The primary difference between the Chinese keli and the Japanese lesson study appears to be that the groups who perform keli include a range of academics and researchers from universities. Participation in a number of keli groups is expected of academics in education. This means that keli is based, to a greater extent than lesson study, in research. The aim of a keli community is to develop an exemplary lesson for a particular topic. The following is a summary of the approach (based on Huang and Bao 2006):

A teacher usually designs the lesson independently and gives the lesson publicly. The first feedback meeting takes place immediately after the lesson, which usually includes the following sections: introduction of the design of the lesson, comment on the lesson, and suggestions for further revision. The aim of this meeting is to find the gap between the teacher's existing experiences and the innovative design suggested by NMCS (National Mathematics Curriculum Standards). Following the first reflecting section, the teacher will revise the design and re-deliver the lesson in other classes at the same grade within the same school. After that, a second reflection meeting will be conducted which focuses on the difference between the new design and effective classroom practice, so as to improve the design further. At the third stage, the teacher gives a lesson by using the revised design and focuses on how students learn in a new style and attain a high quality of learning. All the designs and implementations are focused on the same content and are done by a teacher in different classes of the same school.

In a recent review of teacher preparation and development around the world, Darling-Hammond (2005) affirms these practices in Japan and China, noting that 'schools provide teachers with 20 or more hours each week for collegial work and planning, visitations to other classrooms and schools and demonstrations of teaching strategies'. She adds that, in contrast 'US teachers have almost no in-school time for professional learning or collegial work. Nearly all professional development occurs in workshops or courses held after school, on weekends, or during a small number of professional development days' (Darling-Hammond 2005, pp. 239–40). As *Teachers Matter* reveals, the US pattern is generally the norm around the world. An attempt has been made to introduce Japan's lesson study in the US, but it was found that teachers had difficulty posing rich researchable questions, designing a classroom experiment, specifying the type of evidence to be collected, and interpreting and generalising the results (Fernandez 2002).

The editors of the special issue of *Phi Delta Kappan* in which Darling-Hammond's article appeared highlighted the importance of practitioners engaging in international dialogue and called for more joint research and development projects: 'International research teams are becoming more and more common in science, health and industry, but they remain rare in education and child development'. They urge the creation of institutional partnerships to integrate international content into teacher preparation and leadership development: 'Just as no business can rise to the top today without significant exposure to business practices around the world, so our teachers and educational leaders need to understand how to incorporate an international dimension into teaching and be able to compare our education systems against international benchmarks' (Stewart and Kagan 2005, p. 245).

Synthesising the scenarios

Teachers Matter does not explicitly deal with the teaching profession as it may emerge in the re-schooling and de-schooling scenarios generated in the Schooling for Tomorrow project. Policies and practices are illustrative of schools that continue to operate in a status quo scenario, especially the 'bureaucratic systems continue' option. Consideration is given in this section of the chapter to the implications for school and teacher development if other scenarios emerge. Particular attention is given to the re-schooling scenarios.

Many of the concerns reported in *Teachers Matter* are illustrative of what occurs under the more negative of the status quo scenarios, the so-called 'meltdown'. The report informs us that about half (of the 25 participating countries) 'report serious concerns about maintaining an adequate supply of good teachers, especially in high-demand subject areas' and 'long-term trends in the composition of the teaching workforce (fewer higher achievers and fewer males)' (OECD 2004b, p. 8). There is also concern that 'some countries experience high rates of teacher attrition, especially among new teachers' (OECD 2004b, p. 9). In the 'meltdown scenario' there would be severe teacher shortages in some settings and this would limit capacity to deliver the curriculum. Crisis management would often prevail and a fortress mentality would be evident.

Compare this scenario with the upbeat view of the profession in either of the re-schooling scenarios. As described in Chapter 3, for the 'schools as core social centres' option: 'a core of teachers will enjoy high status but a range of persons from other professions will be involved in different contractual arrangements to support schools'. For the 'schools as focused learning organisations' option, teachers enjoy a high status as professionals and there is extensive use of ICT and partnerships with tertiary education. Teachers are engaged in substantial research and development and continuous professional learning often involves networks, including international networks. Employment arrangements are diverse and offer mobility.

Since the re-schooling scenarios are preferred by the majority of stakeholders, it seems appropriate to work on policies and practices that will nurture and sustain them. Some of these policies and practices should focus on school and teacher development. Approaches considered to be good policy and good practice in *Teachers Matter* should be pursued because they are likely to prove as effective under re-schooling scenarios as they would under status quo scenarios.

Challenging journey or exhilarating adventure?

Practices in schools where the new enterprise logic is evident, as illustrated in this and other chapters in Part B, are more consistent with approaches to professional development in preferred 're-schooling' scenarios than in 'status quo' scenarios. It may take some time before the new enterprise logic is embedded in the profession. Will it be a challenging adventure or an exhilarating journey? It is both of these. Writing in *Creating the Future School*, Hedley Beare concluded an uplifting chapter about those who will work in the school of the future with these words: 'This terrain is *not* for the immature, the shallow, the unworthy, the unformed, or the uninformed, and society needs to be very careful about what people it commissions for this task (Beare 2001, p. 185)'. The scale of change illustrated in these pages confirms that the concept of enterprise is an appropriate one, in the sense that it calls for a 'readiness to engage in daring action'. It is especially so for leaders, and Chapter 11 provides a framework to guide their efforts.

CHAPTER 11

The new leader

Much of the author's work over the last five years has involved the development of a framework for leadership in the 21st century. It has been adapted from time to time and presented in Australia, Chile, China, England, India, Scotland, Singapore, South Africa, Thailand, and the USA (Caldwell 2004). It is summarised in Table 11.1.

Table 11.1: A FRAMEWORK FOR LEADERSHIP IN THE SCHOOL OF THE FUTURE

COMPONENT	ELEMENT
Vision (1): Emerging global consensus on expectations for schools	1. Transformation—significant, systematic and sustained change that leads to high levels of achievement for all students in all settings, thus contributing to the well-being of the individual and the nation
Tracks for change (3): Broad directions for change in schools and school systems	1 Building systems of self-managing schools 2 Unrelenting focus on learning outcomes 3 Creating schools for the knowledge society
Values (2): Defining the public good in education	1 Equity—assurance of access to all students 2 Equality—ensuring high levels of achievement for all students in all settings
Dimensions of leadership (3): Major classifications of approaches to the practice of leadership	1 Strategic 2 Educational 3 Accountable
Domains of practice (3): Areas in which leaders should concentrate their efforts	1 Curriculum 2 Pedagogy 3 Governance
Integrating themes (2): To ensure success in transformation	1 Embedding the new enterprise logic 2 Balancing innovation and abandonment

The framework, which now accommodates the new enterprise logic, may be alternatively styled as a template or a blueprint. Its different parts describe in general terms the areas of work in which leaders should be engaged. It is a frame for the leadership enterprise. It does not describe the particular tasks to be carried out in particular settings in different nations. It does not describe how the work is to be done.

There are six components: vision, tracks for change, values, dimensions of leadership, domains of practice, and integrating themes. There are one or more elements for each of these. Here are brief descriptions of each component and element. In most instances these provide a synthesis of ideas presented in previous chapters.

Vision

Vision is a short statement on a desired future for the school. While it may be expressed in different ways, the key theme is *transformation*: significant, systematic and sustained change that leads to high levels of achievement for all students in all settings, thus contributing to the wellbeing of the individual and the nation. Such a vision should drive the leadership enterprise at all levels of schools and school systems as well as for the nation.

Tracks for change

Three tracks for change were evident at the close of the 20th century and momentum is building in each instance in the first decade of the 21st century. These were described in *Beyond the Self-Managing School* (Caldwell and Spinks 1998) and explained in Chapter 2.

The image of 'track' was selected. Track 1 involves building systems of self-managing schools, Track 2 has an unrelenting focus on learning outcomes, and Track 3 is creating schools for the knowledge society. It is important that leaders have a sense of these movements in education and where their schools and school systems are placed on the three tracks, and above all, where they should move next and how.

Values

The values embedded in the framework are those that ought to underpin a sense of the public good in education. The inclusion of equity and equality are explained in part by the vision of transformation. High levels of achievement for all students in all settings can only be secured if all students have access to the kind of school that will provide such outcomes, and this is the sense in which *equity* is used—equity in access.

The inclusion of *equality* requires explanation. It means 'high levels of achievement for all students in all settings'. It would be preposterous to suggest that all students can achieve at the highest level in an absolute sense. This is where recent progress in developing value-added measures is important and where the achievements of some schools in challenging circumstances should be celebrated. Some of the highest achievements in terms of what value is added have been attained in such settings. Furthermore, it is assumed that achievements lie in different areas of human capacity. Some can achieve at the highest level in music, others in sport, or in business or in languages and so on. The emergence of the specialist secondary school is important to secure such outcomes.

Other values are associated with or are even pre-requisites for the achievement of equity and equality. Examples include choice, reflecting the importance of freedom to choose among schools or other places of learning to ensure that the aspirations and capacities of learners can be satisfied. It may surprise that the value of efficiency should be considered a pre-requisite. It is so in two senses. One is that it is only within a strong economy that resources can be made available to ensure equity in access and equality within the meaning of the terms set out above. The quality of governance is important in this regard, for a capacity for setting priorities among different fields of public and private endeavour is required, as is the need to avoid wastefulness, duplication and corruption. Those seeking moral authority for this view of efficiency and economy will find it in the following statement of Pope John Paul II, set in the context of gross disparities in opportunities between the nations, including those in education. He wrote that 'in today's world, among other rights, the right of economic initiative is often suppressed. Yet it is a right which is important, not only for the individual but also for the common good. Experience shows that the denial of this right…diminishes, or in practice absolutely destroys the spirit of initiative, that is to say the creative subjectivity of the citizen. As a consequence, there arises, not so much a true equality as a "levelling down"' (Pope John Paul II 1988, p. 30).

Dimensions of leadership

There are three dimensions in the framework for leadership in Table 11.1. These are the major classifications of approaches to the practice of leadership. They are connected with each other and with elements in other components of the framework. The classification of strategic, educational and accountable leadership (based on Caldwell and Spinks 1992) is not inconsistent with or exclusive of other ways of describing the role. Sergiovanni's classification of technical, human, educational, symbolic and cultural leadership has stood the test of time, with symbolic and cultural leadership essential for 'excellence' (Sergiovanni 1984). Symbolic leadership involves the focusing of attention of others on matters of importance in the school in the range of words, actions and rewards that are available to the leader. Cultural leadership involves the building of a strong school culture, underpinned by the values described above and directed to a vision of transformation.

Strategic leadership involves:

- keeping abreast of trends and issues, threats and opportunities in the educational environment and in society at large, nationally and internationally; discerning the 'megatrends' and anticipating their impact on education generally and on the school in particular;

- sharing such knowledge with others in the school community and encouraging all leaders in the school to do the same in their areas of responsibility;

- establishing structures and processes which enable the school to set priorities and formulate strategies which take account of likely and/or preferred futures, and being a key source of expertise as these occur;

- ensuring that the attention of the school community is focused on matters of strategic importance; and

- monitoring the implementation of strategies as well as emerging strategic issues in the wider environment, and facilitating an ongoing process of review.

A capacity for strategic leadership has special priority at this time. Higher expectations for schools present challenges that have no counterpart in the history of education if they are to be brought to realisation. It requires every leader at every level to do the things listed above. It is a 'whole-of-government' or 'whole-of-school' approach, with every school leader having a capacity for strategic leadership in the specific meaning of that term: seeing 'the big picture', discerning the 'megatrends', understanding the implications, ensuring that others can do the same, establishing structures and processes to bring vision to realisation, and monitoring the outcomes.

Educational leadership refers to a capacity to nurture a learning community, again defined broadly to include a nation, state, school system, but especially a school. Such leadership is concerned with pedagogy and curriculum, but there is a 'hard edge' to the concept. A 'learning community' or a 'learning organisation' sounds a very comfortable place in which to work, but the stakes are high if the consensus on expectations for schools is to be realised.

With the wide range of learning needs in schools, this kind of leadership calls for helping teachers and those who support them to gain state-of-the-art knowledge about what works for each and every student. It calls for leaders who themselves will have much of this knowledge, but will certainly be able to manage learning and teaching so that knowledge is acquired and successfully brought to bear. Once again, this extends to all levels, including government, as well as for leaders in the local school setting.

Accountable leadership accepts there are many stakeholders who have a 'right to know' how well schools are doing. Its importance is reflected in current interest in 'evidence based leadership'. School leaders will be comfortable in collecting, analysing and acting on data and will be concerned at all times with how their schools 'add value' to the learning experience.

Domains of practice

Domains of practice are areas of work in which leaders should concentrate their efforts. Three are considered here: curriculum, pedagogy and governance. As far as curriculum and pedagogy are concerned, it is sufficient to note that the concept of personalising learning lies at their heart, as it does for the vision of transformation, with its explicit declaration of intention that there shall be high levels of achievement for all students in all settings. Powerful connections must be made between leadership and learning and the pathways have been made clear in recent summaries of research (Leithwood and Levin 2004; Silins and Mulford 2004).

Particular mention is made of the governance domain, for requirements for leadership in this area go far beyond the traditional expectations of the school leader, and they encapsulate much of the new enterprise logic of schools. Governance becomes an important aspect of the work of leaders at all levels. It calls for connections to community and civil society that may be new to leaders where community is largely confined to the school setting (see definition of Governance Working Group of the International Institute of Administrative Sciences 1996). Civil society is considered here to be the network of mutually supporting relationships between government, business and industry, education and other public and private sector services, community, home, and voluntary agencies and institutions. These relationships are essential in the synergy that must be generated around the efforts of schools. The framework for assessment of governance described in Chapter 6 and included in Appendix I was developed in a project for Asia Pacific Economic Cooperation (APEC) on best practice governance in policy formation and service delivery (Department of Education, Science and Training 2005). Elements in the framework included purpose (outcomes), process (engagement), policy (legitimacy, representativeness, accountability, efficiency), and standards (specificity, data, transparency, replication, openness).

Integrating themes

The integrating themes in the framework for leadership must drive the work of leaders in each of the various components and elements described above. Their absence will limit the extent to which the vision of transformation is achieved. One theme is derived from the new enterprise logic of schools. It is important for leaders to embed this logic in the everyday work of the school. In final summary, the major features of the new enterprise logic include the following:

1. The student is the most important unit of organisation – not the classroom, not the school, and not the school system.
2. Schools cannot achieve expectations for transformation by acting alone or operating in a line of support from the centre of a school system to the level of the school, classroom or student. The success of a school depends on its capacity to join networks to share knowledge, address problems and pool resources.
3. Leadership is distributed across schools in networks as well as within schools.
4. Networks involve a range of individuals, agencies, institutions and organisations across public and private sectors in educational and non-educational settings. Personnel and other resources are allocated to energise and sustain them.
5. New approaches to resource allocation are required under these conditions. These take account of developments in personalising learning and the networking of expertise and support.
6. Intellectual capital and social capital are as important as other forms of capital.

The other is balancing innovation and abandonment, in Peter Drucker's view a key leadership challenge for the 21st century (Drucker 1999). He called for the 'organised abandonment' of products, services, markets or processes:

▸ which were designed in the past and which were highly successful, even to the present, but which would not be designed in the same way if we were starting afresh today, knowing the terrain ahead (for example, the majority of school buildings designed in the 19th and most of the 20th century, elements of the curriculum, classes of standard size and certain pedagogies);

▸ which are currently successful, and likely to remain so, but only up to, say, five years—in other words, they have a limited 'shelf life' (for example, some technologies and elements of the curriculum and approaches to learning); or

▸ which may continue to succeed, but which through budget commitments, are inhibiting more promising or necessary approaches that will ensure success well into the future (for example, commitments to the teaching of certain subjects which are no longer connected to the repertoire of knowledge and skills as far as the needs of society are concerned).

Leadership is different but is it more difficult?

At first sight, leadership in the framework described above is daunting, and the question arises as to whether it is possible for school leaders to have the necessary capacities. On the one hand, it is reassuring that schools in which the new enterprise logic is embedded have such leaders. Illustrations have been provided throughout the book. On the other hand, governments in some places have invested substantial sums in an endeavour to meet the need but much remains to be done. The programs of the National College for School Leadership in England are an example of such an investment. The central issue is whether the numbers and capacities of leaders can be built up so that all schools can achieve transformation.

The experience of leaders in charter schools in America can help answer the question. While the new enterprise logic is not comprehensively evident, these schools are 'start up' schools that will succeed or fail on the extent to which learning is personalised and the voices of students and parents are heard. Terrence Deal, Guilbert Hentschke and others provide an interesting account in *The Adventures of Charter School Creators* (Deal, Hentschke et al. 2005). This book has international significance even though it is about a uniquely American project in school reform. There are barely 3000 charter schools in America. Along with magnet schools, they represent a tiny fraction of the total number of schools. Despite this, observers in other countries follow developments with great interest, since the issue of school choice transcends national boundaries, as does concern for how levels of achievement can be raised for large numbers of students in challenging circumstances.

Deal and Hentschke are the lead authors and they are mindful of the range of views about charter schools. They acknowledge that there are many unanswered questions. 'Do partnerships undergirding charter schools portend a new definition of public responsibility and promise new kinds of schooling consonant with 21st century urban America's needs and demands? Or, alternatively, are they precursors of a form of privatisation unresponsive to the welfare of underserved children? Answers to these questions are important but as yet unclear' (Deal, Hentschke et al. 2004, pp. 9–10).

Having framed the book in this manner, Deal and Hentschke leave the stage to leaders of 13 charter schools to tell their stories. These leaders are remarkably frank in their account of the challenges and conflicts. What appeared at the outset to be a shared vision and a common commitment to the way it would be achieved would often give way to debilitating debate that threw doubt on whether the venture would survive. Kathleen O'Connor wrote about this in her story of the Odyssey Charter School in Los Angeles. The charter was approved on 25 May 1999 but 'the first wave of discontent…was in February 2000—by the end of May, there was an attempted mutiny initiated by seven families who enlisted the aid of those who had the power to end our journey' (p. 47). These stories are superb sources for analysis of leadership using frames or lenses that help 'figure out what is going on' in the area of human resources, and at the structural, political and symbolic levels (Bolman and Deal 2003).

Some charter schools enjoy international as well as national renown, notably the Vaughn Next Century Learning Centre in Los Angeles. As she has done on seemingly countless occasions, Yvonne Chan tells how it was achieved. Hers is undoubtedly one of the most remarkable achievements in leadership in any setting. What stood out in her account on this occasion are the kinds of sacrifice that were necessary to get the venture off the ground. 'When no government funds flowed to us in July, when our year-round school began, I mortgaged my house. All staff agreed not to be paid until August' (p. 65).

The book does not set out to provide evidence that the charter school project is a success as far as educational outcomes are concerned. It is essentially a book about leadership under conditions of extraordinary complexity and uncertainty. The final chapter by Deal and Hentschke is one of the most important statements about leadership to appear in recent times. They pose three questions. 'Does starting a charter school from scratch require fundamentally different leadership skills than taking a position in an existing suburban public school? If so, how do those leadership requirements vary? If not, what are the generic characteristics of school leadership relevant across the range of situations?' (p. 247). They conclude that the leadership is different in charter schools to that in regular public schools. It is the opportunity to create and shape that is 'enormously heady and compelling...like the rush that drives an entrepreneur who believes she or he has a novel idea for the marketplace' (p. 250). They complete the analysis with concise descriptions of the kinds of decisions that characterise such leadership: decisions about what business to be in, how to organise and operate service delivery, the kinds of people to employ and their compensation, about customers and clients to be served, and how to allocate operating revenue.

After reading the heroic accounts of leadership in 13 charter schools, the reader might expect Deal and Hentschke to conclude that the role is beyond most people or that few will be attracted to it. This is not the case. They suggest that those who have taken on the role are not the kind of people who are attracted to leadership in a regular school. 'Far from being more demanding and less attractive, charter schools are attracting people to school leadership who seem to thrive on "daunting opportunities"' (p. 256). The challenge for policy-makers and other key stakeholders is therefore to 'extend an invitation to entrepreneurs with a passion for fulfilling the most sacred calling of all—to create places where every child can learn and grow' (p. 250).

This book about leadership in American charter schools has a counterpart in a book of similar genre related to England's specialist secondary schools. Sir Cyril Taylor and Connor Ryan have written a comprehensive account of the latter that is packed with the stories of successful leaders, and offers comparisons with developments in other nations, including the charter school movement in America (Taylor and Ryan 2005). Like Deal and Hentschke, the authors are predisposed to the kind of school they are describing, especially Taylor, who is chair of the Specialist Schools and Academies Trust that advocates and supports the movement. It is timely that such books are written to complement the range of publications that offer a critical perspective. They are strengthened by first hand accounts of leaders who have helped create success.

In search of the new leaders

The case is strong that most programs that seek to prepare people for leadership in schools are designed to suit the old enterprise logic. Expressed another way, they are preparing people for a kind of role that is or should be fading from the scene. Alternatively, given the view of Deal and Hentschke, they may in many instances be preparing the wrong people for these inappropriate roles, and the first challenge is to attract the kind of people who will thrive in an environment shaped by the new enterprise logic.

How can this be achieved? Only so much can be gained by offering higher levels of remuneration or by the glossy promotion of a new and challenging career in school leadership. Some leaders with the right stuff will emerge with time as the new enterprise logic takes hold in an increasing number of schools, especially where synergies with a range of organisations and institutions are created. Leadership is not lonely in these circumstances. It may be that the tipping point will be reached when those who have the power to shape these circumstances—prime ministers and ministers—understand what is needed and can give direction and support to the endeavour. The profession has an important responsibility, and networks of leaders who are adept in the new enterprise logic have important roles to play.

In search of the new leaders

PART C
Exhilarating leadership

CHAPTER 12

Exhilarating leadership

There are paradoxes in the principalship. On the one hand, it is highly satisfying and highly valued work. On the other, there are serious concerns about workload and high levels of stress. It has been documented most clearly in the aptly named *The Privilege and the Price* (Department of Education and Training 2004), a report on principal class workload in government (public) schools in Victoria, Australia, and its impact on health and wellbeing. On workload, for example, the number of hours per week for principals in Victoria was similar to that for headteachers in England and Wales conducted at about the same time, being about 60 hours per week, but well above the average of managers in other fields in several European nations, being about 45 hours per week. Despite the workload, unnecessary paperwork, increasing complexity, and higher levels of responsibility that came with self-managing schools, principals were highly committed to their work, prefer decentralisation to centralisation, and report high levels of job satisfaction.

Good news

It was evident in workshops conducted in Australia, Chile, England and New Zealand, as reported in Part B, that participants found that the positive outweighed the negative when schools had been transformed, or were on a journey to achieving change on this scale. Their leadership was exhilarating in all senses of the word, as reflected in the synonyms provided by Roget's *New Millennium Thesaurus*: animating, bracing, breathtaking, electric, elevating, enlivening, exalting, exciting, eye-popping, gladdening, inspiring, intoxicating, invigorating, quickening, rousing, stimulating, stirring, thrilling, uplifting, vitalising.

The antonyms of exhilarating from the same source are boring, depressing, discouraging, dispiriting. It seems that leaders who are exhilarated may encounter such moments but they have found ways to work around them, or if they cannot do so, their sense of exhilaration overrides them. They acknowledge that there are challenges to be addressed and problems to be overcome, but dealing with them is an aspect of their work they find exhilarating.

Part C is about such leaders. It explores the circumstances under which the balance can be changed to achieve exhilaration. It exhorts policy-makers to create an environment in which this can occur without giving any quarter on an agenda for transformation, that is, change that ensures high levels of achievement for all students in all settings, especially under challenging circumstances. Information is drawn from master classes conducted at the University of Melbourne by leaders in schools that had been transformed, and in five workshops in Victoria and Queensland. The latter were designed to explore more deeply the nature of the leadership experience and to identify the conditions under which that leadership can be exhilarating.

More good news

There is more good news. While more is expected, it is important to acknowledge the contributions that schools have made to success on factors considered important for the future wellbeing of the individual and society, as reflected in the emergence of the 'creative class'.

The importance of 'the creative class' in successful economies has been well-documented by Richard Florida, who reported that there is 'broad agreement among economists and business forecasters that the growth of the overall economy will come in the creativity or knowledge-based occupations and in the service sector' (Florida 2005, p. 29). He documented the growth in the creative sector, especially, and also the service sector, compared to sharp declines in the manufacturing and agricultural sectors, and reported that 'nearly all of the growth in jobs [in the United States] has come in two fields: expert thinking and complex communications' (p. 31). Florida compared the performance of nations as far as creativity is concerned:

- The creative class accounts for more than 40 per cent of the work force in nine countries: Netherlands (47 per cent), Australia (43 per cent); Sweden, Switzerland, Denmark, Norway (all 42 per cent); Belgium, Finland (both 41 per cent); and Germany (40 per cent) (p. 137).

- The Global Talent Index has two dimensions: Human Capital and Scientific Talent. On the Human Capital Index, measured by the percentage of the population with a bachelor's or professional degree, the top-ranked nations are United States, Norway, Denmark, Netherlands and Canada. On the Scientific Talent Index, measured by the number of research scientists and engineers per million people, the top ranked nations are Finland, Japan, Sweden, Norway, United States, Switzerland and Denmark. When the two indices were combined, the top ranked nations are Finland, Japan, Norway, Australia, Iceland, Netherlands, Sweden and Canada. The United States ranked 9th, United Kingdom 13th, Germany 18th and France 22nd (pp. 144–5).

- Along with technology and talent, tolerance is one of three factors in economic growth in the 21st century. The Global Tolerance Index has two dimensions: Values and Self-Expression. Sweden, Denmark, Netherlands, Norway, Japan, Germany, Switzerland, Iceland, Finland and New Zealand are the leaders (p. 151).

- The Global Creativity Index provides a measure of national competitiveness based on the three factors accounting for economic growth: technology, talent and tolerance. The 12 top ranked nations are Sweden, Japan, Finland, United States, Switzerland, Denmark, Iceland, Netherlands, Norway, Germany, Canada and Australia, ahead of the United Kingdom (15th), France (17th) and New Zealand (18th) (p. 156).

- Nations can be 'talent magnets' in respect to the proportion of university students who come from other countries. Top ranked nations are Australia, Switzerland, Austria, Belgium, United Kingdom, Germany, France, Sweden, Denmark, New Zealand, Ireland and the United States (p. 148). [The United States has the highest number of foreign students in absolute terms, accounting for 36 per cent of the world total (p.147).]

Florida contends that 'America will continue to be squeezed between the global talent magnets of Canada, Australia and the Scandinavian countries, who are developing their technological capabilities, becoming more open and tolerant, and competing effectively for creative people; and the large emerging economies of India and China, who rake in a greater share of low-cost production and are now competing more effectively for their own talent' (Florida 2005, p. 238). He argues that reform at the school level is critical to long-term economic success. Writing of the United States, he contends that 'we can no longer succeed—or even tread water—with an education system handed down to us from the industrial age, since what we no longer need is assembly-line workers. We need one that instead reflects and reinforces the values, priorities and requirements of the creative age. At its core, education reform must make schools into places where human creativity is cultivated and can flourish' (Florida 2005, p. 254).

Two observations can be made about Florida's work. First, that schools must be given much of the credit for the capacity for creativity in nations ranked highly in the comparisons above. It is fair to say that schools overall have done astonishingly well, given that so many still operate according to the old enterprise logic, or a 19th century imaginary, of which Florida is so critical. Second, it is likely that efforts to build capacity for creativity will be enhanced if a new enterprise logic shapes the operation of schools.

The new logic of leadership

The bad news about the principalship was summarised in the opening paragraph of the chapter. It is suggested that this dispiriting state of affairs is very much a consequence of efforts to sustain an 'old enterprise logic of schools' when it is no longer appropriate to do so. To use the language of David Hargreaves, it is a consequence of sustaining a '19th century imaginary' when it is a '21st century imaginary' that should be shaping the role of the leader (Hargreaves, D 2004). The 'new enterprise logic' is driving the '21 century imaginary'.

The old and the new enterprise logic of schools can also be described in terms of scenarios generated in the OECD's Schooling for Tomorrow project (OECD 2001), outlined in Chapter 3. Six scenarios described the possible directions for schools over 10–15 years. Elements of the most likely and most preferred scenarios that are concerned with leadership and management are consistent with 'old enterprise logic' and 'new enterprise logic', respectively.

The most likely scenario is that 'bureaucratic school systems continue'. According to David Istance, a leader in the project, 'this scenario is built on the continuation of powerful bureaucratic systems, strong pressures towards uniformity and resistance to radical change. Schools are highly distinct institutions, knitted together with complex administrative arrangements. Political and media commentaries are frequently critical in tone, but despite the criticisms, radical change is resisted (Istance 2003, p. 645). Management and governance are along the following lines: 'priority is given to administration and capacity to handle accountability pressures, with strong emphasis on efficiency. The nation (state or province in federal systems) remains central, but faces tensions due, for example, to decentralisation, corporate interests in learning markets and globalisation' (Istance 2003, p. 646). No matter how well such a scenario is implemented it is, in Hargreaves's terms, a continuation of a '19th century imaginary' or a manifestation of the 'old enterprise logic'. The depressing trends in headship reported at the outset come as no surprise.

For the two preferred 're-schooling' scenarios, the first is known as 'schools as core social centres'. Management in this scenario is more complex and leadership would be widely dispersed. Local decision-making will be important but national and international frameworks of support will be utilised. Additional resources will be secured to upgrade facilities. A core of teachers will enjoy high status but a range of persons from other professions will be involved in different contractual arrangements to support schools. In this scenario 'management is complex as the school is in dynamic interplay with diverse community interests and formal and informal programs. Leadership is widely distributed and often collective. There is a strong local dimension of decision-making while well-developed national/international support frameworks are drawn on, particularly where social infrastructure is weakest' (Istance 2003, p. 647).

Characteristics of the new enterprise logic of schools are evident in this scenario, as they are in the second of the preferred scenarios which sees a strengthening of schools as 'focused learning organisations'. Management and governance in the 'Learning organisation schools' are characterised thus: 'flat hierarchical structures, using teams, networks and diverse sources of expertise. Quality norms typically replace regulatory and punitive approaches. Decision-making is rooted strongly within schools and the profession, with the close involvement of parents, organisations and tertiary education and well-developed guiding frameworks and support systems' (Istance 2003, p. 648).

It seems that the schools described in Part B were already developing along the lines of the two preferred scenarios and their leaders are finding the experience to be exhilarating. One implication is that the key to making the headship more attractive is to accelerate the construction of these scenarios.

Hedley Beare, author of *Creating the Future School* (Beare 2001), has given a glimpse of the scale of change. 'I have just thrown into the recycling bin a heap of textbooks on bureaucracy, structure, corporate culture, organisational behaviour, change theory, and the like. They are all good. I studied them in graduate school [at Harvard], as a chief executive I applied their theories in setting up and leading school systems, I have taught them to principals, lectured and given addresses on them, and supervised research on their topics. Their ideas have been very constructive. I could discard them because they no longer apply. Their frameworks were good but the world has changed radically and they simply do not fit twenty-first century conditions. There is a new world ahead of us' (Beare in Caldwell 2005b, p. 1).

I had a similar experience in mid-2004 when I concluded two terms as Dean of Education at the University of Melbourne. I had a personal professional library of about 900 books, mainly on leadership, management and policy in education. I decided to keep those books that would be most relevant to my continuing work as an education consultant and lecturer in leadership. I kept only about 70 books or about eight per cent. Most of those I kept were published in the last five years.

If these independent acts by two professors of education are a guide, much of what is in print about leadership and management in education does not fit the present or short-term future, let alone the longer term over 10–15 years and beyond. What we were doing was culling books that were relevant to the status quo scenario described above, or those that reflected the old enterprise logic of schools.

This is in no way intended to be a reflection on recent or current research on school leadership. On the contrary, such research is more robust than ever, and it confirms the links between leadership and learning, as summarised by Kenneth Leithwood and Ben Levin in a recent report on the direct and indirect effects of school leadership on student learning for the Department for Education and Skills in the UK (Leithwood and Levin 2004). There is more to be done, of course, and they mapped the terrain for further research. Halia Silins and Bill Mulford (2004) have also illuminated the connections between leadership and learning based on research in Australia. Brent Davies drew on an international panel of researchers in the field to compile *The Essentials of School Leadership* (Davies 2005). Attention is now turning to how leadership that makes these connections and contributes to transformation can be sustained (see also Fullan 2005; Hargreaves A 2005; Hargreaves and Fink 2006).

However, much of the research is dealing with leadership as it is exercised in the context of the old enterprise logic under a status quo scenario. Fullan captures key elements of the new enterprise logic in *Leadership Sustainability* (Fullan 2005), including the building of lateral capacity through networks and networking, but assumes a continuation of a tri-level bureaucratic system (system, district, school). Peter Gronn's comprehensive account of *The New Work of Educational Leaders* (Gronn 2003) describes the challenges faced and the problems encountered by leaders who are working within the 'bureaucratic systems continue' scenario; there are no accounts of leaders whose work reflects the new enterprise logic.

The story that follows

Chapters 13 (Master Class) and 14 (Leader Voice) provide the bookends of knowledge about exhilarating leadership. Chapter 13 reports what was learnt in four master classes conducted at the University of Melbourne in August 2004. The focus in each instance is on how leadership is exercised when transformation occurs. Chapter 14 reports the outcomes of five workshops conducted in two states of Australia from July to October 2005. In each instance, participants were invited to describe aspects of leadership they found exhilarating; aspects they found boring, discouraging, depressing or dispiriting; and to propose courses of action by themselves or others that would help shift the balance to exhilaration. Chapter 15 (Master Strategy) is inspired by Ketan Patel's *Master Strategist* (Patel 2005). It draws on the insights of three people who can be fairly described as 'master strategists' to reflect on what was reported in Chapters 13 and 14. Another kind of master strategist is emerging in England in the role of 'system leader', who cares about and works for the success of other schools as well as their own (Hopkins 2006; Munby 2005). The chapter concludes with a brief reflection on efforts to specify standards for leadership. Chapter 16 (Going Global...Going Faster) describes and illustrates education in a world that is now 'flat' in terms of capacities to network locally, nationally and internationally.

The inspiration for this chapter is the book by triple Pulitzer prize-winning journalist Thomas Friedman entitled *The World is Flat* (Friedman 2005).

Part C does not claim to offer the final word on the topic. While its chapters draw to some extent on research, they are more appropriately described as being based on observations and self-reports by leaders in schools that are being transformed. They are a combination of reporting, advocacy, speculation and challenge. They invite debate. They provide a starting point for research and policy analysis.

CHAPTER 13

Master class

A master class is usually associated with music. The definition of master class in the Merriam-Webster Online Dictionary is 'a seminar for advanced music students by a master musician'. Master classes have been part of leadership programs at the University of Melbourne for several years, and this chapter presents what was learned in master classes in the initial offering of the Master of School Leadership in August 2004.

The University of Melbourne established the degree following consultations with key stakeholders in government and non-government schools in Victoria. Most participants in the first intake in 2004 were from government schools, with fees for 40 participants paid by the Department of Education and Training. Of these 40, 20 were in the young leaders' program, for those holding a position of responsibility and having between five and ten years of experience. Apart from involvement in the master's program, participants have a strong association with the work of the Specialist Schools and Academies Trust and International Networking for Educational Transformation under a contract between the Trust through iNet Australia and the Department of Education and Training.

The master classes described in this chapter were a key component of the subject Leadership for Transformation. On completion, participants are expected to demonstrate (1) understanding of circumstances where the need for transformation is indicated, (2) knowledge of approaches to leadership that have been associated with the successful transformation of schools; and (3) a capacity to design an approach to leadership that will result in successful transformation in settings of professional interest. Consistent with the definition adopted by iNet, transformation is considered to be significant, systematic and sustained change that results in high levels of achievement for all students in all settings, particularly in challenging circumstances, thus contributing to the wellbeing of the individual and society.

The master classes were of 90 minutes duration and were led by the principal of a school where there had been change on the scale of transformation. In each instance they had been identified in earlier research as being outstanding leaders. For each master class, participants received a short description of the school, a description of the major characteristics of the transformation, and a brief biographical statement about the leader. The master class consisted of three parts. The first was intensive dialogue between academic staff, either Professor Brian Caldwell or Dr David Gurr, and the presenter that drew out the major features of the transformation and how it was accomplished, with particular attention to the role of the presenter and other leaders in the school. The second consisted of questions from participants, either seeking further information, or of a 'what if' or 'how' type, such as 'if this needed to be achieved in your [the presenter's] school how would you go about it?' or, for a hypothetical situation or in the participant's own situation: 'how would you proceed if you were faced with these [participant's] circumstances?' The third was a final statement from the presenter summarising his or her knowledge and wisdom about leadership for transformation.

Four of the seven master classes are reported here. Two were led by principals of primary schools, one male and one female, who have contrasting leadership styles. Both schools were in challenging circumstances with dramatic change in each instance. Another was led by the principal of a special school with students spanning the primary and secondary years. She has received many awards for outstanding leadership, with several celebrating her success in relocating from one dispiriting setting to another, with the latter now a spectacular example of transformation, arguably a world-best example of a full-service school. The fourth principal has developed a green field site as a combined primary and secondary school. The setting is exceptional in that it brings together a government and two non-government schools (one Catholic and one independent). She is leading a transformation in governance. Space precludes reports of the other master classes led by principals of two independent schools and one government secondary school.

Master Class 1 with Jan Shrimpton

Jan Shrimpton is principal of Morang South Primary School in the City of Whittlesea north of Melbourne. There has been a primary school at Morang South since 1877. The current buildings are relatively new. About 600 students attend the school.

There was deep concern on a range of indicators at the end of 1998. The levels of student achievement in literacy and numeracy were well below state and like-school levels and the morale of the staff, students and the community was very low. There was little sense of working in teams or of staff supporting one another. The most important transformation since 1999 is that the school now provides a happy and cohesive learning environment with very high staff morale and equally high parent satisfaction. Levels of literacy and numeracy are equal to or above state levels and equal to or better than like-schools.

Shrimpton has been employed by the Department of Education and Training for 39 years and has been a principal for 15 years. At the request of the Regional Director she took up an acting position at Morang South in Term 4 of 1998. She was appointed principal after the position was advertised shortly thereafter.

Shrimpton was asked why she chose to work in challenging circumstances at Morang South and in earlier appointments. She explained that 'my philosophy is about working with people. I very much believe in every child having the opportunity to reach his or her potential. For that reason I was drawn to the more socioeconomically poor areas of Melbourne.' In taking up her current appointment, she noted that it was initially 'a very unhappy place' but she 'did a lot of simple things. They will sound rather corny when I tell you but I think they are really important. I made sure that I was a happy face that everybody saw every day. Because the school community was divided, the school council was divided. People had been leaving the school. Preparatory Grade enrolments were down because people were walking past our school to go elsewhere. I made sure that I was a very visible face for the staff and the community and that I was always smiling. That didn't mean that I didn't sometimes go home and tear my hair out and have the odd tear because it was a very tough task.

'I interviewed every staff member individually and also quite a number of parents on school council. One of the most important questions I asked them that really sort of laid out all of the issues was "What do you want of me as the principal?" One of the powerful messages that I would like to give is that whatever you say you are going to do, you follow it up and that you model what you expect others to do'.

As far as her greatest success is concerned she added 'I would have to say that we are now a really happy and cohesive learning community and that we have really achieved enormously improved outcomes in literacy and numeracy for children'. She identified three factors that explained this success. 'We have a very happy staff that really love working together and really want to do the very best they can for the kids. We have very open and broad ranging communication structures in the school. The staff feel very comfortable and that they can say anything. The third thing is an enormously supportive school council and parent body who, five years ago, were very angry and divided'.

Rather than describe a failure or an action that was unsuccessful, Shrimpton said that 'I really have to be honest and say that I don't think we have had a major failure because it has all been a developmental growth thing'. She admitted to the occasional sleepless night: 'I have the odd one. There is always a stress. They are usually related to "what am I going to do about this person who is having some difficulty or creating some difficulty in the school?" I do have balance in my life—I go to the gym, the ballet, the theatre and I am into lots of sporting activities. I think that is absolutely essential'.

It was evident from Jan Shrimpton's master class that she found her work to be exhilarating, despite the challenging circumstances in which she has chosen to work throughout her career. The dominant themes were optimism, personal modelling, a focus on all children experiencing success, open communication, and attending to the needs, interests and concerns of staff and the community. There were challenges, even to the point of having the occasional sleepless night, but good life-balance meant that stress was manageable.

Master Class 2 with John Fleming

John Fleming was at the time of the master class principal of Bellfield Primary School which serves the Melbourne suburb of West Heidelberg, a community characterised by high levels of aggression, gambling, alcohol and drug abuse. Enrolment is about 220 and remains steady. About 80 per cent of the children's families receive the Education Maintenance Allowance (an indicator of socioeconomic status), nearly 60 per cent of students come from single parent families, and slightly more than 20 per cent are from Non-English Speaking Backgrounds. Many of these students are refugees from Somalia. There is an indigenous (Aboriginal) enrolment of about 20 students. It is one of the most disadvantaged schools in Victoria. The 1996 Triennial Review revealed that over 85 per cent of students were behind state-wide benchmarks in literacy and numeracy.

The transformation at Bellfield Primary School is reflected in the performance of students on tests that shows remarkable improvement, bringing the school close to the essence of the definition of transformation, namely, high levels of achievement for all students in all settings, especially under challenging circumstances. Trends in results on state-wide tests in the Preparatory Grade and in Grades 1 and 2 illustrate what has been accomplished at Bellfield when comparisons are made with schools in similar settings, with all schools across the state, and with results in 1998. The following were reported in the master class in August 2004. Achievement has been sustained since then.

Preparatory Grade: Percentage reading with 100 per cent accuracy at Level 1

BELLFIELD 2004	LIKE SCHOOLS 2004	STATE-WIDE 2004	BELLFIELD 1998
97.4	58.5	67.5	33.3

Grade 1: Percentage reading with 100 per cent accuracy at Level 15

BELLFIELD 2004	LIKE SCHOOLS 2004	STATE-WIDE 2004	BELLFIELD 1998
100	26.3	35.9	34.6

Grade 2: Percentage reading with 100 per cent accuracy at Level 20

BELLFIELD 2004	LIKE SCHOOLS 2004	STATE-WIDE 2004	BELLFIELD 1998
83.3	38.7	47	30.6

John Fleming started teaching in 1977. In 1992, he was promoted to assistant principal at Bellfield. In 1995, he became acting principal and had been the principal since 1996. He has taught every grade level from 1 to 6. In 2005 Fleming was a finalist in the Department of Education and Training Excellence in Education Awards for School Leadership. In 2006 he took up a leadership appointment at Haileybury College in Melbourne.

The master class began with my observation on visiting the school that I had never seen every student in a school so actively engaged in learning. In response to my question about how this had been accomplished, Fleming compared it to the situation when he arrived at the school 13 years ago, when 80 per cent of students were under-performing. He needed to overturn the view that a student's capacity to learn was determined by their home circumstances. 'The children's background has no impact on their ability to learn at school. People find that quite controversial, but it is true, and Bellfield has proved that to be the case. What happens in their home life does not impact on their potential to learn and their ability to learn. Those children at Bellfield have just as great an ability to learn as any kid anywhere. That is what we have set about achieving and people who visit Bellfield now see that the whole staff believes that to be the case'.

High expectations are set. Praise comes from meeting those expectations. It is not about praise like 'The kid who gets 5 out of 20 for his maths in Grade 6 and the teacher comes up and says "Billy, you have tried well today. You have done really well, really tried". What I have said to the teachers at Bellfield is "Billy will feel good about himself when he is getting 20 out of 20 for that test". We don't deal in happy statements at Bellfield'.

Fleming defines his role in terms of the core business of the school. 'The core business of Bellfield Primary School is student achievement. That's it. Everything revolves around that. We should be measured against student achievement. I should be measured against student achievement, so should every classroom teacher. It is all very well to have happy kids in your school but if they are not achieving academically then I think there is a real issue. I think that has been our focus core business'.

Work at Bellfield is underpinned by four pillars. 'I am sure any of the teachers at Bellfield could talk to all of our visitors about the four pillars. The first pillar is that we believe in teacher-directed learning, not child-centred learning. By that, I don't mean that we don't have kids engaged in their learning, of course they are. If they are going to learn effectively they have got to be engaged in it, have an ownership of it and see it as relevant. Teacher-directed learning means we will set minimum standards. Every kid will reach them and as a teacher you are responsible for getting those kids there. That's teacher directed learning—teachers taking accountability for kids reaching standards'.

'The second pillar is that we believe in explicit instruction. We will formally teach kids how to spell, read, write and be numerate. We won't immerse them in curriculum content and hope they pick it up by osmosis'. John illustrated this by referring to what has been accomplished with a different approach to reading. 'We have lost our way a bit with our pedagogy because the whole language people have got us off the trail saying that you learn to read in the same way that you learn to speak. Unfortunately the research states that that is not true, that is not how you learn to read. Learning to read is cracking a code. We have taught our kids to crack a code and the results have been phenomenal. The kids are really, really good readers. Not only have we taught them how to decode effectively, we have taught them to how to recode incredibly effectively too. Our kids comprehend what they read exceptionally well. Their thinking skills are at a really high level'.

'Our third pillar is exceptionally important. We believe in moving kids' knowledge from short-term to long-term memory. Our fourth pillar states that none of the first three will take their place effectively unless you have very good relationships with your kids. Especially in a tough environment like Bellfield—if you don't have that right, then forget it'.

Fleming illustrated the fourth pillar and referred to three important requirements for achieving success. 'We have a kid at school this year that we copped—expelled out of two other schools. He used to be sent home every day. He hasn't been sent home once at Bellfield. His parents haven't been called up to come and get him and they say that is amazing considering he is in Grade 5. Expelled out of two schools but performing really well, working for the first time, enjoying school because he has got those three things. He loves his teacher. The work is at his level, although he has improved significantly because he has gone from a non-reader to quite a good reader. The third thing—he has lots of friends at school'.

John believes that the two most important aspects of change are trust and respect. 'If you flood people with change forget about it, they can't do it, because teachers are hard working dedicated people and they have a whole lot of things to do. When I became principal I thought, no, we can't flood people with change, we need to just focus on one area and that is literacy. For three years that is all we focused on'.

John was asked 'what do you do for a staff member who is not actually performing at the level that you expect them to be at?' He described how he worked with every member of staff. 'From the very start I have always gone into classrooms for the annual performance review and seen them teach, look through the kids' books, listen to the kids read. The staff knew, from the very start, that this is a person who will be looking into what I am doing'.

'Each term I get each teacher's data about their kids and it is quite comprehensive, and we are looking to find kids who are under-performing so that we can make sure that they are on the right track. We did our mid-cycle reviews this morning. The first question I asked each teacher was: "Are you confident that I understand your teaching enough to give you credible feedback?"' He provided what is arguably the most powerful evidence of all that what some may see as a 'big stick' approach is not so, but is one that is professionally very appealing to teachers. 'Since I have been principal the only people who have moved are people who have been promoted out—no one has transferred out. The last time we had a vacancy we had 54 applicants'.

Fleming stressed that learning is personalised at Bellfield. To illustrate he added: 'Vygotsky says the kids have a proximal zone and that is their optimum point of learning, but Vygotsky also says that, with teacher direction, kids can learn above their proximal zone and that is what we are trying to get our teachers to do; to identify the optimum point of learning for every kid and then, with assistance do that—and you can really do it'.

What has been accomplished at Bellfield is transformation in the sense adopted in this book: change that results in high levels of achievement for all students in all settings, especially under challenging circumstances. Knowledge about how this has been accomplished at Bellfield is being networked in powerful ways, with visits from representatives of more than 100 schools in the four terms prior to the master class. There was no doubt that John Fleming and his colleagues found their work to be exhilarating, even though it has been challenging in the extreme.

Master Class 3 with Bella Irlicht

Bella Irlicht is principal of Port Phillip Specialist School (PPSS) that provides a range of educational and other services to about 140 students with moderate to severe disabilities (intellectual, physical, social and emotional). It employs more than 60 staff and receives in excess of $3 million in government funds each year.

Port Phillip Specialist School was established in 1997, re-located from the South Melbourne Special Developmental School (SMSDS), which had about 20 students in a small, cramped, white-ant infested house in Middle Park. Financial support was limited mainly to public funds at SMSDS. PPSS now attracts millions of dollars from a range of public and private sources to enable it to be one of the outstanding full service schools in Australia, offering a range of medical and dental services on site. The school is located in the former Nott Street Primary School that was closed in the early 1990s and was a derelict and unsafe site until it was made available and refurbished to meet the needs of PPSS. A Centre for the Performing Arts was opened in 2005 at a cost of $2.2 million, with funding from the Victorian Government, a range of organisations from philanthropic and private sectors and the Pratt Foundation. A new curriculum model ensures that the arts pervade the curriculum in all areas of learning and teaching. It is noteworthy that each student has a personalised program and is able to use special computer programs to complement their learning. Other facilities include an indoor swimming pool, a technology centre, physiotherapy and dental facilities, and a transition house.

Bella Irlicht was appointed principal of South Melbourne Special Developmental School in 1989. She has served in the Department of Education and Training for 36 years, with appointments in primary as well as special schools. Her work has been recognised in many awards, most recently the Equity Trustees' Not for Profit Chief Executive Officer Award for 2005 for a CEO 'who possesses a distinguished record in the creation of service excellence, partnership success and enhanced organisational image'. Other awards include the Order of Australia (AM) in 2003, a Paul Harris Fellowship of Rotary International in 2000, and a Churchill Fellowship in 1996. She received the Hedley Beare Educator of the Year Award of the Australian Council of Educational Leaders (ACEL) in 2003 and the Sir James Darling Medal from the Australian College of Educators in 2005. An important outcome of the Churchill Fellowship was the opportunity to study full-service schools in England and the United States. She models lifelong learning and has undertaken many graduate and postgraduate programs with her colleagues.

I began the master class by referring to the first time I met Bella in her former school: 'an ant infested old house with twenty students with moderate to severe disabilities'. 'I walked away from that school wondering how you and your colleagues were able to do what you did under those conditions. Then a few years later, you invited me to new premises and my reaction was exactly the same. You had taken possession of a school that had been closed. You took me upstairs to the second floor and I have never seen a building in such disrepair, a building that had been condemned. The walls had the biggest cracks I have ever seen. It had not been occupied for years. There was graffiti on the walls and you said to me: "In this space, I am going to create a new school". On the third occasion I visited, what you said you were going to create was actually there. At that second visit, I asked "How on earth are you and your colleagues going to do this?" You have now created, with your colleagues, what I think is an outstanding model of a full service school'.

In explaining how this was accomplished, Irlicht said that 'I had some fabulous people to work with and I guess the key to it was always surrounding myself by people who were smarter than me; people who had more credibility'. Irlicht was a member of an international study tour to England, Germany and the United States organised by the Faculty of Education at the University of Melbourne in the early 1990s. She acquired a copy of *Full-Service Schools* by Joy Dryfoos (1994). 'I bought every book that had any connotation of a fully serviced school. I went back and, with encouragement from my colleagues, who are a lot smarter than me, I applied for a Churchill Fellowship and travelled through the United States, the UK and different parts of Europe to see how they were handling different issues and marrying the social, welfare, health and the educational needs of children, so that they could make a difference'.

'Very excited, I came back and wrote a huge document and I think it was just my sheer enthusiasm, or ignorance, but I asked for a meeting with three Ministers—Health, Education and Social Services. I actually got the meeting after a lot of jumping up and down by saying, "Look, I've got some fantastic answers; this is what I've seen overseas; this is what I've documented and this is where I think government should go"'.

Irlicht obtained support from government but 'by the time we'd cleaned up the contaminated soil and the lead in the paint, we'd spent the budget. So we went back, cap in hand, and we got a little bit more and things started happening—we didn't dare mention the fact the roof leaked until the opening of the school. The Premier was coming to open the school and that's when I rang the Department and said, 'I hope it doesn't rain because if it does we're in trouble, the Premier will be here and the school will be leaking"; and it was like "What? What are you talking about? Why didn't you fix it?" And we said, "Well, we didn't have the money" and, within two weeks, we had a new roof on the place'.

Port Phillip Specialist School organises several large events each year to raise funds. One example is the 'football breakfast', which features some of the most prominent people in Australian Rules Football. Many people ask: 'How did you get them?' Irlicht's response: 'I just rang them. I told them what we were doing and what we were hoping to achieve and they said "Fine, count me in", and when the question was asked "What did you pay them?" I thought "Pay them? Gosh, I didn't charge them to come in—I thought that was pretty good"'. People are turned away at these breakfasts, as they were at a recent ball that attracted 600 to the Melbourne Town Hall.

'So, there's lots of ways of doing it. There's not just one way. And it's about forming corporate relationships. Sometimes we just have breakfast at school with maybe half a dozen people who could be key sponsors. We tell them the story. It's all about knowing "the story". Knowing where you're going and what you're doing and if you can hook people into your vision and your story, they'll often say "What can I do to help you?"'

I referred to her statement that '"you surround yourself with people who are smarter than you", which is a rather modest and humble view of yourself. That's a rare statement to hear from a leader. I haven't heard John Howard say that. I haven't heard George Bush say that. Or Tony Blair. But you really chose those words carefully'.

Irlicht explained that 'none of us have all the answers. I certainly don't. There's been a lot of people that I have drawn on—consultants—I'm not afraid to call in a consultant and say "Look, what do you think about the way things are running?" When we had some issues at school, I got an outside consultant in. I said, "Tell me—warts and all". I think it's really, really important. If you're going to be successful in any shape or form, surround yourself with smart, capable people and they'll get you through it'.

Irlicht referred to the practice of the National Australia Bank and the Commonwealth Bank in which executives are expected to work in the community for a day. 'We have top bankers coming out to do a day's work experience and we do not make it easy for them. We put them into the high needs areas. One of them came in for a cup of tea and I said, "What are you doing?" He said "Having a cup of tea." I said, "Play time's not over. You're on duty". He looked rather shocked but he went and did his duty. I just wanted him to experience what it's like in the day of the life of a teacher'. This happened to be the CEO of the Southern Region of the National Australia Bank, who has since retired from his position at the bank and has taken on an important voluntary role at the school.

Master Class 4 with Gabrielle Leigh

Gabrielle Leigh is principal in a ground breaking learning precinct where three kinds of school—government, independent and Catholic—are working together with Delfin Lend Lease Property Developers and the Shire of Melton. It is situated on a green field site in Caroline Springs, a new housing development corridor west of Melbourne. When completed, the government school component of Caroline Springs College will have four campuses spanning the Preparatory–Grade 12 continuum. Gabrielle Leigh is the principal of Caroline Springs College. Previously she was principal at Greensborough Primary School for five years. Gabrielle is completing doctoral research into meaningful community links between home and school.

The transformation in this instance is a significant, systematic and sustained change that, through new approaches to governance and cross-sectoral cooperation, is intended to ensure that all students in the Caroline Springs Education Precinct will achieve at a high level. The aim is to ensure a consistency of approach and delivery in achieving the mission of achieving world-class learning. The arrangement is also intended to create community connections and innovative partnerships thereby enhancing the learning environment for students.

In the master class facilitated by Dr David Gurr, Leigh discussed aspects of the different transformations, the first embedded in the principles that underpinned the work of Delfin in developing a new community. 'What they wanted to flag to the community is that education was central in their development. The first people they brought together were the education providers. Those providers worked really hard before I took up my appointment to develop four underlying principles: commitment to lifelong learning, sharing and collaboration between all education providers, commitment to exploring new forms of ownership, and optimal use of ICT in the learning process'. Delfin has drawn on these principles in the development of several new communities in different states in Australia.

Leigh's work in Caroline Springs began with just 68 students in the primary school. At the time of the master class there were 817. She described the second transformation, a groundbreaking partnership of her government school with an independent school which had never been attempted in Victoria. 'Part of the sharing across the different sectors was that, in the 1997 meeting, there were some exciting plans made between the private school (Mowbray College) which wished to establish a satellite campus in Caroline Springs and the Department of Education, which was a fairly brave move. It was decided to share facilities such as the entry to the school. That doesn't sound much but the way everyone enters a school is through a gallery or foyer and both schools were entering through the same foyer. Equally, for the administration and staff area, we decided that was to be shared, so we had six offices, three that we used, three that Mowbray used and then a big combined space in the middle. The staffroom is shared—we take it in turns to supply the tea and coffee and share the noticeboards, so we get to know what is going on in each school. We set up combined staff meetings occasionally too. We share the library. We pay the salary of the librarian and Mowbray College pays the salary of the assistant in the library. We share the performing arts facility, the art room, science room and the full size basketball court. Only the standard classrooms are not shared'.

Catholic Education did not enter a formal sharing arrangement, but Leigh described the warm working relationship. 'The Catholic School started the same day as us but started next door. I had spent a fair time during the holidays working with the principal from the Catholic School. We got to know our leadership styles and started to trust one another and I think that this trust was really important. On the very first day we shared in an extraordinary manner because the Catholic School had a caravan for their administration which was really cold and they would come over and thaw out in our staffroom'.

A decision was made to build four new government schools in the community and agreement was reached to have a common governance structure. 'Instead of creating schools that might compete with one another we wanted to create a situation where you had one approach to governance. You would have separate schools but they would all have the same philosophy, the same educational values and the children would have what we would hope would be a seamless education, as seamless as possible'.

There are regular planning meetings of the leadership team, with careful consideration of appropriate transition points in the primary–secondary continuum. 'In terms of governance we were given a rare opportunity to start from scratch. We are rattling everybody's conception of what should happen in schools. There is nothing normal in our school'.

An important question was how does one create a sense of community in a period of rapid growth. Leigh stressed that it is not only growth. 'There are 47 nationalities alone at our school. So it is a really diverse culture. The good thing that binds people together is that people are coming in hope. They are coming with a positive element that this is a new community—"I'm giving my child the best"'.

It has meant a profound change in her leadership role. 'I was so accessible to everybody when we had 68 kids. I was in classrooms all the time doing things. Now I have 817. I am locked in an office doing administrative things some of the time or else in planning for the next campus. I am that much further removed in terms of my leadership. That's why it is so important to have campus principals, assistant principals and leading teachers in place who can then answer the needs of the community and be responsive'.

Gabrielle and her colleagues have had to accomplish these transformations in a climate of change in the political arena. The school sought self-governing status under a previous government, prior to 1999, but this initiative was abandoned by the incoming Labor Government (it is similar to the decision of the Blair Labour Government to abandon the grant-maintained project of the previous Conservative Government). This meant losing some of the hoped-for flexibility, mending fences with the teachers' union that had opposed the self-governing project, and establishing good relationships with the incoming government. There was success in each instance. 'The notion was that it would be a self-governing school and that would have given it the flexibility, initially, to have had our own budget and a lot more decisions made locally, which would have been a hell of a lot easier in that first couple of years. I was making decisions within a bureaucracy with the private schools and trying to put the two together in terms of monetary decisions and staffing decisions. One of my first huge challenges was to work with the new government to actually support the notion of a private–public partnership because it was quite outside the philosophy of the Labor Party at that point in time. That was a huge challenge. In fact, they have embraced it tremendously now and Premier Steve Bracks has come out and opened most things, which is great. The same with working with the union—Australian Education Union—it wanted to check that we weren't eroding teachers' conditions. And fair enough, that's what the position of the Union is. It took a while again to work with the Union but they have been very supportive over the time in terms of the development and interest in where it goes'.

Gabrielle chose the theme of Part C to describe her work. 'It has been really challenging but a really exhilarating journey also. The thing is to keep going back to your vision and what you are doing, why you are doing things to try and keep focused. You can go off on a tangent and become too big at times, or it seems too big. If you go back to that core purpose it is really important. It doesn't matter what size the school is, if you can keep to the purpose and the vision then you can take the actions that you need to in terms of leading in that environment. Personally, I have had to have incredible levels of energy to do what has happened and I have had to have a little bit of time out every now and again. I think as a leader you need to be able to stand back and look back at what's happening to get a really accurate picture'. One way she did this was to go on an International Networking for Educational Transformation study tour to England in late 2003, attending the annual conference of the Specialist Schools and Academies Trust and visiting schools. 'It is important in your personal journey to keep on learning—that notion of lifelong learning. Keep on researching for yourself and giving yourself challenges but not lose your purpose. Your core purpose is to make a better environment for kids for the best possible education'.

Reflections

It was suggested in Chapter 7 that the work of the enterprising leader is 'difficult, complicated and at times risky, often calling for daring activity which is at all times purposeful. It is an undertaking that is coherent in its intent to achieve transformation. It is an undertaking that is thrilling in its execution'. It describes the work of those who led the master classes reported in this chapter.

Consider the change in culture achieved at South Morang by Jan Shrimpton, who admitted to sleepless nights as she unified a divided community; or the unrelenting determination of John Fleming at Bellfield to reverse a long-held assumption that students in highly disadvantaged settings could not learn well; or the breathtaking achievements of Bella Irlicht who led the creation of one of the world's outstanding fully serviced special schools from two sites, the first infested by ants and the second, an abandoned contaminated school; or the way Gabrielle Leigh has broken the barriers to working across sectors, and successfully navigated what many would consider a political minefield.

The master classes were exhilarating because these leaders were clearly exhilarated by the success of their schools, despite difficulties that many would consider dispiriting. There was pride in what has been accomplished, but also humility. Witness Bella Irlicht's determination to surround herself by people who are smarter than herself. Classical leadership theory on the importance of vision and securing alignment to that vision is affirmed, as is the importance of returning to core purposes in times when the enterprise threatens to go off course. There is something here that warrants deeper exploration, and this was accomplished in five workshops in different settings, as reported in Chapter 14.

CHAPTER 14

Leader voice

Listening to 'student voice' has been a priority in the movement to personalising learning. It is a stepping stone to addressing the first element in the new enterprise logic of schools: 'the student is the most important unit of organisation, not the classroom, not the school and not the school system'. It seems sensible to listen to 'leader voice' if the work of school leaders is to become more exhilarating and less boring, discouraging, depressing or dispiriting. Brent Davies used a similar approach in exploring success and sustainability in the strategically-focused school (Davies 2006).

Listening to leaders and acting on what is heard may be an important stepping stone to addressing the problems of leader stress and premature departure from the ranks. The voices of leaders were heard in the nine workshops over nine weeks in four countries described in Part B. The voices of leaders in the master classes reported in Chapter 13, each of whom achieved success in the transformation of their schools under the most challenging of circumstances, were those of people who found their work exhilarating, despite the countless problems experienced along the way. It was decided to go one step further and listen to the voices of a much larger number and broader cross-section of leaders to help find the key to exhilarating leadership. This is the purpose of Chapter 14.

Five workshops were conducted over twelve weeks in two states of Australia. Most of the 185 participants were principals, with a range of leadership positions among those who were not. They came from a representative cross-section of schools, with most from government or state schools, and the others from non-government subsidised schools, either Catholic systemic schools or independent schools. They came from a variety of socioeconomic settings. There was a balance of male and female participants.

There were two distinctive governance patterns among leaders from government schools. Most were from Victoria, which is one of the most decentralised systems in the world, with a high level of self-management or local management (about 94 per cent of the state's education budget is decentralised to schools). The others were from the south-east corner of Queensland a state which, in contrast to Victoria, has a relatively centralised pattern of governance and only modest levels of local management.

There were two ways in which participants could not be considered a representative sample of leaders. One was that they had volunteered to participate in these workshops. The other was that, with one exception, the workshops were an activity of a network of leaders, that is, they reflected a pattern of operation in the new enterprise logic of schools. In each case it may be said that the leaders were predisposed to continuous professional development. The following is a brief summary of the major characteristics of the workshops.

Workshop 1: Gold Coast (30 participants) This 90-minute workshop was part of the 10th Annual Conference of the Professional Development Network in Queensland (PDN). PDN is a network organised by school leaders for school leaders. Established more than ten years ago, it aims to provide and promote professional development activities for leaders and aspiring leaders in the schools and school districts of south east Queensland. Non-government schools participate as associate members. It has been a financially self-sustaining network since 1998, hosted by the Centre for Leadership and Management in Education at Griffith University. Current membership is 131 schools and school districts in addition to 11 non-government schools with associate membership.

Workshop 2: Crown (50 participants). This one-day workshop was for principals and other leaders from schools in the Inner City network of the Southern Metropolitan Region of the Department of Education and Training in Victoria. This network meets regularly for professional development, and the workshop was part of a two-day event at the Crown Casino organised by Bella Irlicht, principal of Port Phillip Specialist School, who conducted one of the master classes reported in Chapter 13. Most schools are located in middle to upper socioeconomic communities.

Workshop 3: Hume (25 participants). This half-day workshop was organised by iNet Australia and held at the Hume Global Learning Village in a northern suburb of Melbourne. About half of the participants were young leaders from Gladstone Park Secondary College, the first school in Australia to be affiliated with the Specialist Schools and Academies Trust. The other half came from government schools in the Northern Metropolitan Region or from other government and non-government schools that are members of iNet Australia. Most of the participants came from schools in low to middle socioeconomic communities.

Workshop 4: Catholic (25 participants). This two-hour workshop was one of a series conducted by the author for the East Central network of Catholic primary schools in Melbourne. The network has made a special commitment to 'big picture' professional learning. Schools are located in a broad continuum of socioeconomic settings. Even though they form part of a system of schools with a powerful unifying commitment to a Catholic ethos, they are self-managing through a decentralised system of budgeting and a local parish governance arrangement.

Workshop 5: Geelong (55 participants). This three-hour workshop was conducted in Geelong, a city near Melbourne, as part of a three-day professional development program for school leaders in the Southern Metropolitan Region of the Department of Education and Training in Victoria. These leaders are not part of an ongoing network but will come together from time to time over several months in a coordinated series of seminars, workshops and work-related projects. A minority of participants were principals. Schools come from a broad continuum of socioeconomic settings.

The workshops included short presentations by the author on the themes of new enterprise logic and leadership, after which three questions were posed:

1. What aspects of your work as leader are exhilarating?
2. What aspects of your work as leader are boring, depressing, discouraging or dispiriting?
3. What actions by you or others would make your work as leader more exhilarating and less boring, depressing, discouraging or dispiriting?

Participants were given a list of synonyms for exhilarating drawn from Roget's *New Millennium Thesaurus:* animating, bracing, breathtaking, electric, elevating, enlivening, exalting, exciting, eye-popping, gladdening, inspiring, intoxicating, invigorating, quickening, rousing, stimulating, stirring, thrilling, uplifting, vitalising. Antonyms from the same source were included in Questions 2 and 3.

The technology was the same as that used in workshops described in Part B. Each group of participants was able to record its deliberations by keyboard entry, with responses from all groups displayed on a large screen for subsequent analysis. A document with all responses was sent to participants by email in the days following the workshop. Zing, the technology developed by Sydney educator John Findlay, was used. Its use for these five workshops was essentially for research purposes.

Participants were given 5–8 minutes to respond to each question. Groups ranged in size from three to eight. In some instances participants entered their individual responses; in others a group discussion was held and one member of the group listened and entered responses as they were generated. The atmosphere for this part of the workshop was itself exhilarating as participants generated a very large number of responses very quickly, and these were all displayed simultaneously on a large screen so that all could see what was unfolding. The largest number of responses generated in a 5–8 minute period was 162 by the 55 participants at the Geelong workshop for Question 2—one new response on screen every three seconds, with each participant generating on average three responses.

Themes among the responses were identified by the participants as a group when all responses for each question were on screen. After the workshop, the themes were refined by the author who then placed each of the 1413 responses in one of the 21 themes that were generated in this way—seven themes for each question. Summaries are contained in

Tables 14.1, 14.2 and 14.3 and discussed below. Implications for policy and practice are drawn in the final section of the chapter.

Work that is exhilarating

Participants in the five workshops generated 509 responses to the question 'What aspects of your work as leader are exhilarating?' Responses are summarised in Table 14.1. There are some striking features in the pattern of responses. Each of the three top-ranking themes attracted at least 20 per cent of responses, together totalling 67 per cent. Each is concerned with good outcomes. Top ranking (26 per cent) is exhilaration associated with success in a particular project, challenge, problem or grant; second ranking (21 per cent) is associated with good working relationships with and among staff; the third for experiencing and celebrating the accomplishments of students (20 per cent). The dominant pattern is therefore associated with the core purpose of schooling that can be summarised as 'success in tasks related to learning and the support of learning, characterised by fine working relationships with staff, and enjoyment that accompanies good outcomes for students'.

Middle ranking (14 per cent) among the seven themes is a more personal response by leaders to the work situation, with words like passion, challenge, living on the edge, great meetings and reflection. It should be borne in mind that each participant generated on average between two and three responses to this question, so that this theme is unlikely to have been the sole response of any particular person.

The last three themes are associated more with external matters, with community mentioned in 9 per cent of responses and networks by only 1 per cent. Nine per cent referred to exhilaration experienced at being part of or witnessing the collaborative efforts of different stakeholders, conveying a sense of a learning community.

These patterns were generally the same for participants in each workshop. Where there were differences in rankings they were generally of one or two ranks only. It was not possible to discern an explanation for variations when the different locations and characteristics of respondents were taken into account. They are most likely chance variations. Most important, however, is the striking pattern of the three top ranked themes, and some implications are drawn in the final section of the chapter.

TABLE 14.1: ASPECTS OF WORK THAT ARE EXHILARATING

RANK	THEME	ILLUSTRATIVE RESPONSES	NUMBER	PER CENT (%)
1	Success	Achieving success with a particular project; successfully solving a problem or meeting a challenge; realising a vision; preparing a curriculum; winning grants and other resources for school; absence of complaints	130	26
2	Staff	Working with staff; observing staff as they address issues or adopt new practices; mentoring staff including beginning teachers; school-based research and development; dreaming together; having fun together	106	21
3	Students	Experiencing and celebrating the accomplishments of students, especially when needs are met; engaging with students	104	20
4	Personal	Personal development; passion for the moral purpose of schooling; success in the personal exercise of leadership; thinking quickly; personal reflection; receiving positive feedback; being challenged; living on the edge; never a dull moment; diversification in the work; participation in debate; experiencing a great meeting	69	14
5	Collaboration	Witnessing collaborative efforts of different stakeholders: staff, parents, students and others in community; experience in a learning community; enthusiasm of staff working together	47	9
6	Community	Working with parents and other members of the community; winning the support of the community for aspects of the school program; seeing them understand the 'big picture'	46	9
7	Networks	Working with others in a network or cluster of schools	7	1
TOTAL			509	100

Work that is boring, depressing, discouraging or dispiriting

Antonyms for exhilarating are boring, depressing, discouraging or dispiriting, and participants were invited to describe aspects of their work that had these characteristics. A total of 527 responses was received, slightly more than the number of responses about aspects of work that are exhilarating (509). Responses are summarised in Table 14.2.

As in Table 14.1, there is a striking pattern among the themes that are ranked most highly in the analysis. Each of the top three themes attracted at least 20 per cent of responses, with a narrow range of 22–24 per cent, and a total overall of 69 per cent. The top ranked theme is described as 'performance of staff' (24 per cent) and this described the way respondents experienced the work of some of their colleagues: not making an effort, resisting or blocking change, not keeping up to date, or complaining. Second ranking was accorded to 'administrative work' (23 per cent), referring to such matters as form filling, surveys, email, unnecessary meetings and, in one workshop in Victoria, the use of online recruiting procedures. Third rank was accorded the perceived lack of support (22 per cent) from different levels of the system, lack of resources, complexity in bureaucratic arrangements, and lack of feedback.

The middle rank among themes for responses to this question is described as 'external factors' (15 per cent), being a range of matters that were perceived to be outside the control of the school. Reference was made to culture, student characteristics, party politics and imposed curriculum

It is noteworthy that 11 per cent of responses were related to perceptions of self or matters that were immediately concerned with the work of the leader. In some instances, these could well have been characterised as 'administrative tasks' but they were classified as personal in nature if the wording suggested this rather than the alternative. Included here were lack of time, problems in getting a message across, tiredness, absence of challenge, sitting in front of a computer or through meetings, loneliness and the enormity of the workload.

The sixth ranking theme was characterised as 'constraints' (4 per cent), referring to matters related to the performance management of staff, with instances cited of barriers to selection and removal of staff. There were a few references to unions and the overall work environment.

In one of the five workshops, one participant indicated that he found no aspect of his work to be boring, depressing, discouraging or dispiriting. This was the only instance where a participant made a deliberate decision to enter this response. Normally, an 'outlier'

Table 14.2: ASPECTS OF WORK THAT ARE BORING, DEPRESSING, DISCOURAGING OR DISPIRITING

RANK	THEME	ILLUSTRATIVE RESPONSES	NUMBER	PER CENT (%)
1	Performance of staff	Staff not making an effort; resist change; blockers; use outdated pedagogy; make complaints	126	24
2	Administrative work	Filling in forms, reports or surveys, email, including those required for legal purposes; preparing timetables; unnecessary meetings; governance issues; online recruiting procedures (government schools in Victoria)	122	23
3	Lack of support	Lack of support from different levels of the system; poor understanding at higher levels of nature of schooling; unfairness or inadequacy in allocating resources to school; complexity in hierarchy or bureaucracy; lack of feedback	115	22
4	External factors	Factors outside control of school or leader including culture of blame; unmotivated or disengaged students; lack of support from parents; purposeless meetings; death of student; having to reinvent the wheel; party politics; need for marketing to maintain enrolments; imposed curriculum	81	15
5	Personal factors	Lack of time; difficulties in communication; personal judgements not suited to school context; tiredness; absence of challenge; scale of task; workload; loneliness; tough decisions; sitting in front of computer; meetings	59	11
6	Constraints	Constraints on school in performance management; unions; work environment	23	4
7	None	One participant found no aspect of work had these characteristics	1	0
TOTAL			**527**	**99**

of this kind might not be pursued, but the author invited an explanation, which was provided in writing after the workshop on condition of anonymity. The following are excerpts from his explanation:

> Boring—I believe it is not someone else's job to entertain me. If I find something boring I will be active in changing things. So boredom I do not perceive as something others do to me. I control this by the nature of my response. So if at work anything seems to be boring, I would do something positive (for me) about it.

> Dispiriting—my spirit is I believe, fairly resilient and it would take multiple fronts of negativity before I would feel dispirited about things. I guess I take a fairly global view and can safely compartmentalise so I can keep doing whatever it is I need to be doing. Work is only one dimension of possibilities in my life, therefore a setback would not dissolve my spirit. I might get annoyed but would most likely resolve to find another way.

> Discouraging—This seems to be more of a group element, in that if one is individually discouraged you can surmount this by the quality of the people around you. Besides, I believe in equi-finality, there are many paths to the result you want. It may take a bit of compromise.

The respondent is not a principal but occupies a senior leadership role in a school that the author considers to be world-class in its particular field of specialisation. It is noteworthy that at the time he filled this role on a three-day-per-week contract. There is certainly balance in his life that is likely to be exceptional among the 185 participants who participated in these workshops. However, the author senses that the explanations he gives in the three areas would likely be given by those respondents who, on balance, find their work to be exhilarating and are not weighed down by matters that can be boring, depressing, discouraging or dispiriting.

As with the responses to the first question, there were no differences in rankings among participants in the different workshops that warrant observations that could be sheeted home to differences in the characteristics of the five settings.

In general, the over-arching theme is the influence of matters considered by participants to be either outside their control or due to the actions of others. Indeed, 89 per cent of responses are covered by this statement. Some might say there is a familiar pattern here. The early studies of satisfaction and dissatisfaction by researchers such as Frederick Herzberg were sometimes criticised on the basis that it is a human response to attribute satisfaction to achievement of success (as in patterns of response to Question 1) and dissatisfaction to the actions of others (as in patterns of response to Question 2). However, the reader is invited to take the patterns at face value, or suspend judgement, until those for Question 3 are considered. There are some surprises!

Shifting the balance to exhilaration

Question 3 was 'What actions by you or others would make your work as leader more exhilarating and less boring, depressing, discouraging or dispiriting?' The 377 responses were organised according to seven themes, as summarised in Table 14.3.

The biggest surprise, running counter to the criticism of findings of research on satisfaction and dissatisfaction reported above, is that the largest category of response reflected the view that the keys to shifting the balance to exhilaration lay in their own hands. It calls for a personal response. With 33 per cent of responses, this is the strongest theme of any for the three questions posed in the workshops. Items illustrated in Table 14.3 reveal two kinds of personal response. One refers to personal lifestyle to become more tolerant, secure a better balance in life, and have fun. The second referred to the way participants carried out their work. A frequently mentioned item here was to delegate more. Others could see the benefit of mentoring and coaching and seeking greater clarity in their role. There are important implications here, and these are taken up in the final section of the chapter.

The second ranked theme is described as 'professionalism', with 21 per cent of participants seeing the need for greater accountability, enthusiasm, openness, willingness to take risks and innovate, teamwork and a capacity for strategic planning among their colleagues. One might argue that this is another area where the leader can take action without recourse to new policies, although the fourth ranked theme of autonomy does express this view.

Taken together, the two top ranked themes on personal and professional matters account for 54 per cent of responses. The remaining 46 per cent are more clearly connected to actions by others. The third ranked theme is concerned with resources, with 19 per cent calling for additional resources to enable them to give more attention to meeting the needs of students, if necessary shifting more funds from the centre of the system to schools. Resources may be in the form of emotional support, with several participants referring to times of crisis and trauma, as experienced with tragedies that occur from time to time.

It is noteworthy that just 9 per cent of participants called for greater autonomy for the school, especially in respect to personnel matters and freeing the school from 'administrivia' and 'ministrivia', with the latter a term coined in the Gold Coast workshop to refer to demands for action or information that are made by ministers of education. This was one of two themes where a difference among responses at the five workshops seemed to be connected to the characteristics of the setting. While only 9 per cent of 185 participants gave a response that reflected the theme of autonomy, it was the top ranked response from participants at the Gold Coast workshop in Queensland, where schools have limited autonomy compared to their counterparts at the other four workshops in Victoria. At the Gold Coast, 25 per cent of participants gave such a response. In no other workshop

Table 14.3: HOW TO MAKE THE WORK MORE EXHILARATING

RANK (%)	THEME	ILLUSTRATIVE RESPONSES	NUMBER	PER CENT
1	Personal	Achieve better balance in personal life; become more tolerant and sensitive; more time to have fun; study leave; delegate more; improve internal communication and relationships within the school; greater clarity in role and supervision (of self); mentoring; coaching; saying no	125	33
2	Professionalism	There needs to be a higher level of professionalism among some staff, with accountability, enthusiasm, openness, shared values, willingness to take risks and innovate; teamwork; strategic planning	78	21
3	Resources	Additional resources to allow greater focus on students; reduction in class size, shift funds from centre to schools; getting sense of priority; more time; full time deputy; building a capacity to focus on meeting the needs of individual students; support in times of crisis and trauma	73	19
4	Autonomy	Fewer constraints on schools, including industrial; more careful thought at the system level about policies before requiring implementation in schools; separation of education and politics; less administration ('administrivia' or 'ministrivia') unless clearly connected to learning outcomes; greater sensitivity to schools; greater capacity at the school level to select, manage and reward performance of staff	34	9
5	Community	Higher level of support from community in sponsorship, marketing, goodwill and communication	23	6
=6	Recognition	More recognition of achievements of self and school and less blame and cynicism by others toward the school	22	6
=6	Networking	Networking with other schools for mutual support	22	6
TOTAL			377	100

did this number exceed 6 per cent. For the Catholic workshop in Melbourne, the number was 0 per cent. Despite these differences, some caution should be exercised because the workshops were relatively small (30 and 25 for Gold Coast and Catholic, respectively) and, as noted at the outset, the 185 participants are not necessarily a representative cross-section of leaders in the various settings.

The remaining themes drew relatively few responses, with 6 per cent for each of community (for higher levels of support), recognition (of achievements of self and the school) and networking (to seek mutual support). It was for the last of these that another noteworthy difference among participants emerged. For the Catholic workshop, 27 per cent of participants gave a response that referred to more mutual support through networking (it ranked third among the themes). In no other workshop did the number exceed 7 per cent. It is an interesting finding since the East Central network of Catholic primary schools in Melbourne is a close knit group that meets regularly to share information and build their professional capacities. The response may be an affirmation of the value of the network and of a desire among about one-quarter of participants to seek even more support through this process. In contrast, however, no participant in the Inner City network of principals of government schools in Melbourne called for more networking, and this network appears to meet just as often. As before, care should be taken in drawing implications because the numbers of participants are relatively small. There were no other differences in response patterns that were noteworthy to the extent that they appeared to be linked to particular local characteristics.

Implications for policy and practice

Some implications for policy and practice seem to leap off the pages! A large majority of participants (67 per cent) reported that exhilaration was associated with success in the core business of the school, summarised in the statement: 'success in tasks related to learning and the support of learning, characterised by fine working relationships with staff, and enjoyment that accompanies good outcomes for students'. The major implication is the importance of building the capacities of leaders and their colleagues to maximise the probability that they will experience such success. These capacities are concerned with curriculum, pedagogy, strategy formation, vision building, alignment of staff and the community to the vision, working well with colleagues, and having fun along the way. Programs for leadership development and ongoing professional learning should be concerned with these matters.

There was similarly a large majority (69 per cent) in views about aspects of work that participants found boring, depressing, discouraging or dispiriting, with roughly similar numbers reporting concerns about the performance of staff, administrative work, and perceived lack of support. Taken at face value, a major implication is that actions by leaders and others should seek to minimise these concerns through policies that strengthen the hand of the school in selection and performance management of staff, minimising the amount of administrative work, and providing more support, through additional resources and greater sympathy and understanding of those who are in a position to provide support.

While responses to the second question seemed to transfer the burden to others, the keys to shifting the balance to exhilaration, and by implication making the work of leader more attractive and sustainable, lie to a large extent in the hands of leaders themselves, as evidenced in responses to the third question. Getting a better balance in life was important, but equally important was the need to delegate more. An important implication is the need for *serious* distribution of leadership (Harris 2005). The word 'serious' is emphasised here. It is not simply a matter of having more people with designations of authority and responsibility, although this may help. It is about having a very large number of staff having a leadership role and having all work together in common cause. An example of distributed leadership on this scale is Mt Waverley Secondary College in Melbourne where 95 of 140 staff have a leadership role and there is continuing professional development for all. It may be that insufficient attention is given to building a capacity in leaders to distribute leadership in the school.

The issue of school autonomy is an important one. On the one hand, just 9 per cent of participants expressed a wish for more, although this number was 25 per cent in the more centralised Queensland setting. It seems that the amount of autonomy was not a concern for most participants in Victoria. On the other hand, however, there is clearly a wish for more authority in respect to personnel matters, ranging from selection and, where necessary, removal of staff, to the gamut of activities related to performance management. Most important, however, is that there was no indication of any kind that participants sought total autonomy for their schools so that they existed alone and were self-sufficient apart from the provision of a fair share of resources to meet the needs of students. A high level of autonomy and a high level of support from other sources are not mutually exclusive. Such support may come from different parts of the school system through traditional arrangements, or from networks of schools and other entities, or from places that are sourced by the school itself according to its needs and priorities and what is available.

A remarkable development in Victoria is the increasing number of independent non-government (private subsidised) schools that are establishing their own institutes for research and development, with school-based action research linked to the professional learning needs of all staff, networked learning with other sources of professional support, and business arms that make a range of services available to other schools. The author is on the advisory board for the Wesley Institute created within the multi-campus Wesley College, one of the largest schools in Australia, whose principal is Dr Helen Drennen, cited in Chapter 16 for her leadership in the International Baccalaureate Organisation.

These developments in respect to networked support in school systems that enjoy a relatively high degree of autonomy are consistent with key elements in the new enterprise logic of schools:

▸ Schools cannot achieve expectations for transformation by acting alone or operating in a line of support from the centre of a school system to the level of the school, classroom or student. The success of a school depends on its capacity to join networks to share knowledge, address problems and pool resources.

▸ Leadership is distributed across schools in networks as well as within schools.

▸ Networks involve a range of individuals, agencies, institutions and organisations across public and private sectors in educational and non-educational settings. Personnel and other resources are allocated to energise and sustain them.

Responses in these workshops suggest that a broader concept of network is required, and that it should not be restricted to a small formal frequently meeting group. A high level of adaptability and flexibility is required. With this qualification, operating according to the new enterprise logic can be an important factor in ensuring that leadership is exhilarating.

Master strategy

The first part of Chapter 15 provides a reflection on themes in the master classes reported in Chapter 13 and in the workshops, as summarised in Chapter 14. The author sought the assistance of three leaders who epitomise exhilarating leadership and who are now in positions that enable them to place the findings in a broader context. The importance of 'master strategy' emerges from their contributions, and connections are made to Ketan Patel's *The Master Strategist: Power, Purpose and Principle* (Patel 2005). The second part of the chapter shifts the meaning of 'master strategy' to consider how leaders of the kind who gave master classes can influence events on a broader scale, across part or all of a school system. The notion of a 'system leader' is emerging, especially in England, based on the success of the approach in a range of circumstances. Reference is made to the work of David Hopkins and others who are shaping policy and practice in this domain.

More insights from the masters

Further insights were provided by three high profile leaders who are exemplary in the way they communicate a sense of exhilaration in their work. The first was shared in correspondence with Sir Iain Hall, honoured for his leadership at Parrs Wood High School in Manchester, a specialist Arts and Technology College, serving more recently as consultant to the Specialist Schools and Academies Trust and the National College for School Leadership. The others emerged in extended conversations with two leaders who were invited to join the author in the interpretation of responses to Questions 1, 2 and 3 in the workshops described in Chapter 14. One was Steve Marshall, Director of Education and Lifelong Learning for Wales, formerly Chief Executive of the Department of Education and Children's Services in South Australia. The other was Jim Spinks, my co-author in the self-managing school series (Caldwell and Spinks 1988, 1992, 1998). Jim was a successful school principal and is now a skilled consultant on aligning resource allocation in education with expectations for learning, and the nature, needs and aspirations of students. The insights of these three leaders affirmed what was shared in master classes and what emerged in workshops, as reported in Chapters 13 and 14, respectively, and added new perspectives to help shape strategies to shift the balance to exhilaration.

Sir Iain Hall

Sir Iain Hall, former head at Parrs Wood High School in Manchester, and now a consultant on school leadership, affirmed the major themes that emerged in responses to the question: 'What aspects of your leadership are exhilarating?' Sixty-seven per cent of workshop participants associated exhilaration with good outcomes, such as success with a particular project, and high achievement by students and staff who work together to make it all happen. Sir Iain also highlighted the importance of talking up the exhilarating aspects of the role rather than dwelling on workload.

> It is important that we describe leadership as exhilarating, for far too long the negative aspects of workload have obscured the debate and sent out the wrong messages to our developing leaders. I hope that I have always been a headteacher who placed individual learning at the centre of my energies. The real exhilaration comes not when you see your ideas and strategies taken up in school but when you stumble upon them being taken even further than you imagined, with new initiatives and innovations springing from the original thoughts. Suddenly, you see these being laterally transferred across subject boundaries and the excitement growing. No longer are they your ideas but theirs! The 'buzz' in the school and the excitement in the students responding to these new initiatives make it all worthwhile.

Steve Marshall

Steve Marshall held senior leadership positions in Victoria before returning to South Australia as Chief Executive of the Department of Education and Children's Services in South Australia, where he began his career in education. He has a Master of Educational Administration and a Master of Business Administration and is undertaking research on school renewal for a Doctor of Philosophy. He is up to date with current writing about education and the general literature about leadership and change, often exploring the deeper aspects of personal engagement and motivation. He always seems to have a book in hand or in his briefcase. Apart from his track record of successful transformation, he is an exemplar for the second part of his title as Director of Education and Lifelong Learning for Wales. Exuberance and exhilaration are apt descriptions of how others see him, but there is also a steely determination to lead a team that will create a world-class system of public education.

Marshall reflected on the early stages of analysis of responses to Question 1: What aspects of your work are exhilarating?' and Question 2: 'What aspects of your work are boring, depressing, discouraging or dispiriting?' He suggested there was broad consistency with Maslow's hierarchy of needs. Responses to Question 1 indicated that higher order needs were being met (self-actualisation; the esteem needs of self-esteem, recognition and status; and the social needs of sense of belonging and love), while those for Question 2 suggested that lower order needs were not being met (especially safety needs of security and protection). In reference to exhilaration (Question 1) he also noted the sense of moral purpose and the importance of interdependence and alignment with a vision for the school that underpinned the responses. He referred to much of the language in responses to Question 2 as 'toxic' in the sense that there were many references to 'what can't be done'. The dominant theme in responses to Question 3: 'What actions by you or others would make your work as leader more exhilarating and less boring, depressing, discouraging or dispiriting?' was personal; that is, the balance can be shifted to exhilaration through the personal efforts of the leader. Marshall affirmed such a strategy while acknowledging the importance of support that can be provided from within the school system.

The usual interpretation of the Maslow theory is that it is only when lower order needs are satisfied that a person can move up to and attain satisfaction at higher levels. It seems that leaders who presented in master classes reported in Chapter 13 have a capacity to move to higher levels despite unresolved concerns at lower levels. Bella Irlicht is an outstanding example, having transcended the constraints of two settings, the first an ant-infested two-room house; the second a derelict, contaminated building in the 19th century style, to create a world-class full-service special school in Port Melbourne, with state-of-the-art facilities for the performing arts.

Marshall has demonstrated that significant change can occur within current structural arrangements in a school system. He suggests that a 'status quo' scenario in the OECD set of six can be changed organically rather than radically to incorporate elements in the preferred 're-schooling' scenarios ('schools as core social centres' and 'schools as focused learning organisations'). He described how this has been achieved in South Australia with the creation of a Strategic Reform Unit, where different members of the corporate staff move in and out of a range of projects, thus building a central capacity for continuous change. He suggests the same must happen at the school level. 'You have to design and then create it. It won't just happen'.

Jim Spinks

Jim Spinks is also a leader who communicates a sense of exhilaration. Like Bella Irlicht, he transcended a setting that would lead others to be stranded at the lower levels of the

Maslow hierarchy. He served as principal for many years in remote locations in Tasmania, most famously as head at Rosebery District High School, where he developed a model for self-management that underpinned our publications and led to his influential work around the world in recent decades. He has made an important contribution to the transformation of school management. He models an attribute that many participants in workshops believed to be important if they were to shift the balance to exhilaration, namely, a balance in life. He has been a wilderness guide and has travelled to the Antarctic on several occasions.

Spinks affirmed that 'in 27 years as principal I mostly lived on adrenaline through exhilaration'. He was struck by the words of one workshop participant who referred in his response to Question 2 to leadership that is 'emetic', meaning 'an agent that induces vomiting'. While some may read the comment as a devastating reflection on levels of stress in school leadership, Jim Spinks put an entirely different construction on it.

> If you want to experience exhilaration, you've got to do something extraordinary: either you've got to attempt something extraordinary or you've got to achieve something extraordinary. You've also got to be daring, and you've also got to take a risk that you might fail. When you look at leadership in schools, for quite a large percentage of principals, the last thing they want to do is fail, and so they tend to step back from what is courageous, what is daring, what is high risk.

The leader who recorded an emetic experience may have referred to an outcome of attempting or retreating from 'what is courageous, what is daring, what is high risk'. Jan Shrimpton, whose transforming leadership was described in Chapter 13, did not hesitate to admit that, while always maintaining an outwardly positive appearance, 'that didn't mean that I didn't sometimes go home and tear my hair out and have the odd tear because it was a very tough task'.

Spinks referred to the tendency in responses to Question 2 for participants to refer to external factors. He used the example of those who referred to 'party politics'. 'Any principal who thinks that education can take place without it being in a political environment has got rocks in their head!' Without denying the importance of being an active player, he referred to the example of his wife, Marilyn Spinks, also a highly successful principal and now a partner in their consultancy, who displayed the Serenity Prayer of Reinhold Niebuhr on the wall of her office: 'God grant me the serenity to accept the things I cannot change; the courage to change the things I can; and wisdom to know the difference'. He suggested that there were 'people looking for exhilaration but who too often were really focusing on things they had no capacity to change. If you focus on that, you've no time left, no energy left to pursue the things that require courage'. He mentioned two leaders in his experience who never had the opportunity to experience exhilaration, despite successful experience in teaching, one 'who spent 95 per cent of his time decrying decisions made by government and the department', and another who immersed himself in what many participants in the workshops described as 'administrivia', in this instance spending much of his time monitoring power usage in different parts of the school.

Our discussion turned to how people chose to enter or were selected to the principalship. A key question is whether sufficient attention is paid to personal factors. Jim Spinks highlighted the traditional culture of teaching that is now inconsistent with capacities that are required for transformation and leadership that is exhilarating. 'In the past there was a culture where you entered the public service because it was safe and secure. As a kid from the bush, we were encouraged to go into the public service in education because it was a government job, it was secure, with very good holidays, and working conditions were pleasant'. However, 'it attracted people who were not necessarily daring risk takers'. He referred to efforts to attract the right people into the principalship through raising salaries, but the other way 'is to try and change the culture'. He referred to his own experience as principal at Sheffield District High School, following his appointment at Rosebery, when he accepted the challenge of raising levels of literacy, setting a target of 100 per cent of students meeting the standard. Success was achieved through the efforts of a brilliant young team leader on staff. He referred to the reaction of fellow principals: 'Half of them just got so angry. The other half got so excited'. The difference seemed to be associated with views about what was possible and a willingness to set high standards under challenging circumstances, fulfilment of which called for courage and daring action.

Spinks believes that courageous leaders outside education ought to be encouraged to pursue a career in schools but 'they must have some understanding about learning and about teaching. Most of all, they must have compassion for children'. He expressed 'grave doubts' about efforts to set standards for school leaders by developing lists of criteria against which aspirants or incumbents should be measured. He reported on the unsatisfactory experience with the approach in Tasmania. 'None of them talked about courage, none of them talked about risk taking or daring. I think they stepped away from those things and therefore stepped back into mediocrity'.

Master strategist

Sir Iain Hall, Steve Marshall and Jim Spinks can be fairly described as 'master strategists', as reflected in their views on leadership for transformation and leadership that is exhilarating. They gave a 'big picture' view of what is required. There was no place for 'administrivia', even though there was an unrelenting focus on the wellbeing of each learner and the nurturing of each colleague in the enterprise. The notion of a 'master strategist' warrants scrutiny, and a recent book on the topic provides direction.

Ketan Patel's *The Master Strategist: Power, Purpose and Principle* (Patel 2005) is recommended for leaders in education who seek a greater sense of exhilaration in the role. Patel is the founder and head of the Strategic Group at Goldman Sachs.

At the macro level, Patel summarised the challenges that must be addressed. They provide a context for the work of the leader in every field. Challenges 1, 2, 5, 6, and 9 in the list below relate most directly to education:

1. How to deal with the inexorable rise in expectations as barriers are broken.
2. How to find meaning from the confusing and overwhelming volume of information and dis-information.
3. How to survive in a world of ever-rising volume and ever-decreasing prices and an ever-increasing reliance on machines for satisfaction.
4. How to maintain the level of our assets as others instantly copy and exceed us.
5. How to make sense in a world in which people, information and money move freely around the globe.
6. How to avoid ignoring those who live with poverty, brutality and oppression as victims and perpetrators.
7. How to fight those who appear undeterrable in their opposition to our way of life.
8. How to deal with an unlimited capacity to destroy.
9. How to unlock the potential of people.

Patel described the master strategist in language that resonates with insights shared by Hall, Marshall and Spinks, and with those of leaders who conducted master classes, as reported in Chapter 13. The following are a selection of the attributes of the master strategist, listed here with minor adaptation:

▸ The master strategist is open, deliberate and measured. Being open enables influence to enter. Being deliberate enables choice. Being measured enables controlled action.

▸ There is no progress before self-progress; you cannot master strategy before you master yourself.

▸ To be a master strategist one must have the courage to question oneself, the will to persevere, the training to know how to ask, and the mentoring to be effective.

▸ Master strategists create 'golden periods' when their chosen vehicles—personal and organisational—prevail.

▸ The master strategist only pursues ideas and purposes of the highest order.

▸ Positive results require a spirit of compassion. When situations are approached in a spirit of self-interest, negative results are more likely to follow. The master strategist is one who has cultivated compassion in oneself in order to cultivate peace, prosperity and freedom in others (adapted from a list by Patel 2005, pp. 68–9).

There is resonance in this list, and in master classes and the further insights provided by Hall, Marshall and Spinks, with the work of Jim Collins in *Good to Great* (Collins 2001) based on research in enterprises that have gone, quite literally, from being merely 'good' to genuinely 'great'. Collins concluded that a hierarchy of leadership capacity was present, with level 5 calling for an 'executive leader' who 'builds enduring greatness through a paradoxical blend of personal humility and professional will' (Collins 2001, p. 20). These two sides of executive leadership are summarised in Table 15.1.

Table 15.1: THE TWO SIDES OF LEVEL 5 'EXECUTIVE LEADERSHIP'
(Collins 2001, p. 36)

PROFESSIONAL WILL	PERSONAL HUMILITY
Creates superb results, a clear catalyst in the transition from good to great	Demonstrates a compelling modesty, shunning public adulation; never boastful
Demonstrates an unwavering resolve to do whatever must be done to produce the best long-term results, no matter how difficult	Acts with quiet, calm determination; relies principally on inspired standards, not inspiring charisma, to motivate
Sets the standard of building an enduring great company; will settle for nothing less	Channels ambition into the company, not the self; sets up successors for even greater success in the next generation
Looks in the mirror, not out the window, to apportion responsibility for poor results, never blaming other people, external factors, or bad luck	Looks out the window, not in the mirror, to apportion credit for the success of the company—to other people, external factors, and good luck

System leadership

The new enterprise logic of schools includes two elements that have important implications for the way leadership is exercised in a school system: (1) the success of a school depends on its capacity to join networks to share knowledge, address problems and pool resources; and (2) leadership is distributed across schools in networks as well as within schools.

When it comes to the exercise of leadership across a system, the traditional approach has been to appoint successful principals to formal positions in a central office, from where they are expected to influence developments across the system, in whole or in part. It remains the most widely-practised approach to system leadership. It has generally worked well. In terms of the OECD scenarios, it is part of a 'status quo' scenario ('bureaucratic systems continue'). It is an approach that is consistent with the old enterprise logic. As explained in Chapter 5, the preferred scenarios among those developed by OECD ('schools as core social centres' and 'schools as focus learning organisation') call for a high level of professional networking. An approach that is consistent with these preferred scenarios and the new enterprise logic is for successful principals to remain in their posts but exert influence across all or part of a system, rather than leave for an appointment in a central office. This is a new view of the 'system leader', defined by David Hopkins, HSBC iNet Chair in International Leadership at the Institute of Education in London, in the following terms:

> 'System leaders' are those Head teachers [principals] who are willing to shoulder system leadership roles: who care about and work for the success of other schools as well as their own. System leaders measure their success in terms of improving student learning and increasing achievement, and strive to both raise the bar and narrow the gap(s). They look both into classrooms and across the broader system, they realise in a deep way that the classroom, school and system levels all impact on each other. Crucially they understand that in order to change the larger system you have to engage with it in a meaningful way (Hopkins 2006).

Hopkins includes the nurturing of 'system leaders' in a range of strategies that support a vision of 'every school a great school', adapting to education the terminology of Jim Collins in *From Good to Great* cited above (Collins 2001). The role of system leader in this image is already taking shape in England, as illustrated by Hopkins:

▸ Partnering another school which is facing particular difficulties, that is, to run two schools. This role is now commonly referred to as being an *Executive Head* or when more schools are involved in a federation as the *Chief Executive*.

▸ Choosing to lead a school that is in *extremely challenging circumstances* or becoming an *Academy Principal*.

▸ Acting as a '*civic leader*' to broker and shape the networks of wider relationships across their local communities that can support children in developing their potential. In England this role currently relates to leading an Education Improvement Partnership or a cluster of Extended Schools.

▸ Working as a '*change agent*' within the system such as a *consultant leader* with a school leadership team to improve levels of attainment, or operating as one of the new *School Improvement Partners* (Hopkins 2006).

Hopkins does not see every school leader as a system leader. He calls for a segmented approach that visualises a school's capacity to lead reform as increasing as the school succeeds. This does not depart from the element of the new enterprise logic that calls for all schools to join networks to share knowledge, address problems and pool resources.

This example of 'master strategy' elevates the importance of strategic leadership, described by Henry Mintzberg as 'seeing': seeing ahead, seeing behind, seeing above, seeing below, seeing beside, seeing beyond, and above all, seeing it through (adapted from Mintzberg 1995). System leadership goes beyond 'seeing' to 'supporting' in several instances including 'supporting beside' and 'supporting beyond'. It calls for a generic capacity for what Michael Fullan (2005) calls 'system thinking'.

Principal as chief executive

England is rich in the variations to the traditional role of principal (headteacher). Another example of a 'master strategy' that resonates with the notion of a system leader is that of the 'principal as chief executive'. Such a role has been developed by Dr Paul Mortimer, Head of Hollingworth High School, who provided the following account of how it evolved.

In the Autumn of 2004 I was engaged by the National Remodelling Team (described in Chapter 10) to prepare a scoping paper as one of their 'thought leaders'. I developed and led workshops into the changing nature of headship with 35 primary and secondary headteachers in four northern LEAs in the spring of 2005. The idea developed from my own 'experiments' on myself, as I had remodelled my post of headteacher into that of Chief Executive of the Governing Body a year earlier. My 15 years of Headship experience had told me that exasperation was looming given the rapid changes in the nature of 21st Century teaching and learning. The problem was easy to contextualise: the British Government's *Five Year Strategy* (DfES 2004a) would only work if individual schools worked in new and varied partnerships, particularly as LEAs would be responding by redefining themselves in a complementary manner. The nation's responsibility for its children was to be re-engineered through *Every Child Matters* (DfES 2003) with enormous consequences for schools. I modified my own 'post' as I was finding that the capacity or time to draw together or extrapolate from the various (and simultaneous) initiatives was becoming 'un-exhilarating'. My early years of Headship (1980s) did not have such challenges: strategic thinking was 'somebody else's responsibility'. My workshops for the National Remodelling Team revealed that such a view still existed but there was a desire to do something about it.

There is a need now to do two things. Firstly, redefine an acceptable change to the nature of leadership, management and governance of schools so that each school can bring its own coherence to current and future initiatives. Secondly, facilitate experienced school leaders to lead across more than one institution and contribute to system leadership in a manner not unlike the ideas underpinning Putnam's 'bonding' and 'bridging' concepts.

To meet the current needs of pupils, become a future-focused school, and to operate in the evolving new geometric configuration of the school system in the 21st century needs both a headteacher who focuses relentlessly on day-to-day standards and a complementary leader—an experienced educator working strategically at governance level—the role I have created.

Reflection on standards in leadership

The National College for School Leadership in England has embraced the need to prepare and support those who will serve as system leaders (Munby 2006). It is beyond the scope of this book to specify programs for the development of leaders. However, a note of concern is raised about efforts to develop standards for leadership. There is a difference between a high standard of leadership and highly specified standards for leadership. Where such an effort is made, the outcome should be parsimonious. The National Standards for Headteachers in England is a model in this regard: shaping the future; leading learning and teaching; developing self and working with others; managing the organisation; securing accountability; and strengthening community (DfES 2004b). The reader will have little difficulty matching success on these standards with aspects of work that leaders find exhilarating, as reported in Chapter 14. There is fidelity in the experiences of leaders in the master classes reported in Chapter 13 and the views of the master strategists set out in the opening pages of Chapter 15.

Spinks commented on a poorly implemented approach to the detailed specification of standards. The author concurs with his conclusion that: 'None of them talked about courage, none of them talked about risk taking or daring. I think they stepped away from those things and therefore stepped back into mediocrity'.

How can one build a capacity to be a 'master strategist' in education? At the very least, the first step may be summarised in the words of one of the main characters in Paulo Coelho's *The Zahir*: 'All you have to do is to pay attention; lessons always arrive when you are ready, and if you can read the signs, you will learn everything you need to know in order to take the next step' (Coelho 2005, p. 29).

CHAPTER 16

Going global… going faster

The four leaders who conducted the master classes, reported in Chapter 13, achieved dramatic change on the scale of transformation in their schools. The 185 leaders who shared their insights in five workshops in two states in Australia, reported in Chapter 14, provided valuable insights on the circumstances under which leadership can be exhilarating and what it might take to shift the balance of experience in this direction. It is sobering, however, to record that all were still operating in what David Hargreaves calls a '19th century imaginary' when a shift to a '21st century imaginary' is needed if transformation is to be real and sustained. Elements of the new enterprise logic of schools were apparent in the experience of the four leaders in the master classes, but the challenge is how this new logic can be embedded in all schools and to ensure that leadership can be exhilarating under these circumstances.

The purpose of this chapter is to place these experiences and the further analysis provided by master strategists in Chapter 15 in the context of the bigger picture that is emerging in education and in the way work is conducted in all fields of endeavour. The chapter takes a lead from Thomas Friedman's *The World is Flat* (Friedman 2005). The theme is that much of the work is now occurring in a world no longer bound by differences in time, distance, geography or gender. There is no reason why it should be different in education. The implications are profound, because it means that the work of leaders will be more challenging, but it may also be more exhilarating. The insights from exploring an educational world that is flat set the stage for a final word on leadership that is exhilarating.

The starting point is a description of worldwide movements in education in the field of curriculum. Friedman's insights are then explored. Some of the pitfalls are identified. The chapter concludes with a frank acknowledgement that the pace of change is likely to accelerate, so a sturdy sense of values to underpin the leadership effort is essential.

From local to global in curriculum and pedagogy

There was universal acclaim for the UNESCO report entitled *Learning: The Treasure Within* and its famous dictum that 'Education throughout life is based on four pillars: learning to know, learning to do, learning to live together and learning to be' (UNESCO 1996, p. 37). It has become a touchstone for curriculum design in many places.

Some approaches to curriculum and associated pedagogies have a history of success in several nations, including Montessori and Steiner. Whole school designs have been shaped in each instance by underpinning philosophies about learning. Two examples where there is global span are Reggio Emilia and the International Baccalaureate.

The Reggio Emilia approach in the early years has shaped developments in many nations. The Scottish Consultative Council on the Curriculum (1999) provides the following concise account of the approach.

> In educational terms the northern Italian town of Reggio Emilia has become renowned worldwide for its forward thinking and exemplary approach to early childhood education. ...This is a socioconstructivist model. That is, it is influenced by the theory of Lev Vygotsky, which states that children (and adults) co-construct their theories and knowledge through the relationships that they build with other people and the surrounding environment. It also draws on the work of others such as Piaget, Howard Gardner and Jerome Bruner. It promotes an image of the child as a capable participator in his own learning. It is a model where the expressive arts play a central role in learning, where a unique reciprocal relationship of learning exists between teacher and child, and where much attention is given to detailed observation and documentation of learning. It is a model that demonstrates a strong relationship between school and community and provides a remarkable program for professional development (Scottish Consultative Council on Curriculum 1999, p. 1).

Also implemented on a wide scale are the three programs offered by the International Baccalaureate Organisation (IBO). The best known is the Diploma Program (DP), recognised by universities in more than 100 countries. The IBO now offers the Middle Years Program (MYP), introduced in 1994, and the Primary Years Program (PYP) in 1997. These now provide a continuum in primary and secondary education that can be offered in any school in any setting. Helen Drennen, who has played a leading role in the development of the IB curriculum, noted when commenting on a view that the programs are associated in the minds of some people with independent or private schools: 'the majority of schools that offer the programs worldwide are state and government schools' (cited in Tarica 2005, p. 7).

The PYP is framed by consideration of who we are, where we are in place and time, how we express ourselves, how the world works, how we organise ourselves, and sharing the planet. The MYP is framed by subjects of study: humanities, technology, mathematics, arts, sciences, physical education, language A and language B. The DP has six groups of subjects—group 1: first language, group 2: second language, group 3: individuals and society, group 4: experimental sciences, group 5: mathematics and computer science, and group 6: the arts. The core of the DP has three components: theory of knowledge; creativity, action and service; and an extended essay (see IBO 2002 for a summary).

Given its coherence and the aforementioned continuum of curriculum, it seems that the IB programs are the best example of an emerging global curriculum. It is important to note, however, that the IBO recognises the relationship between local and global contexts. 'The content provided in an international curriculum must be both global and local, because each program must be based on the premise that students need to understand themselves and their indigenous local culture before they can appreciate others' (IBO 2002, p. 11).

The World is Flat

It is likely that leadership at the school level will become as much global as local in the decade ahead. Illustrations are provided in a later section of the chapter but a bigger picture is painted before doing this by outlining Friedman's view of the shape of the world.

Writing in *The World is Flat* triple Pulitzer Prize winner Thomas Friedman described ten forces—'the flatteners'—that converged over the last 15 years. The first was the opening of the Berlin Wall in 1989. The others were the release of Netscape in 1995, integration of work flow, out-sourcing, off-shoring, open-sourcing, in-sourcing, supply-chaining, in-forming, and using 'steroids'—building an enhanced capacity in a mobile digitalised world. He suggests that the tipping point was reached around 2000.

> The net result of this convergence was the creation of a global, Web-enabled playing field that allows for multiple forms of collaboration—the sharing of knowledge and work—in real time, without regard to geography, distance, or, in the near future, even language. No, not everyone has access to this platform, this playing field, but it is open today to more people in more places on more days in more ways than anything like it ever before in the history of the world (Friedman 2005, pp. 176–7).

This describes one of three convergences that account for the flattening of the world. The second is that there is stronger alignment between the capacities of an enterprise and the potential that is available as a result of the first convergence. There has been impressive progress in schools over the period that Friedman covers but, in general terms, it is fair to say that it is taking time for work practices in schools to align with the possibilities of a world that is flat.

The third convergence, in Friedman's eyes, is that the flatteners are now at work and alignment has occurred in parts of the world that were previously 'frozen out'.

'Save for a tiny minority, these 3 billion people had never been allowed to compete and collaborate before, because they lived in largely closed economies with very vertical, hierarchical political and economic structures. I am talking about the people of China, India, Russia, Eastern Europe, Latin America, and Central Asia'. He concludes that 'it is this triple convergence—of new players, on a new playing field, developing new processes and habits for horizontal collaboration—that I believe is the most important force shaping global economics and politics in the early twenty-first century' (Friedman 2005, pp. 181–2).

Creating a school in an educational world that is flat

An impressive example of an international approach to curriculum and pedagogy is presented at the 3e International Kindergarten in Beijing that opened in September 2005. The young learners gain from two experiences, one from the west ('child-centred') and one from the east ('direct teaching in a traditional setting'). The former occurs in the morning session and is based on the Reggio Emilia approach described earlier in the chapter. This will be taught mainly by recent graduates from the College of Education at Michigan State University. They experience the latter in the afternoon session and it reflects a Confucian approach that integrates and balances five components: intellectual, physical, aesthetic, communal and moral. Their teachers are Chinese.

The project is an outcome of work in the US–China Centre for Research on Educational Excellence, headquartered at Michigan State University (MSU) and Beijing Normal University. Director of the Centre is Dr Yong Zhao, Distinguished University Professor at MSU. The Centre is supported by a US$5 million grant from Hong Kong-based Sun Wah Education Foundation. The school is built on public land but owned and operated by the Foundation under the leadership of its Chief Executive Gilbert Choy.

The creation of the 3e International Kindergarten is itself a remarkable story. It was conceived following a conference of policy-makers and researchers in the APEC (Asia-Pacific Economic Cooperation) network in Beijing in January 2004, co-sponsored by Sun Wah with a focus on eastern and western aspects of policy and practice in education. The establishment of the US–China Centre for Research on Educational Excellence was announced at the conference. Twelve months of planning followed. The school was built in just four months.

The planning team led by Yong Zhao met on one occasion in the excellent retreat facilities of the George Lucas Skywalker Ranch in California. Contributing to the design was Anne Taylor, Director of the Institute for Environmental Education, School of

Architecture and Planning at the University of New Mexico. An educator in her own right, Taylor has worked for more than 20 years with architect George Vlastos 'researching and designing indoor and outdoor learning environments as functional art forms, places of beauty, and motivational centres of learning. We have used the architecture of the school classroom, museum exhibits, and the landscape as a means of demonstrating how the built and natural environments demonstrate, in real live form, the ideas, laws and principles that we at present are trying to teach children from textbooks' (Taylor n.d., p. 2).

School design matches curriculum and pedagogy in the manner envisaged by the planning team, as captured by Taylor's statement above. Situated adjacent to a park, the rooms are superbly sunlit, with classroom furniture and fittings matching the dual curriculum. 3e refers to 'explore', 'experiment' and 'express'. Running the full length of the school, the level below ground is devoted to a museum of mainly interactive exhibits drawn from both cultures. The main classrooms are on the ground floor. The upper floor features an arts and physical education studio and a library, as well as outstanding facilities for teachers. There is a seminar room for professional learning. Here is a setting in which 'children at 3e International Kindergarten will embark upon their education with multiple perspectives, cultures, and languages. They will enjoy the tremendous advantage of exploring the world with tools from across cultures, and across disciplines' (3e International Kindergarten 2005). It is an exciting integration of international approaches to curriculum, with pedagogy and facilities to match, that has the potential for replication in eastern and western settings. It is intended that the two approaches 'co-evolve' over time.

Textbooks in a world that is flat

There have been notable developments in digitalising books, and there are implications for schools and the educational publishing industry. The image of a student, school or school system with their limited range of recommended books in hard or soft cover is fading from view. Google is moving forward with plans to digitalise books from libraries that include the University of Michigan, Stanford, Harvard, the New York Public library, and Oxford. Yahoo! and Microsoft will make books accessible online through the Open Content Alliance. Microsoft will digitalise 100 000 books from the British Library that are no longer under copyright. Project Gutenberg now has 17 000 digital books in 45 languages. There are between 8 and 10 billion items available online.

Digitalising does not mean that the only item to be downloaded or purchased is the entire book. 'Unbundling' can mean that students can access just a single page or a chapter rather than seeking out or acquiring the whole book. This is what Amazon.com is planning to do with the full blessing of publishers. This development will facilitate the personalising of learning in very powerful ways.

Digitalisation will be delivered through an online service, and there are major implications for point of sale. For example, the book market in the United States grew by just 1.8 per cent per year from 1999 to 2004. Online book sales are growing at 8–9 per cent per year, much faster than book shop sales. 'Few dispute that [online] services will be a boon to the public and that books will eventually go digital' (*The Economist* 2005, p. 66). An indication of trends is that, in 2002, of Florida's high school literature reading list, it was found that over 40 per cent of the books on the list were currently available as e-books, many of them at no cost (Cavanaugh 2002).

These developments do not mean imminent abandonment of books in their traditional form. 'It is difficult to justify eradicating printed text books from the options available to schools' (McGraw et al 2002, p. 2). Textbooks are necessary in a range of circumstances and for many reasons, whether it be their usability, cost, access, and relevance when content is likely to be stable over time, for example, literature of enduring appeal, or material in particular disciplines such as mathematics and science. 'We have had nearly 500 years of experience using printed textbooks, and they not only support a wide range of applications, but users have had such a strong mental model of their generic structure that they can successfully adopt an equally wide range of usage strategies' (McKnight, Dillon and Richardson cited in McGraw et al. 2002, p. 2).

The $100 computer

One of the three convergences in Friedman's description of a world that is now flat is that the flatteners are at work in parts of the world that were previously 'frozen out'. For many, a key issue is whether this can occur in developing countries where few students or schools can afford to have their own computers, and thus have access to a web-enabled world.

A breakthrough is close at hand, as revealed at the World Summit on the Information Society held in Tunis in November 2005. Nicholas Negroponte, head of the Massachusetts Institute of Technology's Media Lab demonstrated a prototype of a US$100 laptop that can be used as a computer, an electronic book, a television, and a writing or drawing tablet. The laptops should start appearing in volume in late 2006, with an estimated production of 100—150 million per year by December 2007. The laptop can be powered with either AC or a wind-up mechanism built into the hinge of the machine. A student can get 10 minutes of use with one minute of cranking. The lab plans to commence distribution in Brazil, China, Egypt, South Africa and Thailand. Governments will need to pay for one million laptops in advance to warrant mass production.

Other developments are also striking. Digital whiteboards are finding their way into classrooms at an increasingly affordable price. Downloading of material through iPods is also relatively common in many countries, with students well ahead of their teachers in their capacity to use them. Pen-top computers have also made their appearance. The Fly, as it is called, is made by LeapFrog, maker of LeapPad, an interactive book reader. The following are illustrations of the Fly at work in an educational setting (Pogure 2005).

> As you tap countries on a world map, the pen pronounces their capitals or plays their national anthems. On a glossy, fold-out mini-poster of a disc jockey's setup, you can tap buttons to trigger music samples…From a website (www.flypentop.com), your sixth-through eighth-graders can download multiple-choice quizzes in PDF format that correspond to the chapters of popular published textbooks…You print them onto the blank paper that comes with this cartridge, and voila: instant interactive tests, specific to the textbook being used in class.

Pitfalls in local and global approaches

Despite such developments, there are substantial costs in digitalisation and online learning that must be borne at some level of a system of education. For example, while the survey did not take account of developments such as the $100 computer, an IBM-funded survey in the Asia Pacific found that, for Australia, with about 23 million people, investments in Kindergarten to Year 12 online learning solutions will increase from AUS$49 million in 2003 to $170 million in 2008 (Watson 2004, p. 54).

There are other pitfalls in a movement to, or rejection of, a global approach. One is the determination of some local authorities to design their own approach when it is more efficient and effective to work with others, both national and international. The second may arise with an excessively specified centralised approach or an uncontrolled decentralised approach.

Australia is one of the few nations in the developed world where constitutional powers in education lie with the states rather than at the national level. The outcome has been that each state has engaged in curriculum reform that is exemplary in process but needlessly expensive, given the results are virtually the same, being shades of difference about the nature of 'essential learning'.

There are three core strands in the Victorian Essential Learning Standards: physical, personal and social learning; discipline-based learning; and interdisciplinary learning (see VCAA 2005). There are many similarities with the coherent continuum in the three programs of the International Baccalaureate, and some state schools in Victoria will soon offer the IB. Across Bass Strait from Victoria is the small island state of Tasmania that developed its own Essential Learnings Framework for curriculum by a similar process of consultation with all stakeholders. International observers must surely ask why common standards and frameworks cannot be established across the country when there has been agreement on the national goals of schooling (MCEETYA 1999) and when successful curricula that balance global and local cultures are at hand. There is, however, little support at any level for creating a national curriculum, as exists in most other countries.

While not denying the forces or even some of the benefits described by Friedman, John Ralston Saul in *The Collapse of Globalism* (Saul, 2005) draws attention to failure in much of the globalisation project, especially its reliance on economists and technocrats and efforts to transcend culture and community within national borders. He contends that 'a prudent approach would have involved remembering that the world is round' (Saul 2005, p. 74). While occurring after he completed the book, the rejection by voters in France and the Netherlands of the proposed new constitution for the European Union supports his contention. This line of argument suggests that there are pitfalls in attempting to do in curriculum what managers have attempted to do with the economy.

There are pitfalls in both centralised and decentralised approaches. Insights may be gleaned from recent work at the interface of nanotechnology, biotechnology and computer technology, as presented in Michael Crichton's science fiction novel *Prey* (Crichton, 2002). Crichton described what happens when scientists create a swarm of micro-robots that are self-sustaining, self-producing and capable of learning from experience. The swarm escapes and preys on humans. The whole endeavour was carefully programmed but the programmers lost control. In a non-fictional introduction on artificial evolution in the twenty-first century, Crichton writes: 'The notion that the world around us is continuously evolving is a platitude; we rarely grasp its full implications. We do not ordinarily think, for example, of an epidemic disease changing its character as the epidemic spreads...But that is what happens' (Crichton 2002, vii).

So how do we control an education epidemic? Some authorities endeavour to do this by regulation. Crichton, in another non-fictional aside, suggests a parallel in older notions in artificial intelligence. 'In the old days, programmers tried to write rules to cover every situation [but] the computer would make mistakes. New rules would be added to avoid mistakes. Then more mistakes, and more rules. Eventually the programs were gigantic. Millions of lines of code, and they began to fail out of sheer complexity. They were too large to debug. You couldn't figure out where the errors were coming from' (Crichton 2002, p. 97).

Sounds familiar? It is certainly familiar to educators in some nations, for example, where centrally determined curriculum involved unnecessarily detailed specification of what shall be taught, or in the multi-volume education codes found in some states in America.

However, the other extreme has high risk. A 'distributed system' that is entirely 'bottom up' rather than 'top down' can lead to the outcome in Crichton's work of fiction when it lacks moral purpose in the behaviour of the swarm: 'we didn't specify reinforcers ...program weights that sustained the goals' (Crichton 2002, p. 120).

Shakespeare's Hamlet observes in Act II Scene II that 'there is nothing either good or bad, but thinking makes it so'. There is nothing inherently good or bad in either a centralised or decentralised approach, or a global or local perspective. Whatever it is, there must be sound moral purpose ('program weights') and it is in this respect that policy-makers and practitioners must make choices. In his final book Pope John Paul II referred to the 'proper use of freedom'—'If I am free, I can make good or bad use of that freedom' (Pope John Paul II 2005, p. 37). Moral purpose and social responsibility are important matters to be addressed in global as well as local approaches.

Fast forward

Developments of a kind described by Friedman, and illustrated in curriculum, digitalisation, pedagogy, and technology, suggest that we are moving forward at breakneck speed. Sir Michael Barber, former head of the Delivery Unit in the Cabinet Office in the UK, now with McKinsey, is fond of quoting Italian-born racing driver Mario Andretti: 'If everything seems under control, you're just not going fast enough'. Andretti also observed that 'Circumstances may cause interruptions and delays, but never lose sight of your goal. Prepare yourself in every way you can by increasing your knowledge and adding to your experience, so that you can make the most of opportunity when it occurs'.

It will be critically important under these circumstances for leadership to be underpinned by powerful moral purpose and a sturdy set of values. Values should endure. Nothing in this book is intended to subtract from them. The challenge is of a different kind. Tony Blair captured its scale in his speech at the annual conference of the British Labour Party on 27 September 2005: 'The challenge we face is not in our values, it is how we put those values into practice in a world fast forwarding to the future at unprecedented speed' (Blair 2005).

Welcome to the world of exhilarating leadership!

Conclusion

CHAPTER 17

The new image of the educational leader

What will education be like 40 years from now? I can't tell you. Nobody can. But I can tell you that it must be totally different because if it is the same as it is today, we're dead. Current approaches will be irrelevant, marginalised, the world will be different. You may want it to be the same, but it can't be the same.

This is a dramatic if not startling way to commence a chapter. The reader may recognise it as a paraphrasing of the remarks of Singapore PM Lee Hsien Loong, cited in the opening pages of Chapter 1. Lee was speaking at a national day rally, highlighting the need to 'remake Singapore – our economy, our education system, our mindsets, our city'. It was a remarkable call to action, especially to leaders in education, given that Singapore students rank first in the world in mathematics and science in Grade 4 and Grade 8, as revealed in the Trends in Mathematics and Science Study (TIMSS). However, as cast above, it could well be a call to action for education in other countries.

The same statement could have been made 40 years ago. Who could have imagined in the mid-1960s what schools would be like in the mid-2000s? Regrettably, the architecture might be recognisable, but the pedagogy has changed dramatically, especially in the use of information and communications technology. In the past, public schools were operating within a more-or-less hierarchical arrangement with few synergies outside their immediate communities. Notions of a knowledge society or globalisation were virtually unknown. Who could have imagined how educational leadership would change in the next 40 years?

The time horizon in the foregoing was set at 40 years, but it could well have been set at 20 or even 10, given the rate of change in the first decade of the century. Leadership is likely to change at the same rate, hence the need to re-imagine educational leadership.

Hitting the wall

If further evidence is required of the need to re-imagine, it may be found in surveys of school principals, either of their views about the role or, in simple statistical terms, about the number of vacancies and the paucity of applicants. In Victoria, *The Privilege and the Price* (Department of Education and Training, 2004) reported on workload in government (public) schools and its impact on the health and wellbeing of the principal class. On workload, for example, as reported in Chapter 12, the number of hours per week for principals in Victoria was similar to that for headteachers in England, as reported in a survey at about the same time, being about 60 hours per week. In both places, this is well above the average of leaders and managers in other professional fields in several European nations (about 45 hours per week). The report contained disturbing evidence of the impact on the emotional and physical wellbeing of principals.

Even more disturbing is the evidence from England about the number of vacancies and the number of acting appointments to the position of headteacher. The issue is not the number of positions falling vacant each year. On average, a school seeks a new head once every seven years, which means about 14 per cent of schools advertise each year. The number of schools advertising in 2005 was 12 per cent. Of deep concern is that more than one-third of schools were not able to make an appointment after the initial advertisement. Education Data Surveys (EDS) reported that re-advertisement reached record levels. EDS's John Howson suggested that: 'the 2005 results are alarming, especially for secondary schools. In all the time I have been conducting this survey, I cannot recall the problem being this bad'. The seriousness of the situation is affirmed in a report of the National Audit Office (NAO) that blamed the shortage of headteachers for holding back progress in the most challenged schools (Smithers 2006).

The interim report of a two-year study conducted by the National Association of Head Teachers (NAHT), the Eastern Leadership Centre (ELC), the University of Cambridge, the National College for School Leadership (NCSL) and the Hay Group (NAHT et al. 2005) found that 'the number of quality candidates to choose from is often seen as too small or nonexistent'. It drew attention to the fact that headteacher salaries had risen on average by 34 per cent between 1998 and 2003. Salaries exceed £100 000 per annum for heads of secondary schools in London; a level likely to make them the highest paid principals of public schools in the world. The report canvassed a range of good practices in recruitment, drawing on approaches from England and other countries. At the same time, it acknowledged that recruitment and appointment of headteachers is an international concern.

One caveat should be included at this point, namely, whether the most appropriate people are being encouraged to seek appointment to a leadership position, especially at the level of principal or headteacher. Reference was made in Chapter 11 to the findings in *The Adventures of Charter School Creators* (Deal, Hentschke et al. 2005) in which the question is posed: 'Does starting a charter school from scratch require fundamentally different leadership skills than taking a position in an existing suburban high school?' Jim Spinks hinted at the same issue when he suggested in Chapter 15 that risk taking is not encouraged in the usual specification of standards for school leaders. It may be that the most appropriate people are simply put off by the prospect of either the traditional or emerging role of principal. A variation of the analysis is that those who serve as deputy heads are typically concerned with the management of core functions in the school, and to achieve a degree of predictability in these, controlling and problem solving along the way. This is essentially a management rather than a leadership role (see the difference between leadership and management proposed by John Kotter, as summarised in Chapter 1). These people see the new and demanding role of the principal and conclude that they are not prepared to take the next step. The issue here is leadership succession.

Developments in England must be deeply disappointing to the government, which has helped fund salaries to the highest levels to be found in any nation, and can show that improvements in learning have been achieved and sustained. Expenditure in schools is at a record high. Particularly noteworthy is the establishment of the National College for School Leadership to support the preparation and ongoing development of those who seek or have been appointed to the headship. Few would argue with the view that it is the most impressive organisation of its kind in the world. The situation in Australia has not been described in such dramatic terms, but the survey in Victoria has sounded the alarm. Of particular concern is that there is no counterpart to the National College for School Leadership, with a fragmented array of programs by principal or leadership centres in each state, and a seriously under-funded national initiative by Teaching Australia (formerly the National Institute for Quality Teaching and School Leadership). Its first program after two years of existence is a seven day residential course in two parts for just 80 principals from around the nation.

Given the foregoing, it is fair to conclude, as signalled in Chapter 1, that educational leadership has 'hit the wall', at least in Australia and England, and that, while incremental improvements may be achieved, nothing short of transformation is required. The good news, of course, lies in Part B and Part C, where leaders who have transformed their schools, or have made a commitment to do so, are exhilarated by the experience. The findings in workshops that provided a forum for 'leader voice', as reported in Chapter 14, were clear in what made the work boring, discouraging, depressing or dispiriting, and the implications for policy and practice were also clear.

Self-management affirmed

Some observers, including those who have been critical of the approach from the outset, might argue that there should be a re-centralisation of authority and responsibility, that is, abandonment of the concept of the self-managing school. However, this is not the preference of principals. *The Privilege and the Price*, while reporting high workloads and serious levels of stress, included a powerful statement of support for self-management. Surveys conducted from time to time in England and New Zealand, where there have been similar patterns of decentralisation, have yielded the same point of view. This is understandable, not because principals have sought or seek to maintain a high level of personal power, but because they recognise that there must be local decision-making to ensure that the unique mix of learning needs in each school is addressed. This educational argument is supported by findings in PISA and TIMSS that there is a strong association between school level decision-making and results on these international tests of student achievement (Schleicher 2004; Woessmann 2001). Criticisms of school-based or site-based management in Canada and the United States (Fullan 2005) may be valid in these countries, where the educational focus of the process is not as powerful or as long-standing as in Australia, England and New Zealand.

Reviewing the evidence

Several directions on the way forward stand out from the evidence presented in preceding chapters. There is no one best way to proceed that will suit every setting and, even when one is determined, it is certain to change in a relatively short time. This is what Bentley and Wilsdon (2004, p. 16) called 'the adaptive state'—'we need new systems capable of continuously reconfiguring themselves to create new sources of public value'. One thing is certain: 'the era of the large, slow moving, steady, respected, bureaucratic public services, however good by earlier standards, is over' (Barber 2004, p. 115).

Support

In the developed economies, which are the main focus of this book, the centralised arm of the public service must henceforth be conceived of almost exclusively as an agency of support—deep support—for schools. Small parts of the agency will help develop the framework within which schools in a system of public education will operate. The framework will be largely concerned with standards, mechanisms for resource allocation to schools, and accountabilities. Increasingly, if best practice reported in this book is a guide, deep support for schools from a central agency is likely to be just one of many sources of support. A central role ought to include support for schools as they endeavour to locate and deploy support from other agencies. As the former head of the public service in Australia has declared: 'the goal of government should be to build stronger communities, not bigger bureaucracies' (Keating 2004, p. 5). The need to take this advice to heart is evident in

Australia, where the Productivity Commission found that the size of bureaucracies at the state level increased by 82,700 or 24 per cent in the five years to 2003–04, with wage rates increasing by 25 per cent in real terms over this period (Nahan 2006, p. 10).

Peter Hyman expressed it another way in *1 out of 10: From Downing Street Vision to Classroom Reality*. Hyman left 10 Downing Street after many years as speech writer and advisor to the prime minister to work as an assistant at Islington Green School. 'For lasting change to occur in public services, politicians need to show more humility and bring on board the professionals' and 'governments must take the need to let go more seriously, and to empower the frontline. It must produce a climate where frontline public servants do not become risk-averse. This means less dictating, less putting up pots of money to be bid for— ambitious targets yes, accountability yes, but also back creativity and imagination' (Hyman 2005, p. 390 and p. 385).

Principals everywhere resent the mountain of paperwork they are required to deal with. It goes without saying that this must be reduced to an absolute minimum, but the larger issue of approaches to knowledge management of schools is raised. Part of the deep support to be expected of centralised services is to furnish every school and every leader with a state-of-the-art computer-based system to assist every aspect of school operations, including curriculum, pedagogy, accounting and accountability. Some schools are doing this well from their own resources but it is a capacity that ought to be built for all. School leaders are lagging far behind their counterparts in health care and airline services when it comes to managing information about the individual. How much more important it is in schools where the focus is on personalising learning. The principal's office ought to be a paperless office.

A related issue is the amount of support for principals. There can be few enterprises as large as a typical secondary school or a large primary school where the chief executive does not have a personal assistant and several managers to deal with business and finance. Why not such support for principals of these schools or for principals in networks of smaller primary schools, or however networks of schools are configured? It is inexplicable that such support is not included in the basic package of support for leaders of schools in the public sector, when it is taken for granted for their counterparts in the private or independent sector. The notion of a 'package' is stressed, because the way in which the resource is used will vary from school to school. Some principals may not seek additional personal assistance or require a business manager, or they may choose to outsource the support.

Some governments or systems of education have failed to come to terms with scenarios for the future of schools such as those formulated in OECD's Schooling for Tomorrow project. Take-up is limited to barely a handful of countries. Most are still determined to ensure that 'bureaucratic systems continue' when it is patently clear that they have reached a plateau in what they can achieve, despite the best efforts of highly committed people. Such systems have literally 'hit the wall'. The best of such systems ought now to be planning their own transformation to another scenario such as 'schools as core social centres' or 'schools as focused learning organisations'. It is worth re-reading the descriptions of the leadership and management aspects of these scenarios, as described by Istance (2003) and summarised in Chapter 12.

Networks

Networks are central to the logic of the preferred scenarios, and this book contains many examples of networks in action, along with evidence now starting to emerge that there is a positive impact on learning. Networks are not simply bureaucratically organised clusters of schools for geographic convenience in disseminating information and securing compliance. They are powerful learning communities in their own right, sharing knowledge, solving problems and pooling resources. They are needed and can thrive in the most challenging circumstances, as illustrated in Chapter 8 in the case of the Doveton Endeavour Hills cluster in south-east metropolitan Melbourne.

The notion of 'system leadership' is emerging in England where networking is proceeding apace through the networked learning communities of the National College for School Leadership and the Specialist Schools and Academies Trust. System leadership calls for leadership to be distributed across schools as well as within a school. This is an element in the new enterprise logic. This might be leadership in a network of schools, or across a system of schools, in a particular area where a leader, or her or his school, has expertise, as in the twinning of schools in efforts to raise the achievement of one. At first sight there is a contradiction, or at least the potential to add to the workload or stress levels of already fully engaged principals. This was not the experience of leaders in schools where transformation had been achieved. However, it is important that system leadership be supported by other approaches described above.

Governance

Each of these matters raises the question of the governance of a system of public education. It has been raised in several chapters, notably in the context of proposals by Michel Fullan (2005) for sustainability in a 'tri-level' system. How many levels should there be in a school system? Some may contend that it doesn't matter so long as a school is not unduly encumbered and is powerfully supported as it goes about its work. The counter is that there ought to be as few layers as possible in a hierarchy of authority between the principal and the minister of education. What is construed as a 'level' in the provision of support is best described as a 'locus' of support within the system. As demonstrated in several places, the schools that are leading in transformation view agencies of government as just one of many sources of support.

These matters are not an issue in countries where the provision of basic education is still to be achieved, and where capacities at the school level are rudimentary, or in countries like China or India, where the sheer scale of the education enterprise demands several levels of authority and responsibility.

Specifying different levels may be helpful in describing the operations of a school system. Six levels are used by the OECD in describing patterns of centralisation and decentralisation, including trends from year to year and place to place (OECD 2004a). However, the case is strong that, in policy terms, in places like Australia, England and New Zealand, there ought to be just two levels of authority: the level of government where constitutional authority for education lies, and the school. In the longer term the two levels may be the level of constitutional authority and the family, as is the case with home schooling, one of the fastest growing sectors of education in several countries, including the United States. Indeed, the greatest challenge may be faced by the United States, which has functioned under a 'tri-level' system for well over a century. Constitutional authority lies with the states and, in each state except Hawaii, the system is organised into districts which operate the schools. The number of districts has shrunk from about 85 000 to 15 000 but many of these are very small. Some may say there are four levels in the United States, if the federal government is included. While it does not have constitutional authority, it makes substantial grants available to the states, under strict conditions of compliance, as is the case in Australia with grants from the federal government. A tri-level system operates in Canada and there has been similar consolidation, even in recent times in some provinces, especially Alberta. In each of these countries, why not two layers, the state or the province, and the school, in a system of self-managing schools?

In the final analysis, however, there is nothing inherently 'right' or 'wrong' about particular configurations in the balance of centralisation and decentralisation. The most important consideration is the quality of governance, and there are robust frameworks for its assessment. One is contained in Appendix A, and it warrants close scrutiny. Introduced in earlier chapters, it was developed in a project of Asia Pacific Economic Cooperation (APEC) on 'best practice governance' as reflected in education policy and service delivery (Department of Education, Science and Training 2005). It was developed from indicators devised by the World Bank Group (2001). There are four domains (purpose, process, policy, and standards). For each domain there is at least one element and for each element there is at least one indicator. For 'purpose', the single element is 'outcomes', for which there are three indicators: Is there a contribution to the public good? Is there a contribution to economic development? Is there a contribution to social development? For standards, there are four elements: specificity, data, transparency, replication and ownership, with indicators for the first three listed in Table 17.1. It was in the domain of standards in governance that the main differences were apparent in the APEC project, especially in respect to data and transparency. Economies that were particularly strong were Australia, Canada, New Zealand, Singapore and the USA.

Table 17.1: CRITERIA FOR ASSESSING STANDARDS IN A FRAMEWORK OF GOVERNANCE
(based on DEST 2005)

ELEMENT	INDICATOR
Specificity	Expectations and intended outcomes are clearly specified
Data	Information to be gathered in the implementation of policy is of a kind that will enable judgements to be made on the effectiveness of delivery
	There is a capacity to gather information about the implementation of policy
	Data that are gathered in the course of implementation are of high quality to the extent that they are valid, timely, understandable and capable of effective use in decision-making
	Data are gathered across the range of intended outcomes
	Approaches to the gathering of data are designed to ensure accuracy
	There are incentives in place to ensure that data are gathered and utilised in the manner intended
	Data are used in making decisions in the formulation of policy and in making judgements about the effectiveness of policy
Transparency	Information about policies and associated regulations and procedures is readily available to all stakeholders, as is information about implementation, having due regard to the ethical use of such information

It is the inclusion of standards in this authoritative framework for assessment of governance that challenges the view of Hargreaves and Fink (2006, p. 10), cited in Chapter 1, that the 'educational standards bubble is about to burst'. No government will retreat from its commitment to standards. The challenge is to ensure that the means of addressing standards does not constrain the achievement of purpose. The publication of 'league tables' of results on tests, with or without a correction to determine the 'value added' by the school, may serve as a constraint to the extent that it results in the delivery of a narrow curriculum. The approach in Finland provides a contrast to approaches in England and the United States, and to a lesser extent, Australia. Finland is a top-performing nation in the Program for International Student Assessment (PISA). Finland does not publish results of school performances. The only measurement of different achievements among students that is publicly available is the national rather than local result in PISA. School performance is assessed by the local municipal school board. The results of performance reviews are provided only to the school in question. It seems that this practice fosters high levels of trust between schools and the governing school bodies and high rates of participation in school evaluations (Välijärvi 2005). It is noteworthy that education in Finland is conducted on a two-level model: municipal and the school, with the centre (state) having the most limited role, after the Netherlands (where all decisions are taken at the school level) as reported in the OECD survey of 25 nations (OECD 2004a).

Knowledge

One of several factors accounting for the success of Finland in PISA is the quality of its teachers. Finnish teachers are highly valued and well paid professionals who are expected to have high levels of pedagogical expertise and flexibility in order to achieve learning success with all students in heterogeneous groups. Applications to tertiary education studies are so high that just 10–12 per cent of applicants are accepted in teacher education programs (Linnakylä and Välijärvi 2003). Only students who demonstrate outstanding academic ability and personal qualities are accepted. All teachers are required to have a master's degree in either pedagogy or the subject that they wish to teach.

It will require leadership of the highest order at every level of government and in universities to achieve an expectation that all teachers should hold a master's degree before taking up their appointments. In the absence of such a qualification, and the assumed capacities that follow, schools must become powerful learning communities if teachers are to be at the forefront of professional knowledge. They should remain so, even when these standards of initial teacher education are achieved. Illustrations in government (public) and non-government (private or independent) schools were provided in Chapters 5, 8 and 10, illustrating an element in the new enterprise logic of schools about sagacity and the importance of intellectual and social capital. Principals and other school leaders will require a capacity to develop a comprehensive approach to knowledge management. Sample indicators of such an approach are contained in Appendix B.

Infrastructure

One of the most distressing aspects of the educational scene are the structural constraints on schools that seek to address the new enterprise logic and achieve transformation ('high levels of achievement for all students in all settings'). This refers to the deplorable state of school buildings in many nations. For the most part these reflect the judgement of David Hargreaves that schools are 'a curious mix of the factory, the asylum and the prison' (Hargreaves, D 1994). While some improvements have been made since he made that statement, it is nigh on impossible for some schools to personalise learning using appropriate technologies in a pleasant environment for students and staff. England, Scotland, and Singapore have, to their credit, declared a national priority on the replacement, refurbishment or re-design of schools, but there is little evidence that a commitment has been made in most nations, including Australia. A 'third way' approach is required if improvements are to be made for very large numbers of schools in a relatively short time. A combined public-private effort along the lines of England and Scotland is one such approach. It requires strong and determined leadership in government to do this in the face of opposition from those who believe that public schools must be entirely funded, built, owned and operated by government.

Implications for policy and practice

The major dimensions in the new image of the educational leader are set out above. There are other important elements such as curriculum and pedagogy, and these were included in the framework for leadership in the school of the future set out in Chapter 11. Integrating themes are embedding the new enterprise logic and balancing innovation and abandonment. The emotional aspects of leadership are important and these have been addressed in engaging style by David Loader in *The Inner Principal* (Loader 1997). The book makes clear that success in leadership is 'as much about discovering self as discovering strategy' (Foreword). Resourcing schools for personalising learning is taken up in other publications (Caldwell 2006b; Spinks 2006).

What are the implications of these matters for policy and practice in educational leadership? There are many, but it is important to bear in mind that schools and school systems will continue to change, albeit at a faster rate, in the decade ahead, and that approaches to leadership will change accordingly. What follows is based on current practice in several nations where transformation has been achieved and leaders are exhilarated by the experience. The intent is to provide a framework that can help all schools and all leaders achieve these outcomes at the same time that new practices emerge and the nature of schools and leadership changes. Approaches to governance will continue to evolve, consistent with the notion of 'the adaptive state'.

Government and the public service

Governments and their ministers for education should immediately prepare a scenario to transform the way the system of public education supports its schools. While a small part of the public sector in education will be concerned with setting policies, allocating resources, determining standards and ensuring accountability, the overwhelming majority of staff should be engaged unambiguously and unrelentingly in the support of schools. This support may be deployed from a central office, or it may be dispersed in a geographic sense, close to schools.

Schools should be self-managing, with most moving as close to autonomy as possible while still operating within a system that prides itself on good governance. Governments will be comfortable with the notion that the public service is just one agency of deep support for schools, who ought to be encouraged and supported to draw assistance from a range of sources, public and private, in education and other fields. The government and its public service will appreciate that its chief role is to provide this deep support, and to help build powerful communities rather than larger bureaucracies. 'Whole-of-government' approaches will be reality not rhetoric, and there will be no place for the public servant who cannot operate in this manner.

The best systems of knowledge management will be set up in schools. The aim is the support of personalised learning and a profession at the forefront of knowledge. Public servants shall play their part in ensuring that the principal's office is a paperless office. A support package will ensure that principals and other school leaders have appropriate executive and management support.

Ministers and public servants will be accountable for ensuring that most schools are replaced or re-built to make them proper places for learning and teaching and the support of learning and teaching in the 21st century. Leaders will be courageous in the true sense of the word, brooking no ideological opposition to the use of all of the resources of society to achieve this end. The failure to involve the private sector in this aspect of education has done grave harm to the working conditions of staff and students in many settings.

There will be acknowledgement in reality and not just rhetoric that transformation across the system will not occur with top-down and bottom-up approaches. Powerful networks to support the lateral transfer of knowledge will be nurtured and supported. They will not be another mechanism for distributing information and ensuring compliance. These networks will be resourced in substantial and not trivial ways. System leadership by school leaders will be encouraged and rewarded. Creative entrepreneurial risk-taking leadership will be nurtured in the early stages of a career. These qualities will be a normal expectation for those appointed to the principalship.

Schools and their leaders

There are implications in the foregoing for those who take up leadership positions in schools, especially at the level of principal. Each of the capacities specified above will be taken up at the school level, including the deployment of a wide range of mechanisms for support, tailoring to the needs of the school an advanced capacity for knowledge management, building a powerful learning community to ensure that staff are at the forefront of knowledge, participating in and sharing the leadership of networked learning communities and in other ways serving as a system leader, and accepting and utilising a support package to ensure that the balance is on leadership rather than management. As far as possible, the principal will have a paperless office and will build a personal capacity to use computer-based management information systems. The school will set a limited number of priorities among the many demands for change that are made. Distributed leadership will be taken seriously so that most staff take on a leadership role of one kind or another. The principal will actively seek and accept a higher level of authority and responsibility as the school moves closer to autonomy.

Creative entrepreneurial risk-taking leadership is nurtured and staff who demonstrate such attributes should be appointed to senior positions. Personal health and wellbeing are priorities. If either suffer, then re-consider the role or make adjustments to approaches to leadership and management in the light of the above, insisting on and utilising support from outside the school as necessary.

These implications are important for leaders in non-government, private or independent schools that do not operate in a system of education, even if they are wholly or partly funded from the public purse. High priorities are placed on personalising learning, an approach that such schools have typically prided themselves on. Particular attention should be given to knowledge management, taking the lead from schools of this kind that have established their own institutes as part of a strategy to build and sustain a powerful learning community for staff as well as students. System leadership is important, although its limitations are acknowledged in networks of schools that are in competition.

Leaders at the system level and in all kinds of schools are strategic, following Mintzberg (1995) in 'seeing ahead, seeing behind, seeing above, seeing below, seeing beside, seeing beyond, and above all, seeing it through'. They are comfortable with, although inevitably challenged by, their role in one of the most significant transformations of society in the history of humankind.

Universities and other providers of professional education

Bodies responsible for professional standards in teaching will seek the transformation of initial teacher education, with serious consideration to approaches that have proved successful in Finland, where a masters degree is required before appointment. Programs for the preparation and ongoing professional development of leaders will be transformed, drawing more heavily than ever on the work of leaders who have transformed their schools and school systems. Master classes of the kind described in Chapter 13 will be a major feature. Much of the professional literature will be discarded, following the lead of Hedley Beare and the author, as described in Chapter 12. This in no way detracts from its value in the past.

Higher priority will be given to research on leadership, as exercised by those who are succeeding in transforming their schools and who have helped make the link to learning. Current research along these lines is robust and it needs to be supported and expanded.

Coaching and mentoring have their place but those who provide the service must be those who have transformed their schools and school systems in the manner illustrated in these pages, and who have come to terms with the new enterprise logic of schools.

The tipping point

Is the new image of the educational leader attainable? Some may have asked the same question of self-managing schools when the concept was developed in the 1980s, but it is now simply 'the way things are done around here' in some countries. Similarly, for the embrace of information and communications technologies on a global scale. The 'tipping point' has been reached. The same is certain to occur in the adoption of the new image of the educational leader, as described in these pages. One thing is certain. The image will continue to change. Re-imagining educational leadership will be a continuing and indeed exciting endeavour.

Appendix A: A framework for the assessment of governance in education

(Department of Education, Science and Training 2005)

DOMAIN	ELEMENT	INDICATOR
Purpose	Outcomes	There is a contribution to the public good
		There is a contribution to economic development
		There is a contribution to social development
Process	Engagement	There is interaction between formal institutions (constitutions, legislature, executive, judiciary) and institutions, agencies, organisations and units in the public and private sectors in the wider community
Policy	Legitimacy	Policies are derived from or reflected in legislation and are implemented within a legal framework
	Representativeness	Policies are formulated to meet the needs of the whole of society and are not discriminatory to the extent that learners in the same circumstances will be supported in the same manner in the course of their learning
	Accountability	Authorities and responsibilities are specified and information is gathered and made available to provide a basis for assessing the extent to which intentions have been realised through the actions of those who are so empowered
	Efficiency	Mechanisms are in place to ensure that outcomes are optimised in the context of available resources
Standards	Specificity	Expectations and intended outcomes are clearly specified
	Data	Information to be gathered in the implementation of policy is of a kind that will enable judgements to be made on the effectiveness of delivery
		There is a capacity to gather information about the implementation of policy
		Data that are gathered in the course of implementation are of high quality to the extent that they are valid, timely, understandable and capable of effective use in decision-making
		Data are gathered across the range of intended outcomes
		Approaches to the gathering of data are designed to ensure accuracy

DOMAIN	ELEMENT	INDICATOR
Standards (cont.)		There are incentives in place to ensure that data are gathered and utilised in the manner intended
		Data are used in making decisions in the formulation of policy and in making judgements about the effectiveness of policy
	Transparency	Information about policies and associated regulations and procedures is readily available to all stakeholders, as is information about implementation, having due regard to the ethical use of such information
	Replication	Implementation has demonstrated the feasibility of policy to the extent that implementation is likely to be successful in other similar settings
	Ownership	There is a strong sense of commitment to the policy and approaches to its implementation on the part of stakeholders

Appendix B: Knowledge management— Sample indicators

The following are illustrative items, adapted for schools, drawn from a self-assessment instrument developed by Rajan, A. et al. (1999) as reproduced in Bahra (2001). Twelve of 38 items are included in the following excerpts, each concerned with a knowledge culture that fosters a systematic approach.

Item 1 Benchmarking: Identifying and implementing outstanding practice
Item 2 Groupware/intranet: Using technologies across the school to assist the knowledge-sharing process
Item 3 Search engine: Creating a substantial, systematic and sustained capacity for acquiring and sharing knowledge
Item 4 Knowledge coordinators: Giving individuals the responsibility for coordinating knowledge within a department or unit within the school
Item 5 Staff selection criteria: Ensuring that new staff are able to subscribe to the values conducive to knowledge sharing
Item 6 Competencies: Ensuring that knowledge-sharing competencies are part of training and developmental initiatives
Item 7 Contractual obligations: Getting senior management to actively endorse knowledge management
Item 8 Virtual teams: Bringing together teachers and other professionals from different departments or units and in different locations via video conferencing to offer different approaches to thinking and working
Item 9 Communities of practice: Promoting self-organised groups where teachers and other professionals exchange ideas and thoughts on common issues, practices, problems and possibilities in the workplace
Item 10 Team-based rewards: Recognising and rewarding teamwork
Item 11 Metrics: Measuring the impact of knowledge sharing in different areas of the school
Item 12 Balanced scorecard: Ensuring that the impact of knowledge management is assessed in terms of learning and other outcomes

References

Adler, PS and Kwon, S-W 2000, 'Social capital: The good, the bad and the ugly' in Lesser, EL (ed) *Knowledge and Social Capital: Foundations and Applications*, Butterworth Heinemann, Boston, Chapter 5.

Bahra, N 2001, *Competitive Knowledge Management*, Palgrave, Basingstoke.

Barber, M 2002, *The Next Stage in Large Scale Educational Reform in England*, IARTV Seminar Series, no 116, Incorporated Association of Registered Teachers of Victoria (IARTV), Melbourne.

Barber, M 2003, 'Deliverable goals and strategic challenges—A view from England on reconceptualising public education' in OECD *Networks of Innovation: Towards New Models for Managing Schools and Systems*, OECD, Paris, Chapter 7.

Barber, M 2004, 'Delivery: Why it Matters, What it Means?', Presentation at a conference on 'Tackling Inequalities in Newham to Improve Health' organised by Your Newham Local Strategic Partnership, Newham Primary Care Trust, Newham Council and University of East London, 22 January.

Beare, H 2001, *Creating the Future School*, Routledge Falmer, London.

Beare, H 2003, 'The school of the future', in Davies, B and West-Burnham, J (eds) *Handbook of Leadership and Management*, Pearson Longman, London, Chapter 61.

Beare, H 2006, *How We Envisage Schooling in the 21st Century: The New 'Imaginary' in Practice*, Specialist Schools and Academies Trust, London.

Bentley, T and Miller, R 2003, *Possible Futures: Four Scenarios for Schooling in 2030*, National College for School Leadership, Nottingham.

Bentley, T and Wilsdon, J 2004, 'Introduction: The Adaptive State' in Bentley, T and Wilsdon, J (eds) *The Adaptive State: Strategies for Personalising the Public Realm*, Demos, London, Chapter 1.

Blair, T 2003, 'Radical Reform is the Route to Social Justice', Remarks by the British Prime Minister at the Official Opening of the Bexley Business Academy.

Blair, T 2005, Address to the Annual Conference of the Labour Party, Brighton, 27 September.

Board of Teacher Registration (Queensland) 2002, *Networks@Work*, Board of Teacher Registration, Toowong.

Bolman, L and Deal, T 2003, *Reframing Organisations*, Jossey-Bass, San Francisco.

Broder, JM 2006, 'Humbled Schwarzenegger apologises for '04 election, and then proposes a centrist agenda', *The New York Times*, 6 January, Section A, p. 16.

Bukowitz, WR and Williams, RL 1999, *The Knowledge Management Fieldbook*, Financial Times Prentice Hall, London.

Caldwell, BJ 2002, 'Autonomy and self-management: Concepts and evidence' in Bush, T and Bell, L (eds), *The Principles and Practice of Educational Management*, Paul Chapman Publishing, London, Chapter 3, pp. 24–40.

Caldwell, BJ 2003, 'A theory of learning in the self-managing school' in Volansky, A and Friedman, I A (eds) 2003, *School-Based Management: An International Perspective*, Ministry of Education, Israel.

Caldwell, BJ 2004, 'A strategic view of efforts to lead the transformation of schools', *School Leadership and Management*, vol. 24, no. 1, pp. 81–100.

Caldwell, BJ 2005a, *School-Based Management*, no. 3 in the Education Policy Series of the International Academy of Education, International Institute for Educational Planning (IIEP) of UNESCO, Paris.

Caldwell, BJ 2005b, *The New Enterprise Logic of Schools*, Specialist Schools and Academies Trust, London.

Caldwell, BJ 2006a, *Exhilarating Leadership*, Specialist Schools and Academies Trust, London.

Caldwell, BJ 2006b, *Resourcing Schools for the 21st Century 1: Principles*, London: Specialist Schools and Academies Trust.

Caldwell, BJ and Spinks, JM 1986, *Policy-Making and Planning for School Effectiveness*, Education Department, Hobart, Tasmania.

Caldwell, BJ and Spinks, JM 1988, *The Self-Managing School*, Falmer, London.

Caldwell, BJ and Spinks, JM 1992, *Leading the Self-Managing School*, Falmer, London.

Caldwell, BJ and Spinks, JM 1998, *Beyond the Self-Managing School*, Falmer, London.

CAN (Community Action Network) 2003, 'The CAN Academy', Unpublished document prepared for the Community Action Network by Christine Megson and Kevin Davis, 31 July.

Catholic Education Office Melbourne (CEOM) 2003, 'The School as a Core Social Centre'. Catholic Education Office, East Melbourne, November.

Cavanaugh, T 2003, 'Is this the future of print accommodation', *Teaching Exceptional Children*, vol. 35, no. 2, pp. 56–61.

Cheng, YC 2001, 'New education and new teacher education: A paradigm shift for the future'. Cheng, YC, Chow, KW and Tsui, KT (eds) *New Teacher Education for the Future*, Hong Kong Institute of Education and Dordrecht, Kluwer Academic Publishers, Hong Kong, Chapter 2.

Coelho, P 2005, *The Zahir*, HarperCollins, London.

Cogan, JJ and Baumgart, N 2003, 'Views of Educators and Policy Makers in the Asia-Pacific Region Towards Schooling for the Future: Survey Findings', Presented at the OECD Forum on Schooling for Tomorrow, Document no. 08, *Futuroscope*, 12–14 February, Poitiers, France.

Cole, P 2004, *Professional Development: A Great Way to Avoid Change*, IARTV Seminar Series, no. 140, Incorporated Association of Registered Teachers of Victoria (IARTV), Melbourne.

Collarbone, P 2004 *Remodelling Schools for Tomorrow*, IARTV Occasional Paper Series, no. 88, Incorporated Association of Registered Teachers of Victoria (IARTV), Melbourne.

Collins, J 2001, *Good to Great*, Random House, London.

Confederation of British Industry (CBI) 2005, *The Business of Education Improvement*, CBI, London, viewed 1 May 2006, <www.cbi.org.uk/pdf/leareport0305.pdf>.

Crichton, M 2002, *Prey*, HarperCollins, London.

Crossley, D 2003, 'The role of the private sector in the UK in turning around a failing school: A case example' in Davies, B and West-Burnham, J (eds.), *Handbook of Educational Leadership and Management*, Pearson Publishing, London, Chapter 33.

Crossley, D 2005, 'Raising Achievement Transforming Learning', Unpublished paper of the Achievement Networks of the Specialist Schools and Academies Trust, Specialist Schools and Academies Trust, London.

Darling-Hammond, L 2005, 'Teaching as a profession: Lessons in teacher preparation and professional development', *Phi Delta Kappan*. vol. 87, no. 3 (November) pp. 237–40.

Davies, B (ed) 2005, *The Essentials of School Leadership*, Paul Chapman, London.

Davies, B 2006, *Leading the Strategically Focused School*, Paul Chapman, London.

Deal, TE, Hentschke, GC with Kecker, K, Lund, C, Oschman, S and Shore, R 2004, *Adventures of Charter School Creators*, Scarecrow Education, Lanham, Maryland.

Department for Education and Skills 2003, *Every Child Matters*, presented to Parliament by the Secretary of State for Education and Skills, DfES, London.

Department for Education and Skills 2004a, *Five Year Strategy for Children and Learners*, presented to Parliament by the Secretary of State for Education and Skills, DfES, London.

Department for Education and Skills 2004b, *National Standards for Headteachers*, DfES, London.

Department of Education and Training (Victoria) 2004, *The Privilege and the Price*, Department of Education and Training, Melbourne.

Department of Education, Science and Training (DEST) (Australia) 2005, *Best Practice Governance: Education Policy and Service Delivery*, Report for the Human Resource Development Working Group of Asia Pacific Economic Cooperation (APEC), DEST, Canberra.

Drucker, PF 1993, *Post-Capitalist Society*, HarperBusiness, New York.

Drucker, PF 1999, *Leadership Challenges for the 21st Century*, Butterworth Heinemann, Oxford.

Dryfoos, J 1994 *Full-Service Schools*, Jossey-Bass, San Francisco.

Duncan, M, Leigh, A, Madden, D and Tynan, P 2004, *Imagining Australia*, Allen & Unwin, Crows Nest.

Earl, L and Katz, S 2005, *What Makes a Learning Network*, National College for School Leadership, Nottingham. (Available along with other papers on networked learning communities at www.ncsl.org.uk/nlc).

Fancy, H 2005, *Schooling Reform: Reflections on New Zealand Experience*, IARTV Seminar Series, no. 142, Incorporated Association of Registered Teachers of Victoria (IARTV), Melbourne.

Fernandez, C 2002, 'Learning from Japanese approaches to professional development: The case of lesson study', *Journal of Teacher Education*, vol. 53, no. 5, pp. 393–405.

Florida, R 2005, *The Flight of the Creative Class*, HarperBusiness, New York.

Friedman, T 2005, *The World is Flat: A Brief History of the Globalised World in the 21st Century*, Allen Lane, London.

Fukuyama, F 1995, *Trust: Social Virtues and the Creation of Prosperity*, Hamish Hamilton, London.

Fullan, M 2004, *Leading the Way from Whole School Reform to Whole System Reform*, IARTV Seminar Series, no. 139, Incorporated Association of Registered Teachers of Victoria (IARTV), Melbourne.

Fullan, M 2005, *Leadership Sustainability*, Corwin Press, Thousand Oaks, California.

Fundación Minera Escondida 2003, *From Antofagasta…A Commitment to Chile*, Annual Report for 2003, Fundación Minera Escondida, Antofagasta.

Gladwell, M 2001, *The Tipping Point*, Abacus, London.

Goh, CT 1997, 'Shaping our Future: Thinking Schools, Learning Nation', speech by the Prime Minister of Singapore at the 7th International Conference on Thinking, 2 June, Singapore.

Gronn, P 2003, *The New Work of Educational Leaders*, Paul Chapman Publishing, London.

Hannon, V 2004, 'Intelligent Networks', in *The Future is Networked: How Schools are Working Smarter Together*, National College for School Leadership, Nottingham.

Hargreaves, A (ed) 2005, 'Sustaining Educational Leadership', *The Educational Forum*, vol. 69, no. 2. Winter. (This issue was devoted in its entirety to articles on the theme of leadership sustainability.)

Hargreaves, A and Fink, D 2006, *Sustainable Leadership*, Jossey-Bass, San Francisco.

Hargreaves, D 1994, *The Mosaic of Learning: Schools and Teachers for the New Century*, Demos, London.

Hargreaves, D 2003, *Education Epidemic*, Demos, London.

Hargreaves D 2004, *Personalising Learning: Next Steps in Working Laterally*, Specialist Schools and Academies Trust, London.

Harmer, J 2004, Letter to the author in his former role as Dean of Education at the University of Melbourne, describing measures to address the findings and recommendations of the Review of Teaching and Teacher Education in Australia, Dr Jeff Harmer, Secretary, Department of Education, Science and Training, 5 July.

Harris, A 2005, *Distributed Leadership*, Specialist Schools and Academies Trust, London.

Hislop, D 2004, 'The paradox of Communities of Practice: Knowledge sharing between communities' in Hildreth, P and Kimble, C (eds), *Knowledge Networks: Innovation Through Communities of Practice*, Idea Group Publishing, London, Chapter 4.

Hopkins, D 2006, *Every School a Great School*, Specialist Schools and Academies Trust, London.

Huang, R and Bao, J 2006, 'Towards a model for teacher professional development in China: Introducing keli', *Journal of Mathematics Teacher Education*, vol 9, no 3.

Huntington, SP 2002, *The Clash of Civilisations and the Making of a New World Order*, Free Press, New York.

Hyman, P 2005, *1 out of 10: From Downing Street Vision to Classroom Reality*, Vintage, London.

International Baccalaureate Organisation (IBO) 2002, *A Continuum of International Education*, IBO, Geneva. (A regularly updated PDF version may be downloaded from www.ibo.org)

International Institute of Administrative Sciences 1996, *Governance: A Working Definition*, Report of the Governance Working Group, The Global Development Research Center, viewed 1 May 2006, <http://www.gdrc.org/u-gov/work-def.html>.

Istance, D 2003, 'The OECD scenarios' in Davies, B and West-Burnham, J (eds), *Handbook of Leadership and Management*, Pearson Longman, London, Chapter 62.

Istance, D and Kobayashi, M 2003, 'Introduction' in OECD *Networks of Innovation: Towards New Models for Managing Schools and Systems*, OECD, Paris.

Jesson, D 2004, *Educational Outcomes and Value Added by Specialist Schools*, Specialist Schools and Academies Trust, London.

Johansson, Y 2003, 'Schooling for tomorrow—Principles and directions for policy' in OECD *Networks of Innovation: Towards New Models for Managing Schools and Systems*, OECD, Paris, Chapter 9.

Keating, M 2004, *Who Rules? How Government Retains Control of a Privatised Economy*, The Federation Press, Sydney.

Kerr, D, Aiston, S, White, K, Holland, M and Grayson, H 2003, 'Networked learning communities', Paper presented at the National Foundation for Educational Research (NFER), Council of Members Meeting, London, 3 October.

Kotter, JP 1990, *A Force for Change: How Leadership Differs from Management*, The Free Press, New York.

Leadbeater, C 2004, *Learning about personalisation: How Can We Put the Learner at the Heart of the Education System*, DfES, Memos and National College for School Leadership, London.

Lee, HL 2005, National Day Address at National University of Singapore (NUS), 21 August.

Lee, HL 2006, 'The Singapore Way', *Newsweek*, Special Edition on 'The Knowledge Revolution: Why Victory will go to the Smartest Nations & Companies', January–March.

Lee, KY 2000, *From Third World to First: The Singapore Story 1965–2000*, HarperCollins, New York.

Leigh, G 2002, 'Education Triggers Community to Spring to Life', Paper contributed to a web-based symposium of the Technology Colleges Trust (now Specialist Schools and Academies Trust) on the theme 'What Future—What Learning—What Teachers—What Schools?' (Available from Gabrielle Leigh, Principal, Caroline Chisholm College, Caroline Springs, Victoria, Australia).

Leithwood, K and Levin, B 2004, *Understanding Leadership Effects on Pupil Learning*, A Report for the Department for Education and Skills (DfES), DfES, London.

Lesser, EL 2000, 'Leveraging social capital in organisations' in Lesser, E L (ed.), *Knowledge and Social Capital*, Butterworth Heinemann, Boston, Chapter 1.

Linnakylä, P and Välijärvi, J 2003, *Finnish students' performance in PISA—Why such a success?*, Published as 'Das erfolgreiche abschneiden von finnischen schülern bei de PISA-Studie. Welche erklärungen gibt es dafür?' *Forum Jugendarbeit International*, Hänisch, D und Schwalbach, R. (toim), Internationaler Jugendaustausch und Besucherdienst der Bundesrepublik Deutschland, Bonn, pp. 284–95, Paper presented in English at the 'Finland in PISA-Studies–Reasons behind the Results' Conference, 14–16 March 2005, Helsinki, viewed 2 May 2006, <http://www.oph.fi/info/finlandinpisastudies/conference2005/jounivalijarvi.doc>.

Loader, D 1997, *The Inner Principal*, Falmer, London.

MCEETYA 1999, *The Adelaide Declaration on National Goals for Schooling in the Twenty-First Century*. (Available on the MCEETYA website at www.mceetya.edu.au).

MacGilchrist, B, Myers, K and Reed, J 2004, *The Intelligent School*, 2nd edn, Paul Chapman, London.

McGraw, TM, Burdette, K, Seale, VB, and Ross, JD 2002, 'Using Imperceptible Digital Watermarking Technologies to Transform Educational media: A Prototype', ERIC ED 477 706.

Midgley, S 1998 'Third Way: A challenge for all in education', *Times Educational Supplement*, 26 June, pp. 44–5.

Ministry of Education (Singapore) 2005, *Nurturing Every Child: Flexibility & Diversity in Singapore Schools*, Ministry of Education, Singapore.

Mintzberg, H 1995, *The Rise and Fall of Strategic Planning*, Free Press, New York.

Mitchell, J 2002, *The Potential for Communities of Practice to Underpin the National Training Framework*, Australian National Training Authority, Melbourne.

Munby, S 2005, *Leadership in Complex Schools*, advice to the Secretary of State for Education and Skills by Steve Munby, Chief Executive, NCSL, October, National College for School Leadership, England, viewed 2 May 2006, <www.ncsl.org.uk/media/897/OA/leadership-in-complex-schools.pdf>.

Nahan, M 2006, 'Taxpayers cheated by bloated bureaucracy', *The Australian*, 2 February.

National Association of Head Teachers (NAHT), Eastern Leadership Centre (ELC), University of Cambridge, National College of School Leadership (NCSL), and Hay Group (2005) *Leading Appointments: A Study into and Guidance on Headteacher Recruitment*, Interim Report. (Available on the NAHT website at www.naht.org.uk).

National College for School Leadership 2005, 'Making the difference: The evidence from the networks', *Nexus*, Autumn, pp. 14–15.

OECD 2001, *What Schools for the Future?* OECD, Paris, Chapter 3, 'Scenarios for the future of schooling'.

OECD 2003, *Networks of Innovation: Towards New Models for Managing Schools and School Systems*, OECD, Paris.

OECD 2004a, *Education at a Glance*, OECD, Paris.

OECD 2004b, *Teachers Matter: Attracting, Developing and Retaining Effective Teachers*, OECD, Paris.

Ojeda JMF 2002, *Towards a Sustainable Mining: Building Up Human and Social Capacities*, Fundación Minera Escondida, Antofagasta.

Papert, S 1993, *The Children's Machine: Rethinking School in the Age of the Computer*, Basic Books, New York.

Patel, KJ 2005, *The Master Strategist: Power, Purpose and Principle*, Hutchinson, London.

Peters, T 2003, *Re-imagine!* DK, London.

Peters, TJ and Waterman, RH 1982, *In Search of Excellence*, Harper and Row, New York.

Pogure, D 2005, 'The fine points of a high-performing pen', *International Herald Tribune*, 19–20 November, p. 16.

Pope John Paul II 1988, *Sollicitudo Rei Socialis (On Social Concerns)*, Encyclical Letter, St Paul Publications, Homebush, NSW.

Pope John Paul II 2005, *Memory and Identity*, Weidenfeld & Nicolson, London.

Prime Minister's Delivery Unit 2003, 'Key Stage 4 Priority Review: Final Report', PMDU, London.

Putnam, RD 2000, *Bowling Alone: The Collapse and Revival of American Community*, Touchstone, New York.

Queensland Consortium for Professional Development in Education 2004, *The Way Forward: The Future for Teacher Professional Associations and Networks*, Board of Teacher Registration, Toowong.

Quinn, N 2005, 'Islington's education success highlighted at CBI conference', media release, Islington Council, 16 March. (Available online at www.islington.gov.uk).

Rajan, A, Lank, E, & Chapple, K 1999, *Good Practices in Knowledge Creation and Exchange*, Create, Tunbridge Wells.

Saul, JR 2005, *The Collapse of Globalism: And the Reinvention of the World*, Camberwell, Viking.

Schleicher, A 2004, 'I resultati dell'Italia nell'indagine OCSE "Education at a Glance"', OECD, Paris. (PowerPoint available at www.oecd.org/dataoecd/33/33/33732967.ppt).

Scottish Consultative Council on the Curriculum 1999, *The Reggio Emilia Approach to Early Years Education*, Learning Teaching Scotland: The Council. (PDF version may be downloaded from www.ltsscotland.org.uk/earlyyears/resources/publications/ltscotland/reggioemilia.asp).

Scotland 2003, *Partnership for a Better Scotland*, Joint Statement by the Leaders of the Scottish Labour Party and the Scottish Liberal Democrats, Scottish Executive. (Available online at www.scotland. gov.uk/Resource/Doc/47095/0025772.pdf).

Scotland 2005, *Key Findings from the National Evaluation of the New Community Schools Pilot Program in Scotland*, A report of the evaluation conducted by the Institute of Education, University of London, Scottish Executive.

Sergiovanni, TJ 1984, 'Leadership and excellence in schooling', *Educational Leadership*. vol. 41, no. 3.

Shanmugaratnam, T 2005, Speech by the Minister for Education in Singapore, Mr Tharman Shanmugaratnam, at the 8th appointment ceremony for principals in Singapore, 29 December.

Silins, H & Mulford, B 2004, 'Schools as learning organisations: Effects on teacher leadership and student outcomes', *School Effectiveness and School Improvement*, vol. 15, nos 3–4, September–December, pp. 443–6.

Smith, AK & Wohlstetter, P 2001, 'Reform through school networks: A new kind of authority and accountability', *Education Policy*, vol. 15, no. 4, September, pp. 499–519.

Smithers, R 2005, 'Facelift for primary schools in "education to 18" package', *The Guardian*, 17 March.

Smithers, R 2006, 'Headteacher vacancies expose schools crisis', *The Guardian*, 12 January.

Spender, D 1995, *Nattering on the Net: Women, Power and Cyberspace*, Spinifex, North Melbourne.

Spinks, JM 2006, *Resourcing Schools for the 21st Century 2: Models*, Specialist Schools and Academies Trust, London.

Stewart, TA 1997, *Intellectual Capital: The New Wealth of Organisations*, Nicholas Brealey, London.

Stewart, TA 2002, *The Wealth of Knowledge: Intellectual Capital and the Twenty-First Century Organisation*, Nicholas Brealey, London.

Stewart, V and Kagan, SL 2005, 'A new world view: Education in a global era', *Phi Delta Kappan*, vol. 87, no. 3. pp. 241–5.

Tarica, E 2005, 'Working harder and smarter', *The Age* (Melbourne), 8 August (Education Supplement pp. 6–7).

Taylor, A n.d. *The Ecology of the Learning Environment*, New Horizons for Learning, viewed 1 May 2006, <www.newhorizons.org/future/Creating_the_Future/crfut_taylor.html>.

Taylor, C 2004, *Modern Social Imaginaries*, Public Planet Books, Durham, North Carolina.

Taylor, C and Ryan, C 2005, *Excellence in Education: The Making of Great Schools*. David Fulton, London.

The Economist 2005, 'Pulp Fiction'. 12 November, pp. 65–6.

3e International Kindergarten 2005, *3e International Kindergarten*. (More information is available at www.3eik.com).

Tobin, M 2004, 'Schools as Core Social Centres Project', Paper presented at the 2nd OECD Forum on Schooling for Tomorrow, June, Toronto.

UNESCO n.d. *UNESCO and Education*, UNESCO, Paris.

UNESCO 1996, *Learning: The Treasure Within*, report to UNESCO of the International Commission on Education for the Twenty-First Century (Highlights), Jacques Delors (Chair), UNESCO, Paris.

Välijärvi, J 2005, 'The system and how does it work: Some curricular and pedagogical characteristics of the Finnish comprehensive school', *Education Journal*, vol. 31, no. 2 and vol. 32, no. 1, Special Issue.

van Aalst, HF 2003, 'Networking in society, organisations and education' in OECD *Networks of Innovation: Towards New Models for Managing Schools and Systems*, OECD, Paris, Chapter 1.

VCAA (2005). (All papers related to the Victorian Essential Learning Standards can be found on the website of the Victorian Curriculum and Assessment Authority (VCAA) at http://vels.vcaa.vic.edu.au).

Warner, D 2006, *Schooling for the Knowledge Era*, ACER Press, Melbourne.

Watson, H 2004, 'Classrooms of the future', *Teacher*, November, pp. 54–5.

Wenger, E, McDermott, R & Snyder, W 2002, *Cultivating Communities of Practice: A Guide to Managing Knowledge*, Harvard Business School Press, Boston.

Woessmann, L 2001, 'Why students in some countries do better: International evidence on the importance of education policy', *Education Matters*, Summer, pp. 67-74.

Wohlstetter, P, Malloy, CL, Chau, D & Polhemus, JI 2003, 'Improving schools through networks: A new approach to urban school reform', *Education Policy*, vol. 17, no. 4. September, pp. 399–430.

World Bank Group 2001, 'Public Sector Governance'. (Available on the World Bank website at http://www.worldbank.org/html/extdr/thematic-alpha.htm).

Zuboff, S & Maxmin, J 2004, *The Support Economy*, Penguin Books, New York.

Index

Centre for Leadership and Management in
   Education (Griffith University)   150
Centre for Research and Innovation (CERI)
   (OECD)   43
Chan, Y   124
charter schools   123, 124
Chau, D   58, 206
Cheng, YC   67, 68, 200
Chile   10, 35, 64, 70, 79, 80, 83, 93, 99, 100,
   109–112, 117, 129
China   34, 64, 113, 114, 117, 131, 175, 177, 189
China Hong Kong   34
Chinese Taipei   34
Choy, G   175
Christ the Priest Catholic Primary School
   45
Churchill, Sir W   82
Cisco   53, 83, 108
Cisco Systems Network Academy   83
City of London Academy   92
civil society   69, 70, 121
Clarke, C   29
Claxton, G   108
Coelho, P   171, 200
Cogan, JJ   34, 200
Cole, P   110, 200
Colegio Antonio Redic School   109
Coles, M   92, 93
Collaborative School Management   19
Collarbone, Dame P   107, 200
Collins, J   168, 169, 200
Comberton Village College   88, 111
Commonwealth Bank (Australia)   144
Commonwealth Schools Commission (Australia)
   17
Community Action Network (CAN)   37, 42–44,
   47, 53, 200
computers   22, 78, 177, 178
Confederation of British Industry (CBI)   104,
   200
Copernicus   49
Core Education (Christchurch)   80
'core social centres' scenario   33, 34, 55, 106,
   115, 132, 164, 169, 188
Craig, W   104
creative class   130
Crichton, M   179–180
Crossley, D   45, 92, 102, 200
cultural leadership   119, 120
curriculum   4, 5, 18–21, 23, 32, 33, 35, 48, 51,
   57, 63, 66, 71, 72, 85, 89–91, 98–100, 107, 108,
   114, 115, 117, 120–122, 140, 142, 153–155,
   159, 172–176, 178–180, 187, 190, 192

Dalton, J   89
Darling-Hammond, L   114, 200
Davies, B   9, 134, 149, 199–202
Deal, T   123–125, 199, 202
decentralisation   16, 17, 24, 33, 64–66, 70, 71,
   129, 132, 186, 189
   link to learning   24
Delfin Lend Lease   45, 145
Demos   31, 199, 202
Denmark   64, 130
Department for Education and Skills (DfES)
   (UK)   53, 97, 105, 201
Department of Education and Training (DET)
   (Victoria), Northern Metropolitan Region
   104, 156
Department of Education, Science and Training
   (DEST) (Australia)   69, 121, 189, 196, 201
digital whiteboards   177
digitalisation   177, 178, 180
Diploma Program (DP) (International
   Baccalaureate)   173
distributed leadership   19, 82, 160, 193
Distributed Staff Leadership Model (Mt
   Waverley Secondary College)   108
Doveton-Endeavour Hills Cluster (Victoria)
   89–91, 188
Drennen, H, 160, 173
Drucker, P   27, 28, 63, 122, 201
Duncan, M et al.   4, 201

Earl, L   58, 201
East Central Network (Catholic Education
   Melbourne)   150, 159
Eastern Europe   175
Economist, The   177, 205
Edmonton   63
Education Epidemic   62, 110, 179
'education imaginary'   7, 64, 67
Education Reform Act 1988 (UK)   17, 38
educational leadership   8, 35, 120, 183, 185, 192,
   195
Educational Leadership Centre (ELC) (England)
   184
Effective Resource Allocation in Schools Project
   (ERASP)   17
Egypt   64, 177
Eltham College of Education (Victoria)   108
enterprise   10, 36, 48, 49, 53, 67, 75, 76, 82, 93,
   116, 174
enterprise logic
   new   10, 30, 71, 75, 76, 79–81, 83, 85, 87–89,
      91–96, 101–103, 106, 108–110, 116–118,
      121–123, 125, 132–134, 149–151, 168, 169,
      172, 188, 191, 192, 194

social   67
imagination   3, 5, 7, 82, 110, 187
India   64, 117, 131, 175, 189
iNet   9, 80, 100, 109, 136, 147, 169
iNet Australia   85, 136, 150
iNet Australia Principals Reference Group   85
informed prescription   51
informed professionalism   50, 51
innovation   43, 44, 51, 54, 58, 60, 88, 89, 92,
   111, 112, 117, 122, 192
Innovation Unit (DfES)   31, 53, 97
intellectual capital   40, 42, 59, 60, 72, 79, 88, 93,
   94, 99, 122
International Baccalaureate (IB)   160, 173, 174,
   178
   Diploma Program (DP)   173, 174
   Middle Years Program (MYP)   173, 174
   Primary Years Program (PYP)   173, 174
International Baccalaureate Organisation (IBO)
   160, 173, 202
International Centre for Classroom Research
   (ICCR) (University of Melbourne)   113
International Conference on Thinking   5
International Institute of Administrative Sciences
   69, 121
International Networking for Educational
   Transformation (iNet)   9, 80, 100, 109, 136,
   147, 169
Investors in People   83, 108
iPhase (George Spencer Foundation School and
   Technology College)   108
Irlicht, B   46, 142–144, 148, 150, 164
Islington Council   104, 105
Islington Green School   82, 187
Istanbul   30, 81
Istance, D   32, 36, 44, 132, 133, 188, 202

Japan   34, 43, 64, 113, 114, 131
Jesson, D   37, 202
Johansson, Y   55, 202
John Cabot City Technology College   84
Jones, D   104
Jowatt, S   108

Kagan, SL   115, 205
Katz, S   58, 201
Keating, M   30, 48, 49, 186, 202
keli (China)   114
Kelly, R   101
Kempton, J   105
Kennett Coalition Government (Victoria)
   17
Kerr, D et al.   57, 202
King, J   89

Kings College for the Arts and Technology   45,
   92
knowledge management   36, 59, 60, 72, 187,
   191, 193, 194, 198
knowledge society   21–23, 28, 41, 44, 67, 117,
   118, 183
knowledge-based networks   51, 62, 106
Knowsley (Education Authority) (England)   104
Kobayashi, M   44, 202
Korea   34, 43, 64, 65
Kotter, J   6, 185, 202

Lanyon Cluster (Australian Capital Territory)
   98, 99, 111
Latin America   175
Latin American Heads Conference   80
Leadbeater, C   31, 32, 203
leader voice   11, 134, 149, 185
leadership
   accountable   119, 121
   cultural   119, 120
   dimensions of   117–119
   domains of practice in   117, 118, 121
   educational   8, 35, 120, 183, 185, 192, 195
   essentials   9, 134
   executive (level 5) (Collins)   82, 168
   exhilarating   11, 12, 129, 134, 149, 162, 180
   for Transformation (University of Melbourne)
      11, 136
   framework for   117, 119, 122, 192
   responsive (accountable)   19, 119, 121
   standards for   134, 171
   strategic   120, 170
   sustainability in   7, 134
   sustainable   7, 9
   system   168–170, 188, 193, 194
Leading Edge   97
Leading the Self-Managing School   16, 19, 63
learning networks (scenario)   34, 63
Learning: The Treasure Within (UNESCO)   173,
   205
Learning to Learn (L2L)   84, 88, 108–110
Lee, C   97
Lee, HL   4, 5, 183, 203
Lee, KY   4, 203
Leigh, A   4, 201
Leigh City Technology College   83
Leigh, G   45, 145, 148, 203
Leithwood, K   121, 134, 203
Lesser, EL   60, 203
lesson study (Japan)   113, 114
levels (of a school system)   8, 95, 134, 188, 189
Levin, B   121, 134, 203
Linnakylä, P   191, 203